Restoring Sustainable Macroeconomic Policies in the United States

Restoring Sustainable Macroeconomic Policies in the United States

Barry W. Poulson and John Merrifield

LEXINGTON BOOKS

Lanham • Boulder • New York • London

Published by Lexington Books
An imprint of The Rowman & Littlefield Publishing Group, Inc.
4501 Forbes Boulevard, Suite 200, Lanham, Maryland 20706
www.rowman.com

86-90 Paul Street, London EC2A 4NE

British Library Cataloguing in Publication Information Available

Library of Congress Cataloging-in-Publication Data

Names: Poulson, Barry Warren, 1937- author. | Merrifield, John, 1955- author.
Title: Restoring sustainable macroeconomic policies in the United States / Barry W. Poulson and John Merrifield.
Description: Lanham : Lexington Books, [2022] | Includes bibliographical references and index.
Identifiers: LCCN 2022032924 (print) | LCCN 2022032925 (ebook) | ISBN 9781666916607 (cloth) | ISBN 9781666916614 (ebook)
Subjects: LCSH: Debts, Public—United States. | Fiscal policy—United States. | Monetary policy—United States. | United States—Economic policy—21st century.
Classification: LCC HJ8101 .P68 2022 (print) | LCC HJ8101 (ebook) | DDC 336.3/40973—dc23/eng/20220728
LC record available at https://lccn.loc.gov/2022032924
LC ebook record available at https://lccn.loc.gov/2022032925

Contents

List of Figures and Tables

FIGURES

TABLES

Preface

RESTORING SUSTAINABLE MACROECONOMIC
POLICIES IN THE UNITED STATES

Can the United States restore sustainable macroeconomic policies? Macroeconomic policies are unsustainable when governments incur unconstrained growth in spending, accompanied by deficits and debt accumulation. Debt sustainability is an area of economics where conceptual clarity meets practical fuzziness. Conceptually public debt cannot exceed the present value of future budget surpluses (net of interest payments). But accumulating debt is a sovereign decision, reflecting many political as well as economic factors. This book explores public debt in the United States from a public choice perspective.

For two centuries the United States pursued sustainable macroeconomic policies. The federal government might incur deficits and accumulate debt in periods of war, but the government was expected to balance the budget and use surplus revenue to repay the public debt in peacetime. It is only in the last half century that the federal government has consistently incurred deficits and accumulated debt in periods of peace as well as war. The United States is not alone in pursuing unsustainable macroeconomic policies; debt has been increasing at an unsustainable rate in many countries in recent decades. The United States has emerged as one of the most heavily indebted countries in the world, with a ratio of debt relative to national income second only to that of Japan.

As the burden of public debt increased in the western nations over the past half century, citizens responded by imposing new fiscal rules designed to constrain fiscal decisions. The first generation of new fiscal rules was enacted in the European countries. The most successful of these fiscal rules is the Swiss "debt brake." The Swiss debt brake is a constitutional fiscal rule enacted through referendum with overwhelming support from Swiss citizens. It requires the federal government to balance the budget over the business cycle and constrain the growth of spending to the growth in national income in the long run. The debt brake allowed Swiss citizens to cut the ratio of debt to national income by half over the past two decades. The Swiss debt brake was copied at both the national and supranational level in the European Union. The new fiscal rules enabled most of these countries to respond to recent economic crises without a massive accumulation of debt, but in some European countries the fiscal rules proved to be less effective, and this led to the second generation of fiscal rules.

Over the past half century, citizens in the United States also enacted new fiscal rules. The tax revolt was most successful at the state and local level. Beginning in California in the 1970s, citizens enacted tax and expenditure limits (TELs) limiting the power of state and local governments to increase revenue, spending, and debt. Thirty-two states have enacted some form of tax and expenditure limit. In some states, such as California, TELs have proven to be ineffective in constraining fiscal decisions in the long term; in other states, such as Colorado, TELs continue to limit increases in revenue, spending, and debt at both the state and local level.

New fiscal rules were also enacted at the federal level mandating a balanced budget and limiting debt, and in the 1990s Congress was able to balance the budget and reduce debt burdens. In those years discretionary monetary policy was replaced by rules-based monetary policy to stabilize prices. Unfortunately, this "Great Moderation" in macroeconomic policy came to an abrupt end; over the past two decades the United States has virtually abandoned rules-based fiscal and monetary policies. Congress has evaded and suspended statutory fiscal rules and has responded to economic crises with massive increases in public debt. The Fed has pursued accommodative monetary policies, lowering interest rates and purchasing government securities.

The challenge in the coming years is whether the United States can restore a Great Moderation in macroeconomic policy. This book explores the failures in fiscal and monetary policies that have led the nation to a fiscal cliff. New fiscal and monetary rules are explored that could put the nation back on track toward sustainable macroeconomic policies. Statutory fiscal rules have proven to be ineffective, and reforms in these rules must be enacted to improve their effectiveness. Avoiding a fiscal cliff may require the second-generation fiscal rules, such as those enacted in Switzerland and other European countries. Some of the proposed fiscal rules set quantitative targets for deficits and debt, and these proposals are examined more rigorously.

A dynamic simulation model is introduced to estimate whether the proposed fiscal rules achieve quantitative targets within a given time frame.

Enacting second-generation fiscal rules will also require fundamental reforms in our fiscal and monetary institutions. Congress can of course enact statutory rules constraining fiscal and monetary policies. But given the failure of statutory fiscal and monetary rules over the past two decades, citizens in the United States must now follow the lead of European countries and incorporate new fiscal and monetary rules in the constitution. The Swiss enacted their debt brake as a constitutional rule through referendum. The U.S. Constitution does not provide for a referendum, but Article V provides for amendments either through Congress or through an amendment convention. This book introduces a model fiscal responsibility amendment and explores issues of political economy in enacting such an amendment.

Ultimately, enacting effective fiscal rules, either as statutory or constitutional provisions, depends upon the will of the people. An ethos of fiscal responsibility in America can be traced to the founding fathers. The commitment to balanced budgets is clear in the federalist papers, and especially in the writings of Thomas Jefferson. For Jefferson, repaying one's debt was a moral obligation. Jefferson considered it immoral for governments, as well as individuals, to incur debt and then pass the debt along to future generations. For two centuries American citizens and their elected representatives remained committed to this "Old Time Religion" of balanced budgets.

As Milton Friedman argued, the ethos of balanced budgets began to shift in the twentieth century. He points to a major shift in this ethos in the New Deal policies pursued during the Great Depression, and the Great Society policies of the post-World War Two era. A progressive ideology preached greater dependence on government and less reliance on individual responsibility to meet the challenges of the twentieth century. As the government assumed an expanded role in the economy, increased government spending was accompanied by continuous deficits and debt accumulation. Much of this debt has been incurred as unfunded liabilities in the major entitlement programs—Social Security and Medicare.

Today there is an even greater threat to rules-based fiscal policy in the increased demands on the public sector. Progressives argue that the federal government must fund infrastructure investments, transition to a carbon-neutral economy, and redistribute income and wealth. The credibility of the federal government commitment to sustainable debt and stable prices is now in doubt, and failure to meet these two commitments will make it difficult if not impossible to meet the new demands on fiscal policy.

The challenge will be to normalize fiscal and monetary policies without doing further damage to the economy.

Constraining policy makers' discretion through rules-based fiscal and monetary policies has become even more important in this post-pandemic economy. Effective fiscal and monetary rules may now require fundamental reforms in institutions, and perhaps even a new economic constitution as Milton Friedman argued. This book offers a starting point for considering new macroeconomic frameworks that could preserve policy credibility and show resilience in meeting the new challenges of our time.

Acknowledgments

We wish to thank Kurt Couchman for reviewing the manuscript. We also wish to thank the team at Lexington for their work in editing and publishing the book.

Introduction

The COVID-19 pandemic is a tail event that has had an unprecedented impact on the economy. The United States has experienced the worst economic downturn since the Great Depression. The economy is recovering more rapidly than originally forecast, due primarily to the massive fiscal stimulus policies pursued in 2020 and 2021, and continued recovery is forecast for 2022. Tail events like the COVID-19 pandemic require unprecedented coordination of monetary and fiscal policy to provide the macroeconomic policy response required for stabilization. Large purchases of financial assets by the Federal Reserve created the fiscal space required for countercyclical fiscal policy. Monetary or fiscal policy alone could not have provided the level of support required in responding to the crisis.

As the COVID-19 pandemic ends, the burning question is when and how to restore normal monetary and fiscal policies. The coordination of monetary and fiscal policy works only if the credibility of the two commitments to stable prices and sustainable debt levels is not questioned. During the "Great Moderation" of the late 1980s and 1990s, the United States made significant progress in fulfilling these commitments. In those years, John Taylor and others formalized benchmarks for prudent monetary and fiscal policy. While Taylor-style monetary and fiscal rules were never adopted as formal rules, they served as benchmarks for prudent policy. Empirical studies reveal that fiscal and monetary policies approximated, and in some years exceeded, these benchmarks.

However, over the past two decades monetary and fiscal policies no longer approximated the rules-based policies pursued during the Great Moderation. The commitment to sustainable debt was abandoned long before the COVID-19 pandemic. During the 2008 financial crisis, debt roughly doubled from $5 trillion to $10 trillion and doubled again to $20 trillion in the years prior to the pandemic. The Congressional Budget Office forecasts that by midcentury the total debt will exceed 200 percent of gross national product. Elected officials are now demanding massive new spending programs that will require even more debt, and they are demanding that the Fed buy more treasury bonds or "print" the sovereign currency required to finance these programs. The commitment to sustainable debt has virtually disappeared in both political parties.

The major discontinuity in monetary policy occurred during the 2008 financial crisis when the Fed began to pursue unorthodox monetary policy. Since then the Fed has failed to normalize monetary policy, it greatly expanded its balance sheet and left the crisis-era operating system in place. The Fed's policy response to the COVID-19 pandemic has further blurred the lines between monetary and fiscal policy. The Fed is in danger of becoming a pawn of Congress, forced to finance government expenditures in a manner that endangers the legitimacy of both monetary and fiscal policy.

The United States has emerged from the pandemic as one of the most indebted nations in the world. Debt fatigue in the United States has occurred over the last half century and is projected to continue in the coming decades. Over the past two decades, each major economic shock has been accompanied by a sharp discontinuous increase in debt. In years of economic recovery as well as recession, the United States exhibits debt fatigue in which debt continues to increase relative to gross domestic product (GDP). The fiscal rules and fiscal policies now in place are flawed in that they have failed to prevent an unsustainable growth in debt. Future generations of Americans will bear the burden of debt fatigue in the form of direct taxation, the hidden cost of inflation, higher borrowing costs, or some combination of the three. The debt incurred to finance stimulus spending has triggered higher interest rates and inflationary pressures, and Democrats have proposed higher taxes to finance more stimulus spending.

Debt fatigue in the wake of the coronavirus pandemic is a worldwide phenomenon. Public debt has increased sharply, and in many countries it is increasing more rapidly than GDP. Legislators across the globe have responded to economic shocks by authorizing massive fiscal stimulus policies. Central banks have followed the lead of the U.S. Federal Reserve Bank in pursuing unconventional monetary policies, cutting interest rates and buying securities in the open market. These macroeconomic policies were designed to shore up the financial system and stabilize their economies. But much of the money created by global governments in response to the coronavirus pandemic has now leaked into asset prices. The appetite for risk and irrational exuberance is evident across a wide range of asset classes. The speculative bubble includes stocks, real estate, commodities, and esoteric assets such as bitcoin. Investors have poured unprecedented amounts of money into mutual and exchange-traded funds tracking global stocks. Stock values in Europe and Asia as well as the United States have hit all-time highs. Even in Japan where stocks have been depressed for decades, the Nikkei index increased above 3,000 for the first time in thirty years.

Despite the massive stimulus programs launched in the United States in response to the financial crisis and the coronavirus pandemic, the United States continues to experience retardation in economic growth, and the economy is projected to continue to experience retardation in productivity change and economic growth in the long term. The underperformance of the U.S. economy appears increasingly like Japan's lost decades. For three decades, Japan has experienced retardation in economic growth. The Japanese government has incurred deficits over this entire period, leaving it with the highest debt levels in the world. The Bank of Japan has pursued unconventional monetary policies, purchasing massive quantities of public and private securities, and pushing interest rates well into negative territory. These macroeconomic policies have failed to jump-start the Japanese economy, and the Bank of Japan appears to have reached the limit in pursuing an unconventional monetary policy.

It is now clear that the culprit in Japan's economic stagnation over the past three decades is zombies. The Japanese government has accumulated massive debt, attempting to jump-start the economy. The macroeconomic policies designed to promote private investment have in fact created generations of zombie enterprises. Zombie firms are inefficient and unprofitable enterprises that rely on direct transfers and subsidized loans to avoid bankruptcy. Weak banks with nonperforming loans find it cheaper to roll over or "evergreen" these loans because of government subsidies and guarantees. In the absence of zombie lending, these firms would default on their debt, and either restructure or leave the industry. The impact of this zombification is a misallocation of resources that are retained by inefficient firms rather than flowing to more efficient uses.

Economic stagnation is also evident in European countries and other developed countries in recent years. These countries have also experienced deflationary pressures, characterized by low interest rates and zombie lending. Indeed, recent empirical studies suggest that many governments have allowed their total debt to increase to levels that expose them to the risk of insolvency and default. The growing risk of debt default has required a fundamental reevaluation of debt sustainability. Debt fatigue does not necessarily end with the bankruptcy of zombie firms and debt default, as in the Argentine case. Debt solvency is an area of economics where conceptual clarity meets practical fuzziness. Conceptually, public debt cannot exceed the present value of all future surpluses (net of interest payments). But, in practice, predicting future budget surpluses is uncertain, and in the near term these countries will likely continue servicing their debt. However, debt fatigue is putting these countries on a path of secular stagnation similar to that in Japan. There is growing evidence that zombification contributes to a "climacteric" or retardation in economic growth.

In the final analysis, the failure to fulfill fiscal commitments is a political failure. As Yared (2019) argues, "Normative economic theories cannot deliver a complete justification for the increase in public debt across all advanced economies. This suggests that the widespread increase in debt partly represents a political failure."[1] There is extensive literature exploring the reason for the bias toward deficits and debt. In the public choice literature, the culprit is time inconsistency. Politicians, focusing on the next election, find that expenditures generating immediate benefits for their constituents are more valuable than future expenditures, or present outlays whose benefits are visible in the future. Government budgets are ultimately the translation of a political platform. This means that fiscal policy is determined by political factors that make it difficult to solve the "commitment problem."

The problem of the fiscal commons is crucial in understanding the debt crisis. The benefits of government spending are concentrated in special interest groups, while the costs are spread over all taxpayers, either through taxes or debt. While the burden of additional public spending is hardly noticed by the average taxpayer, special interests capture a significant share of the benefits of those expenditures. Citizens demand government services up to the point at which the marginal utility obtained from an additional dollar of spending equals the marginal cost incurred by additional taxes and debt. Thus, government spending is increased, and public revenues (fiscal commons) are overused.

Given the bias toward deficits and debt, the question is how to constrain fiscal policy decisions to achieve sustainable debt. This book is a starting point in understanding how the United States can normalize fiscal and monetary policies in the post-COVID-19 era. It offers new ways to think about the macroeconomic frameworks needed to solve the commitment problem. The government must preserve policy credibility while showing resilience in meeting the challenge of economic shocks. Constraining policy makers' discretion will be even more important in this new era than it was during the Great Moderation. The recent economic crises have provided a learning experience, and the rules-based macroeconomic framework required for this new era may be significantly different than that of the past.

NOTE

1. Yared, Pierre (2019), "Rising Government Debt: Causes and Solutions for a Decades-old Trend," *Journal of Economic Perspectives*, 33(2): 115–40.

Chapter 1

Debt Fatigue and Debt Sustainability in Historical Perspective

THE "OLD TIME FISCAL RELIGION"

The "Old Time Fiscal Religion" was part of an ethos of fiscal responsibility that emerged during the Renaissance. In America, this ethos reflected the unique experience of a country dominated by small family farms. During Colonial times the patterns of settlement depended on the availability of land. When older settlements were filled up, a new town would be established with each colonist entitled to a share of the land. Colonists in America benefited from a unique form of property ownership referred to as "allodial." When the courts granted land to a group of settlers the land was divided into individual private property rights, protecting each colonist from infringement of their property. Each property owner was able to use the property to maximize family welfare, relatively free from government interference in the form of taxation or regulation (Poulson 1981).

The system of inheritance in America contributed to an ethos of fiscal responsibility. In contrast to the inheritance system in England, based on primogeniture, inheritance in America was based on a relatively equal distribution of property among heirs. The major form of wealth transferred from one generation to the next was in the form of land. In the older settled parts of the colonies, where new land was not available, older children were expected to inherit the land and provide for elderly parents. An ethos of equal inheritance often required the family to take out a mortgage that provided younger children with liquid assets they could use to purchase land, invest in a business, and so on. Thus, debt was perceived as part of a moral obligation in colonial families to give each child a start in life comparable to their own. Debt allowed farm families to share in the growth of wealth and prosperity from one generation to the next; the expectation was that each generation would repay any of the debts they incurred (Poulson 1981).

Thomas Jefferson's ideas were influenced by the classical economists, including Adam Smith and David Hume. These economists translated the ethos of fiscal responsibility into principles of fiscal responsibility in the public sector. Jefferson's principles were the basis for the Old Time Fiscal Religion that influenced public policy in America over several centuries. The best way to understand Jeffersonian debt principles is to follow his own writing (Poulson 2021).

Jefferson lays out the principles for public as well as private debts. Each generation has a responsibility to repay their debts; failing to repay debts and passing debts along to the next generation is considered immoral.

> Then I say, the earth belongs to each of these generations during its course, fully and in its own right. The second generation receives it clear of the debts and incumbrances of the first, the third of the second, and so on. For if the first could charge it with debt, then the earth would belong to the dead and not to the living generation. Then, no generation can contract debts greater than may be paid during the course of its own existence. (Thomas Jefferson to James Madison, 1789. ME)
>
> I sincerely believe . . . that the principle of spending money to be paid by posterity under the name of funding is but swindling futurity on a large scale. (Thomas Jefferson to John Taylor, 1816. ME 15:23)

Jefferson recognized that emergency expenditures during wartime may require the government to incur debt, but he argued that debt should be repaid by that generation in peacetime. He maintained that this principle of repaying debts during periods of peace should be incorporated in the constitution. As president, Jefferson fulfilled the commitment to repay the debts incurred during the Revolutionary War, until the last year of his presidency when hostilities that led to the War of 1812 required him to increase military spending. This principle of repaying public debt in periods of peace was followed by the federal government until well into the twentieth century.

> I wish it were possible to obtain a single amendment to our Constitution. I would be willing to depend on that alone for the reduction of the administration of our government; I mean an additional article taking from the Federal Government the power of borrowing. (Thomas Jefferson to John Taylor, 1789. ME 10:64)
>
> With respect to future debts, would it not be wise and just for a nation to declare in its constitution that neither the legislature nor the nation itself can validly contract more debt than they may pay within their own age, or within the term of 19 years? (Thomas Jefferson to James Madison, 1789)

To meet the commitment to repay public debt Jefferson supported the concept of a sinking fund, that is earmarking taxes and other revenues to pay both principal and interest on the debt within a finite amortization period.

> It is a wise rule and should be fundamental in a government disposed to cherish its credit and at the same time to restrain the use of it within the limits of its faculties, never to borrow a dollar without laying a tax in the same instant for paying the interest and principal within a given term; and to consider that tax as pledged to the creditors on the public faith. (Thomas Jefferson to John Wayles Eppes, 1813, ME 13: 269)
>
> We should now set the example of appropriating some particular tax for the loans made" sufficient to pay the interest annually and the principle within a fixed term, less than nineteen years. (Thomas Jefferson to John Wayles Eppes, 1813. ME 13: 273)

While Jefferson recognized that the emergency of war could necessitate incurring public debt, he argued that the principle of repaying the debt within one generation would act to curb military spending and discourage expansionist foreign policies.

> The natural right to be free of the debts of a previous generation is a salutary curb on the spirit of war and indebtment, which, since the modern theory of the perpetuation of debt, has drenched the earth with blood, and crushed its inhabitants under burdens ever accumulating. (Thomas Jefferson to John Wayles Eppes, 1813, ME 13: 272)

Jefferson was unsuccessful in convincing his colleagues to incorporate a provision limiting debt in the constitution; nonetheless, he argued that this principle was grounded in natural law. Even though the constitution places no explicit constraints on debt, this "unwritten constitution" was part of the Old Time Fiscal Religion that would guide fiscal policy for many generations. This principle was less effective in constraining debt at the state level. Many states pursued imprudent fiscal policies that resulted in unsustainable debt. During the economic crises of the Jacksonian period, a number of states defaulted on their debt. In those years most states did in fact incorporate provisions in their state constitutions requiring a balanced budget and limiting debt.

For most of our history elected officials perceived themselves as guardians of the nation's wealth and patrimony. Repaying public debt was part of the ethos of fiscal responsibility, limiting government and maximizing individual freedom. As citizens prospered, this provided a growing revenue base and prosperity for communities. The outcome of this Old Time Fiscal Religion was rapid economic growth, and limited growth in government spending and debt, especially at the federal level. Jeffersonian debt principles meant that the government played a minimal role in the economy and was a neutral bystander in the distribution of income and wealth. Some government policies, such as tariffs and infrastructure investment, had distributional effects that benefited special interests. On the other hand, the transfer of land and resources from the public to the private sector created greater equality in the distribution of income and wealth, especially during the latter nineteenth century as land policies became less restrictive, culminating in the Homestead Act. But redistribution of income and wealth per se was not perceived to be within the government's remit (Poulson 1981).

THE NATION'S FIRST DEBT CRISIS

The new government formed after ratification of the constitution in 1789 faced a debt crisis. The state and federal debt issued under the Articles of Confederation would today be classified as junk bonds. It was not clear that the new nation could pay the interest, let alone the principal on this debt. Not surprisingly, the debt inherited by the new government was heavily discounted in credit markets. The new government had to convince creditors of its commitment to meet these obligations. The problem was one of time inconsistency, how to convince creditors that the debt would be serviced, not only by the current government but by future governments as well (Poulson 1981).

To solve the commitment problem the new government created sinking funds. Sinking funds are a commitment mechanism designed to convince creditors that the securities they purchase will be redeemed by contractual commitments according to a schedule for repayment (Ross 1892). A sinking fund is unique in that the contract provides for the amortization of a portion of the debt prior to maturity. These provisions of the sinking fund are designed to make the securities more attractive to lenders. The origin of sinking funds can be traced to early eighteenth-century England. The precedent established at that time was to pledge specified tax revenues at the time securities are issued, to not only reduce the debt but to eliminate it entirely.

The concept of a sinking fund was first introduced in America by Robert Morris, as Superintendent of the Treasury, in 1782. Morris' plan provided that surplus revenue from import duties and taxes on polls, land, and whiskey would be earmarked for a sinking fund to pay interest and principal on public debt. At that time the federal government failed to enact laws providing for taxation and continued to rely on discretionary transfers of revenue from the individual states. As a result, Morris' proposal for a sinking fund was never enacted. However, a resolution was passed to create a sinking fund whenever the federal government had the power to impose import duties (Sylla 1999).

Alexander Hamilton became the first secretary of the Treasury shortly after the federal government was established under the constitution in 1789. The first Congress enacted tariffs as the major source of revenue, which made sinking funds a viable commitment option. Hamilton proposed sinking funds in two reports on funding the U.S. debt, in 1790, and again in 1795 shortly before he resigned as secretary of the Treasury. In his 1790 report, Hamilton proposed a sinking fund to retire the public debt, by issuing 6 percent bonds to replace older bonds issued by the states and by the federal government. The sinking fund would be financed from post office revenues, and Congress would be authorized to borrow funds to finance debt reduction. Congress modified Hamilton's proposal, substituting surplus revenues from duties on imports and tonnage, for post office revenues. However, very little surplus revenue was available at that time so very little debt redemption occurred in those early years (Swanson and Trout 1992).

By 1795, the U.S. economy was prospering, and significant surplus revenue was available for debt redemption. In the plan that Hamilton submitted in 1795, he proposed redeeming the entire national debt in thirty years. Sinking fund revenues would be augmented to include interest on securities purchased and held by the sinking fund, land sale proceeds, and all surplus revenue. The funds would be placed in trust under the direction of commissioners, and the commitment of the funds to redeem the debt would be part of the contract with creditors. The contract called for the markdown each year of the capital value of a security holder's property by the excess of payments, equal to 2 percent annually, over the stipulated interest rate on the security (Edling 2007).

From the very outset, Hamilton's plans for redeeming the public debt were opposed by Jefferson, Madison, and other Republicans. They argued that Hamilton's sinking fund proposals were designed not so much to redeem the public debt, but rather to secure the public credit and issue more debt. Given that very little revenue was available in the early years to finance the sinking fund, this criticism was valid. But the criticism was not valid for Hamilton's report in 1795. By that time, surplus revenue could be earmarked for a viable sinking fund. Hamilton's report in 1795 became the blueprint for the sinking fund to eliminate public debt over the next three decades (Sloan 1995).

Hamilton had a nuanced understanding of public finance. He argued that a sinking fund provided a more stable commitment to debt redemption, rather than relying on the discretion of Congress. In the long run, the lower cost of debt service with a sinking fund in place would permit more rapid redemption of the public debt. He understood that Congress was always under pressure from special interests to increase spending and reduce taxes rather than pay down public debt, especially when surplus revenue was available. He perceived that a conditional sinking fund with provision for suspension in periods of war and emergency would be politically more viable in the long run (Sylla 1999).

Hamilton's views of the sinking fund and public debt would prove to be prescient. Jefferson, Madison, and the antifederalists argued that Congress' hands should not be tied by the constraints imposed by Hamilton's sinking fund. In the years leading up to the War of 1812, Jefferson did allocate more surplus revenue to debt redemption than that called for in the sinking fund. But with the onset of hostilities, Jefferson had to increase borrowing and taxes in order to finance military spending. During the war, Madison found it difficult to issue new debt to finance military spending and was forced to resort to an inflationary printing of near monies to finance the war. Had Jefferson allocated surplus revenue to the sinking fund rather than to debt reduction, this would have provided for more stable debt redemption in the long term and would have enabled the government to finance military expenditures during the War of 1812 without resorting to distortionary increases in taxes or inflationary printing of money (Sylla 1999).

In the nineteenth and early twentieth centuries, sinking funds were of declining importance (U.S. Secretary of the Treasury). After the War of 1812, Congress replaced Hamilton's sophisticated funding mechanism with a fixed annual appropriation from ordinary government revenues. The various commitment mechanisms in the original sinking fund were eliminated, leaving funding to the discretion of Congress. Congress chose to redeem debt by less than that called for in the original sinking fund; nonetheless, the entire debt was eliminated by 1835, a decade later than that called for in Hamilton's 1795 report (Sylla 1999).

During the Civil War and again during World War I, new sinking funds were enacted to finance military spending. In these years, Congress used discretionary fiscal policy to make annual appropriations to the sinking fund accounts. In separate transactions, the Treasury issued new debt and rolled over the old debt. Thus, the commitment mechanisms and constraints on debt incorporated in Hamilton's original sinking funds were abandoned, and reduction in public debt was left to the discretion of Congress. In peacetime, Congress did reduce the debt, and the debt/GDP ratio declined in the long term. The commitment to sustainable debt was complemented by the commitment to stable prices under the gold standard (Poulson 1981).

The Great Depression launched an era of debt fatigue in which the public debt has trended upward continuously over time. There have been several periods when the debt/GDP ratio declined, most notably after World War II, and during the Great Moderation in macroeconomic policy in the 1980s and 1990s; the decrease in debt burdens in these years reflected not a commitment to reduce and eliminate debt by the legislature, but rather years of rapid economic growth in which the growth in GDP outpaced the increase in debt. It is not surprising that in these years, reports on sinking funds disappeared from Treasury reports altogether (Merrifield and Poulson 2016b, 2017a).

Hamilton's conditional sinking funds may appear to be a relic from America's history. Progressives dismiss the idea of a conditional sinking fund as irrelevant in modern monetary and fiscal policy, but later in this study we make the case for a conditional sinking fund to address the current debt crisis.

ABANDONING THE OLD TIME FISCAL RELIGION

The commitment to reduce and eliminate public debt was part of the Old Time Fiscal Religion, accepted by elected officials as well as citizens. The founding fathers may have debated how rapidly to eliminate the public debt, but there was a consensus that they had an obligation to do so (Merrifield and Poulson 2016b, 2017a).

Today the United States has abandoned the Old Time Fiscal Religion; elected officials have chosen not to commit to balanced budgets and sustainable debt levels, as they did over most of our history. Public choice economists explain this deficit bias as a problem of time inconsistency; elected officials cannot commit future governments to pursue fiscally responsible policy. But the abandonment of the Old Time Fiscal Religion reflects a more fundamental change in the ethos of fiscal responsibility. Over time the ethos of fiscal responsibility shared by citizens in Jefferson's time has been replaced by a Progressive ethos, undermining individual fiscal responsibility, and the responsibility of elected officials to balance the budget and reduce debt to sustainable levels.

The change in the ethos of fiscal responsibility reflected the transformation of the United States from a primarily rural agricultural society of individual farm families to an urban industrialized society. By the end of the nineteenth century, the United States had displaced Great Britain as the dominant industrial economy and center for international finance and trade. Rapid economic growth was accompanied by significant improvements in incomes and standards of living, but it also resulted in fundamental changes in the welfare of the different classes of society (Poulson 1981).

In the United States, as in other developed countries, the early industrial revolution was accompanied by greater inequalities in the distribution of income and wealth. Some aspects of urban industrial society diminished the welfare of working classes, including poor sanitation, pollution, and crowded living conditions. The Progressive ethos can be traced to the muckraker literature written in the late nineteenth and early twentieth centuries in which critics exposed the worst aspects of urban industrial society, and dangerous working conditions. By the end of the nineteenth and early twentieth centuries, these problems could no longer be ignored, and over time citizens learned how to better cope with poor working conditions in urban industrialized society.

Over the past century, the Progressive ethos has evolved in response to war, economic instability, and most recently a major pandemic. A major turning point in the evolution of this ethos was the Great Depression of the 1930s. It is at that point that the government began to abandon its commitment to balanced budgets and sustainable debt. While Franklyn Roosevelt paid lip service to balance the budget during the Great Depression, that was the first peacetime decade in which the federal government consistently incurred deficits and accumulated debt. The debt could not be explained by military spending in response to war as in the past; in fact, defense spending fell as a share of total government spending during the 1930s. Most of the increase in spending in that decade financed the social and welfare programs created by the New Deal. An ethos of individual fiscal responsibility was increasingly replaced by a Progressive ethos, best expressed in Franklyn Roosevelt's second inaugural address (Poulson 1981).

> Instinctively we recognized a deeper need—the need to find through government the instrument of our united purpose to solve for the individual the ever-rising problems of a complex civilization. Repeated attempts at their solution without the aid of government had left us baffled and bewildered. For without that aid, we had been unable to create those moral controls over the service of science which are necessary to make science a more useful servant instead of a ruthless master of mankind. To do this we know that we must find practical controls over blind economic forces and blindly selfish men. (Roosevelt 1937)

The presupposition of this Progressive ethos is that the capitalist system not only fails to provide opportunities for individuals to improve their welfare from one generation to the next, but it also exploits the working class and creates great inequalities in income and wealth between classes.

In the Progressive ethos, the Old Time Fiscal Religion is turned on its head. In the Old Time Fiscal Religion fiscal responsibility meant providing for one's family, including providing an inheritance to give one's children a start in life at least equal to one's own. Inheritance allowed families to share in their prosperity from one generation to the next. Wealth accumulation also allowed families to make charitable bequests at a time when private charitable institutions provided the societies a safety net.

For Progressives, individuals who accumulate wealth, and who are successful in fulfilling these fiscal responsibilities, are guilty of cupidity. The accumulation of wealth to be passed from one generation to the next generation is not viewed as a moral commitment, but rather a source of inequality in income and wealth distribution. Progressives view taxes on income and wealth, and especially on inherited wealth, as essential to achieving a more equitable distribution of income. Some Progressives would prohibit the inheritance of wealth altogether. Progressives see Jeffersonian principles of fiscal responsibility as relics of the past, irrelevant to the fiscal policies that should be pursued in a modern government.

The Progressive ethos provided the rationale for New Deal social and welfare programs. If redistribution of income and wealth through the public sector could not be financed entirely from taxation, then the government had a moral obligation to finance these transfers through deficits and debt accumulation. The ethos of public sector fiscal responsibility fundamental to the Old Time Fiscal Religion was abandoned.

The Progressive ethos that provided the rationale for the New Deal did not go unchallenged. Advocates for the Progressive ethos, such as the Fabian Socialist in England, were challenged by the Austrian economists, Friedrich Hayek and Ludwig Von Mises. The Keynesian paradigm was challenged by Milton Friedman and monetarist economists, and by James Buchannan, Gordon Tulloch, and public choice economists. These ideological battles surrounding the Progressive ethos continue down to the present day and will be further explored later in this study.

THE CURRENT DEBT CRISIS, DOES DEBT MATTER?

Since the Great Depression of the 1930s, public debt has grown continuously in periods of peace as well as war. Public debt now exceeds national income and is projected to grow to more than double national income by midcentury. The debt fatigue that began in the Great Depression culminated in an explosive growth in deficits and debt over the past two decades. This debt fatigue has had a profound impact on our economy, society, and institutions.

Does the current debt crisis matter? Posing this question seems to be an oxymoron; surely the massive debt accumulated in the United States is of serious concern. Some economists and a growing number of elected officials from across the political spectrum claim that public debt is not a problem and that we should stay calm and carry on with business as usual. It is important to understand why Progressives now take this view of public debt.

Modern monetary theorists maintain that as long as the interest rate on the public debt is below the rate of economic growth, there is no limit on the amount of debt the country can incur (Sawyer 2021). As a mathematical statement, this is true, but it is also a tautological statement assuming debt impacts neither the rate of interest nor the rate of economic growth. But, as debt increases relative to gross national product, this increases the risk of default on that debt, even in reserve currency countries such as the United States. After several decades of financial market repression in which the Fed has held interest rates on public debt well below the natural or market rate of interest, we are beginning to see the increased risk of default on U.S. debt reflected in higher inflation and higher interest rates (Merrifield and Poulson 2020; Poulson et al. 2022).

The view that public debt doesn't matter in the near term is held by many economists (Bloomberg Government 2022). For example, Furman and Summers (2020) argue that an epochal decline in the real interest rate in the United States and around the world requires a reassessment of public debt. They maintain that low interest rates are likely to persist in the aftermath of the coronavirus pandemic.

Furman and Summers (2020) offer three reasons why we should not worry about public debt in the near term. In a low interest rate, environment monetary policy is less effective as a countercyclical tool. There are limitations on how far interest rates can be reduced given a zero lower bound. Further, low interest rates may result in excessive leverage and financial market instability. On the other hand, fiscal policy may improve fiscal sustainability by increasing output and employment. In a low interest rate environment with excess capacity, there is likely to be less crowding out of productive private investment. They maintain that carefully designed fiscal policies that focus on productive expenditures and promote productivity advance and economic growth can justify deficit finance. They conclude that the issue is not how much debt is incurred, but rather how the borrowed funds are used. When deficit-financed expenditures increase GDP more than they raise debt and interest payments, this can improve fiscal sustainability.[1]

Unfortunately, we are beginning to see the negative impact of unsustainable debt accumulation on U.S. economic growth. The rate of economic growth over the past two decades has been significantly below the long-term average, and this retardation in economic growth is projected to continue in the coming decades. The federal bailouts during each economic crisis have created zombie enterprises and zombie state and local governments that survive only due to these federal transfers. The U.S. economy is looking more like the Japanese economy, which has experienced zombification and retardation in economic growth for two decades (Merrifield and Poulson 2020; Poulson et al. 2022). It remains to be seen what the post-pandemic economy will look like. Even if the sanguine view of Furman and Summers is correct and the United States achieves a soft landing, citizens will be left with a massive debt burden and a debt trajectory that is unsustainable under current law.

AMERICA SHOULD NOT ABANDON
JEFFERSONIAN DEBT PRINCIPLES

Progressives argue that we should abandon Jeffersonian debt principles. Furman and Summers (2020) defend increasing the public debt burden as fiscally responsible, using the analogy of a family that accumulates equity by owning a home rather than renting the home in which it lives, or a business that owns rather than leases its headquarters. In their view, the government faces the same choice when it borrows to finance appropriate categories of federal expenditures that pay for themselves in federal budgeting terms.

Jeffersonian debt principles suggest a different analogy than that used by Furman and Summers. If a family takes out a mortgage for a home that it can't afford, the costs may be borne by future generations of that family, as well as the current generation. If a business takes out a loan for a facility that it can't afford, the costs are borne by investors. In the private sector, irresponsible decisions to borrow may result in bankruptcy in which the burden of debt is imposed on the individuals who make the decisions.

When the federal government incurs debt, the burden is imposed on future as well as current taxpayers. The federal government is not subject to bankruptcy law; this means that when the federal government fails to repay debt, the burden of that debt is passed on to future generations of taxpayers. The failure of the federal government to be fiscally responsible is evident in unfunded liabilities accumulating not only in Social Security and Medicare but also in other federal programs as well. For example, Congress is now considering forgiving $1.6 trillion of debt in the federal student loan program (Committee for a Responsible Federal Budget 2022). Significant shares of the loans in this program are now in default, and a program of loan forgiveness would convert the entire student loan program into a new unfunded liability. Loan forgiveness has perverse incentive effects, resulting in a misallocation of resource to post-secondary education. Students would have an incentive to take on more loans anticipating federal forgiveness. Universities would have more room to increase tuition, anticipating that much of the increase would be paid for by the federal government. Loan forgiveness also has perverse distributional impacts. The major beneficiaries of loan forgiveness are middle- and upper-income families who can afford to send their children to college. Students who benefit from these loans often earn lifetime incomes far above that of the average American family. Thus, loan forgiveness is regressive, redistributing income to middle- and upper-income families from all taxpayers, including low-income families. Such an inegalitarian redistribution of income is difficult to defend on equity grounds. As Jefferson argued, this redistribution of income is especially repugnant when the burden of debt is shifted from the current generation of taxpayers to future generations of taxpayers, who have no say in the matter.

At the end of the day, we must confront the moral challenge posed by Jeffersonian debt principles. For Jefferson and the founding father, repayment of debt within one's own generation is a moral as well as an economic issue. Progressives dismiss this moral issue with the bromide that public debt is a debt we owe to ourselves. But, as James Buchannan argued, the citizens who pay taxes are different than the citizens who extend credit, including foreign creditors. Fiscal responsibility means that as individuals we are responsible for the debts incurred over our lifetime. As citizens, fiscal responsibility means that the public debt that we incur should be paid for by our generation, and not passed on to our children and grandchildren.

Before Congress fully abandons Jeffersonian debt principles, it should understand how European countries have addressed their debt challenges. In a referendum, Swiss citizens with an overwhelming majority approved an amendment to their constitution that requires the government to bring expenditures into balance with revenues over an economic cycle. The government may incur deficits in some years but must offset those deficits with surpluses in other years. Enabling legislation to satisfy this amendment constrained the growth in spending to the long-term growth of the economy. A "debt brake" was enacted, reducing the growth in spending required to balance expenditures and revenues. The "debt brake" has allowed Switzerland to cut the ratio of debt to national income in half. Today Switzerland has the highest credit rating, the second highest per capita income of any country. In short, the Swiss enacted new fiscal rules satisfying Jeffersonian debt principles, even though Switzerland is a neutral country that has avoided participating in wars. Similar fiscal rules have been enacted in other European countries and are incorporated in European Union fiscal rules. These new fiscal rules that focus on limiting deficits and debt levels as a percentage of GDP allowed European countries to respond to recent economic crises without massive accumulations of debt. We will explore this new era of fiscal rules and its relevance for the United States later in this study (Merrifield and Poulson 2016a, 2016b, 2017a, 2017b, 2020; Poulson et al. 2022).

The current debt crisis has renewed interest in fiscal rules in the United States including amendments to the constitution. The U.S. Constitution does not provide for a public referendum, as in Switzerland, but it does provide alternative routes to amending the constitution. Article V provides that Congress, with two-thirds votes, can propose amendments. Over the years many resolutions have been introduced in Congress calling for a balanced budget, and other fiscal responsibility amendments, but none of these resolutions has received the two-thirds votes required for Congress to submit the amendment to the states for ratification (Herrel 2022).

Article V also provides that citizens can propose amendments to the constitution through an amendment convention. "The Congress . . . on the Application of the Legislatures of two-thirds of the several States, shall call a Convention for proposing Amendments . . . to the Constitution." Article V provides that when two-thirds of the state legislatures (thirty-four states) approve a resolution calling for an amendment convention, Congress must call the convention. With a subsequent ratification of a proposed amendment by two-thirds of the states (thirty-eight states), the proposal becomes an amendment to the constitution.

In 1979, the Legislature of the State of Nevada passed the 34th Article V Application for the purpose of imposing fiscal restraints upon the Federal Government stating, To date 42 States have submitted related applications, calling for a convention for proposing amendment(s) related to imposing fiscal restraints on the Federal Government. New resolutions have been introduced in the states calling on Congress to fulfill its commitment under Article V to call for an amendment convention. This year, a Congressional resolution supporting this call for a fiscal responsibility amendment to the constitution, proposed by Representative Evette Herrel, Republican from New Mexico, and supported by the Republic caucus, appears to be gaining traction (Herrel 2022).

An Article V amendment convention would give citizens an opportunity to address the debt crisis directly, rather than through Congress. It is not surprising that Congress is reluctant to be constrained in its discretion over the budget by fiscal rules incorporated in the constitution. But that may be the only way that citizens can restore Jeffersonian debt principles. American citizens, like their Swiss counterparts, should have a say in addressing our debt crisis. In the concluding section of this study, we will explore this alternative route to rules-based fiscal policy in greater depth. Appendix C has model legislation for a fiscal responsibility amendment to the U.S. Constitution.

NOTE

1. The increased spending and debt incurred in recent years by both Democrats and Republicans has apparently been too much even for a Progressive like Larry Summers. He now argues that "These are the least responsible fiscal macroeconomic policies we have had for the last 40 years." https://Blomberg.com/news/articles/2021 -03-20/summers.

REFERENCES

Bloomberg Government. 2022. "Even Hawks See Room for Deficits-If Congress Could Curb Itself," https://about.bgov.com/news/.

Committee for a Responsible Federal Budget. 2022. "Cancelling Student Debt Would Add to Inflation," https://www.cfrfb.org/canceling-student-debt-would-add-inflation.

Edling, M. 2007. "An Immense Power in the Affairs of War: Alexander Hamilton and the Restoration of Public Credit," *The William and Mary Quarterly,* Third Series, Vol. 64, No. 2, April 287–326.

Furman, J., and L. Summers. 2020. "A Reconsideration of Fiscal Policy in the Era of Low Interest Rates," Draft, Brookings Institute, November 30, https://www.Brookings.edu

Herrell, E. 2022. Calling an Article V Convention of the States for Proposing Amendments and Stipulating Ratification by State Conventions, a Vote of the People, House Concurrent Resolution, 117th Congress 2nd Session.

Merrifield, J., and B. Poulson. 2016a. "The Swedish and Swiss Fiscal Rule Outcomes Contain Key Lessons for the U.S.," *Independent Review,* Vol. 21, No. 2 Fall, 251–274.

Merrifield, J., and B. Poulson. 2016b. *Can the Debt Growth be Stopped? Rules Based Policy Options for Addressing the Federal Fiscal Crisis,* Lexington Books, New York.

Merrifield, J., and B. Poulson. 2017a. *Restoring America's Fiscal Constitution,* Lexington Books, New York.

Merrifield, J., and B. Poulson. 2017b. "New Constitutional Debt Brakes for Euroland Revisited," *Journal of Applied Business and Economics,* Vol. 19, No. 8, 110–132.

Merrifield, J., and B. Poulson, editors. 2020. *A Fiscal Cliff: New Perspectives on the U.S. Federal Debt Crisis,* Cato Institute.

Poulson, B. 1981. *Economic History of the United States,* Macmillan Publishing.

Poulson, B. 2021. "Restoring a Jeffersonian Vision for U.S. Debt," Academia Letters, Article 3989.

Poulson, B., J. Merrifield, and S. Hanke, editors. 2022. *Public Debt Sustainability: International Perspectives,* forthcoming, Lexington Press.

Ross, E. 1892. "Sinking Funds," The Economic Journal, Vol. 3, No, 9, March 102–104.

Roosevelt, F. 1937. 2nd Inaugural Address, Franklyn D. Roosevelt Presidential Library and Museum.

Sawyer, M. 2021. "Keep Calm and Carry On: Responding the Higher Public Debt After the Pandemic," *Academic Letters,* Article 276.

Sloan, H. 1995. *Principal and Interest: Thomas Jefferson and the Problem of Debt,* Oxford University Press, New York.

Summers, L. 2021. "These are the Least Responsible Fiscal Macroeconomic Policies We Have Had for the Last 40 Years," https://Blomberg.com/news/articles/2021-03-20/summers.

Swanson, D., and A. Trout. 1992. "Alexander Hamilton's Sinking Fund," *The William and Mary Quarterly,* Vol. 49, No. 1 (January), 108–116.

Sylla, R., and J. Wilson. 1999. "Sinking Funds as Credible Commitments: Two Centuries of National-Debt Experience," *Japan and the World Economy,* Vol. 11, 199–222.

U.S. Secretary of the Treasury. Annual Reports. *Financial Report of the United States Government,* U.S. Government Printing Office, Washington DC.

Chapter 2

Understanding the U.S. Debt Crisis

DEBT FATIGUE

Debt fatigue in the wake of the coronavirus pandemic is a worldwide phenomenon.

Public debt has increased sharply, and in many countries it is increasing more rapidly than gross domestic product (GDP). In the Euro area, the average public debt-to-GDP ratio increased from 63 percent to 76 percent in 2020 and is forecast to increase to 79 percent in 2021. The primary deficit-to-GDP ratio in the Euro area averaged 7.2 percent in 2020, compared to a small surplus in 2019 (Organization for European Cooperation and Development 2021).

Debt fatigue in the United States has occurred over the last half-century and is projected to continue in coming decades. Figures 2.1 and 2.2 show the extent of the changes in the ratio of debt and deficits-to-GDP in the post-World War II era and long-term projections (Congressional Budget Office 2021).

The debt/GDP ratio fell during the post-World War II era until the mid-1970s. But although the government ran deficits in most years, these deficits were modest and more than offset by growth in GDP. From the mid-1970s until the early 1990s, the U.S. government consistently incurred deficits, with growth in debt exceeding the growth in GDP.

During the Great Moderation of the 1990s, the government incurred lower deficits and generated surplus revenue from 1998 to 2001. The debt/GDP ratio was actually reduced to levels comparable to the 1970s.

Current debt levels are a historical anomaly. Over the last two decades, the growth in U.S. debt has occurred alongside substantial economic shocks. Countercyclical fiscal policy in these years boosted deficits and the debt/

Federal Debt Held by the Public

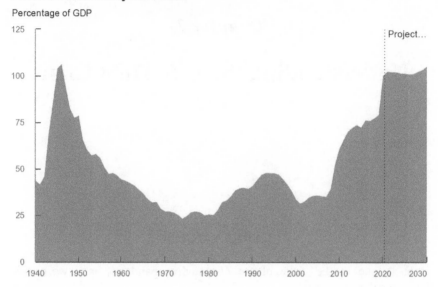

Figure 2.1 **Debt as a Share of Gross Domestic Product (percentage).** *Source*:
Congressional Budget Office (2020a).

Total Deficits and Surpluses (Adjusted for timing shifts)

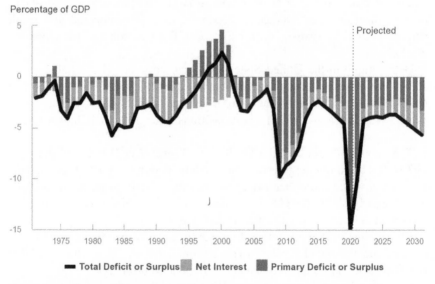

Figure 2.2 **Primary Balance as a Share of Gross Domestic Product (percent).** *Source*:
Congressional Budget Office (2020a).

GDP ratio. In the wake of the relatively mild 2001 recession, the first economic shock during this period, deficits were reduced and debt-to-GDP was stabilized.

This experience stands in contrast to the financial crisis of 2008, another major inflection point during the last two decades. This sharpest recession of the post-World War II era incurred greater deficits than any other during the period and resulted in a sharp discontinuous increase in debt as a share of GDP. In the years following that recession, deficits were reduced, but not eliminated, and debt continued to increase accordingly. The fiscal footing of the United States was not particularly strong even before the response to the 2020 COVID pandemic.

The Congressional Budget Office's (CBO) most recent forecast captures the impact of the pandemic on the budget and the economy (Congressional Budget Office 2022). The CBO estimates debt as a share of GDP equal to 98 percent in 2022, increasing to 107 percent in 2031. In the long term, the CBO projects that debt as a share of GDP will exceed 200 percent by midcentury.

The CBO estimates deficits as a share of GDP equal to 3.9 percent in 2022. In the long-term CBO projects that by midcentury deficits as a share of GDP will be 11.1 percent. Updates based on the most recent CBO data.

Over the past two decades, each major economic shock has been accompanied by a sharp discontinuous increase in debt; in years of economic recovery as well as recession, the United States has seen debt continue to increase relative to GDP. The fiscal rules and policies now in place have failed to prevent debt fatigue.

A Climacteric in U.S. Economic Growth

CBO (2021) forecasts that higher debt levels in the coming decades will be accompanied by retardation in economic growth. Potential output is now growing at a significantly lower rate than it did during the Great Moderation of the 1990s. This means that even when the gap between actual output and potential output is reduced, the economy will grow more slowly than it did two decades ago. This climacteric in economic growth is making it more difficult to bend the debt/GDP curve downward.[1]

From a historical perspective, the CBO long-term forecast appears to be very optimistic. The CBO forecasts assign probabilities of recession in every future year. However, these projections are based on current law and do not include policies that Congress might pursue in response to a major recession. The CBO does assume that actual output will fall somewhat short of potential output over the forecast period, but that is not the same as assuming a major recession. In recent decades, after each major recession, the United

States has recovered more slowly, with long periods when actual output was significantly below potential output. Each major recession has left the federal government with higher debt levels and with less fiscal space to pursue countercyclical fiscal policy.

IT'S THE SPENDING, STUPID

It is not a mystery why the United States has accumulated so much debt. Although many contemporary conversations about the national balance sheet may highlight the impact of deficit-producing tax cuts, data in figure 2.3 shows that spending dwarves them in terms of overall impact. In fact, the share of outlays in GDP grows significantly over time, while the share of revenues is relatively stable (Congressional Budget Office 2021).

The CBO estimates federal outlays equal to 31 percent of GDP in 2021. The high level of outlays in that year reflects federal spending in response to the coronavirus pandemic. This spending as a share of GDP is comparable to that incurred during World War II. The CBO projects that federal outlays as a share of GDP will fall in the next few years as the economy recovers from the pandemic and then increase to 23 percent of GDP in 2032. By midcentury the CBO projects that federal spending will increase to 31 percent of GDP.

Total Revenues and Outlays (Adjusted for timing shifts)

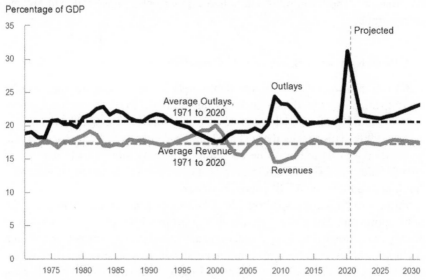

Figure 2.3   Total Revenues and Outlays as a Share of Gross Domestic Product (percent). *Source*: Congressional Budget Office (2020a).

Figure 2.4 shows mandatory spending accounts for a growing share of federal spending in GDP over the past decade and is projected to continue to do so in the coming decades. Mandatory spending as a share of GDP is estimated at 22 percent in 2021, reflecting the impact of the coronavirus pandemic. That is more than double the average over the past half-century. Mandatory spending is projected to fall in the next few years as the economy recovers from the pandemic. In the long term, however, mandatory spending is projected to continue to increase as a share of GDP.

The long-term growth in mandatory spending is driven mainly by the growth in entitlement programs: Social Security, Medicare, Medicaid, and many smaller programs. This entitlement spending reflects an aging population with a growing share of the population eligible for entitlement benefits. The growth in Medicare and Medicaid spending also reflects the fact that health care costs per beneficiary are increasing more rapidly than GDP.

Discretionary federal spending has been declining as a share of GDP over the past half-century and is projected to continue to do so in coming decades. Discretionary spending was boosted to 7.4 percent of GDP in 2021 due to the coronavirus pandemic. The CBO projects that discretionary spending will fall to 5.7 percent of GDP in 2031. This forecast for discretionary spending must be questioned because of the constraints imposed on CBO forecasting by the Deficit Control Act. The act requires that the CBO base its projections for discretionary spending on the most recent funding and then apply the appropriate inflation rate to project funding for future years. These projections assume that the rate of inflation will be below the rate of economic growth, an assumption that is questionable.

Interest spending as a share of GDP has been low for several decades, reflecting low interest rates. The CBO estimates interest spending as a share

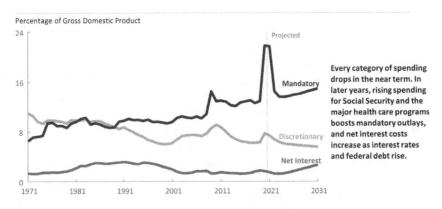

Figure 2.4   Mandatory, Discretionary, and Interest Spending. *Source*: Congressional Budget Office (2021).

of GDP at 1.5 percent in 2021, increasing to 2.7 percent in 2031. In the long term, interest costs are projected to increase due to both increased levels of debt and rising interest rates. By midcentury the CBO projects interest costs equal to 8 percent of GDP. Some economists forecast even higher interest rates and interest costs over this forecast period (Federal Reserve Bank of St. Louis 2018).

DEBT FATIGUE AND RISK OF DEFAULT

Future generations of Americans will bear the burden of debt fatigue in the form of direct taxation, the hidden cost of inflation, and higher borrowing costs. Higher inflation has emerged, and interest rates are now projected to increase and diverge even further from that in low-debt countries (Congressional Budget Office 2021). The CBO forecasts that the interest rate on ten-year Treasury notes will increase from 0.9 percent in 2020 to 4.8 percent by 2050 (Congressional Budget Office 2021). The CBO forecasts do not reflect recent increases in the federal funds rate by the Federal Reserve.

The higher interest rates reflect increased uncertainty and risk associated with U.S. debt. The CBO (2019) estimates that the average long-run effect of interest rates ranges from about two to three basis points for each one percentage point in debt as a percentage of GDP. The existing literature on this topic posits a nonlinear relationship between yields and debt levels (Turner and Spinelli 2012). Yields may not rise smoothly with increases in the debt levels; instead, they may rise gradually at first but eventually increase in a steep nonlinear way. At some point, credit markets respond by denying borrowers credit. Turner and Spinelli (2012) estimate that each percentage increase in government debt as a share of GDP raises the interest rate differential by about five basis points.

The impact of debt on interest rates depends on whether it is financed domestically or externally. In the United States, the share of debt financed externally has increased; as a result, the impact of higher debt on interest rates has also increased. This relationship holds even when considering the effects of quantitative easing on interest rates. Like the heavily indebted countries in Europe that are dependent on external finance, the United States has become more vulnerable to a financial crisis (Poulson et al. 2022).

The CBO notes that as debt levels continue to rise, a major uncertainty is the willingness of lenders to purchase U.S. debt (Congressional Budget Office 2019, 2020c). This has not really been tested in recent recessions because the unorthodox monetary policies the Fed pursued expanded the share of U.S. debt in the Fed portfolio. However, there is growing evidence that debt levels in the United States have increased to levels that risk default.

For example, some credit agencies have downgraded U.S. debt. S&P Global Ratings downgraded U.S. debt to AA+ in 2011 (https://www.spglobal .com/ratings/en/). In July 2020, Fitch Ratings downgraded U.S. debt from stable to negative, citing "deterioration in the U.S. public finances and the absence of a credible fiscal consolidation plan." Fitch questions whether U.S. policy makers will be able to consolidate public finances sufficiently to stabilize public debt after the pandemic shock. "Treasury flexibility, assisted by Federal Reserve intervention to restore liquidity to financial markets, does not entirely dispel risks to medium—term debt sustainability" (https://www .fitchratings.com/). Fitch further notes that the United States has the highest debt of any AAA-rated sovereign. Fitch has become pessimistic regarding U.S. debt even though the country has a higher debt tolerance level than other AAA sovereigns (https://www.fitchratings.com).

High debt levels often lead to debt crises, but there is considerable uncertainty regarding the debt levels where a country risks default (Reinhart and Rogoff 2009, 2010, 2012; Reinhart et al. 2003). IMF guidelines (2013) set public debt benchmarks at 85 percent of GDP for advanced countries, suggesting that debt in the United States has now increased to levels that risk default.

DEBT SOLVENCY AND SUSTAINABILITY

In the most basic definition, solvency means the ability to meet financial obligations in full and on time. When individuals and private firms become insolvent, they may face legal sanctions or be forced into bankruptcy. Governments can also become insolvent when they fail to meet their financial obligations.

The economic definition of solvency is based on a mathematical proposition. If the rate of economic growth exceeds the rate of interest, debt can grow without limit. In the United States, total debt now exceeds GDP, and Keynesians argue that even if total debt grows to some multiple of GDP, this is not a problem if economic growth exceeds the rate of interest. The flaw in this view is that higher levels of debt impact both the rate of economic growth and the rate of interest. Indeed, CBO (2021) projects that as the ratio of debt-to-GDP continues to increase in the long term this will be accompanied by higher interest rates and a slowing in the rate of economic growth. CBO also points out that printing more money that leads to hyperinflation is not a solution to our debt crisis.

The literature on debt tolerance suggests that debt in the United States has increased to levels that negatively impact economic growth (Poulson et al. 2021). For example, a study by the Bank for International Settlements (2011) finds that "At moderate levels, debt improves welfare and economic growth. But high levels are damaging." The BIS study found that when government debt exceeds 85 percent of GDP, economic growth slows. The report also found that beyond this threshold, a country is less able to respond to economic shocks.

An alternative approach to solvency is suggested by the market discipline hypothesis.[2] A crucial proposition in this approach is a nonlinear relationship between yields and debt levels. Yields may not rise smoothly with increases in the debt levels. Yields may rise gradually at first, but eventually, yields increase in a steep nonlinear way, and at some point, credit markets respond by denying borrower's credit.

We can dismiss a proposition in modern monetary theory that sovereign governments are immune from insolvency. The proposition states that sovereign governments can incur deficits and accumulate debt of any size. The proposition assumes that sovereign governments can meet their debt obligations by simply printing more money. We have seen the outcome when sovereign governments print money without constraint, in the hyperinflations experienced in Germany following World War I, and more recently in Argentina.

A pragmatic approach to debt sustainability focuses on the predicted public debt trajectory in the medium term. This is the approach the IMF uses in its Debt-Sustainability Analysis.[3] Basically, this methodology assesses whether the debt-GDP ratio is on a dynamically stable path. A debt limit is defined as a debt/GDP ratio where yields increase in a steep nonlinear way, and credit markets respond by denying borrower's credit.

Given the uncertainties in these estimates, a pragmatic policy maker would want to target a debt threshold well below the debt limit. Hitting a debt threshold should trigger fiscal policy reforms designed to reduce and maintain debt levels below the threshold to avoid the risk of default.

Debt thresholds are highly country specific. Some countries may default when the debt/GDP ratio is less than 40 percent. A major factor is a country's experience with debt default. Countries with a long history of debt default, such as Argentina, experience a deterioration in institutions, especially in institutions performing financial intermediation, and are likely to default at low debt/GDP ratios (Abbas et al. 2019; Badia et al. 2020; Debrun et al. 2019; Turner and Spinelli 2012; Poulson et al. 2022).

Empirical studies use historical records to estimate debt limits for individual countries, including countries that have experienced financial crises involving debt default. In the modern era, these empirical studies include countries experiencing fiscal stress forcing them to restructure debt through an IMF program, referred to as the early warning literature (Debrun et al. 2019; Abbas et al. 2019; International Monetary Fund 2013; Reinhart et al. 2003; Reinhart and Rogoff 2009; Reinhart and Rogoff 2010).

The Climacteric in Economic growth in Japan and the United States

Unsustainable debt levels have been observed in other countries, but further study is required to ascertain the levels at which the United States will experience similar stress. In this section, we explore the empirical evidence for unsustainable debt trajectories in Japan and the United States (International Monetary Fund 2020; Congressional Budget Office 2020a, 2020b, 2020c, 2021).

Figures 2.5 and 2.6 trace the trend in the debt/GDP ratio and economic growth in the two countries. In the early 1980s, the debt/GDP ratio in Japan drifted above 50 percent, but in the late 1980s, Japan was able to reduce this ratio. As shown in the following figure, during the 1980s, Japan experienced one of the highest rates of economic growth among developed countries, with average annual rates of growth close to 5 percent. In the United States, the debt/GDP ratio was also rising but was well below 50 percent. The United States also enjoyed rapid economic growth at rates near the long-run average of 3 percent for the post-World War II period.[4]

In the 1990s, there was a clear divergence in the debt trajectories of Japan and the United States. In Japan, that period marked the start of an unsustainable debt trajectory that continues down to the present. It is not surprising that in the 1990s, Japan also began to see slower economic growth. The average annual rate of GDP growth fell to about 1 percent, and Japan had several recessions with negative economic growth.

In contrast, the 1990s saw the United States restore a sustainable debt trajectory. It was an era of moderation in U.S. fiscal and monetary policies. At the end of that decade, the United States balanced its budget and reduced its debt/GDP ratio. Orthodox monetary policies reduced the inflation rate significantly. In that decade, the average annual growth rate was above the long-term average for the post-World War period (Debrun and Jonung 2019).

But over the past two decades, debt has been on an unsustainable trajectory in both Japan and the United States.[5] The debt/GDP ratio rose continuously in both countries, with sharp increases during the financial crisis and the coronavirus pandemic. The debt/GDP ratio in Japan reached 250 percent, the highest among developed countries. In the United States, the debt/GDP ratio now tops 100 percent, double the 2001 ratio. Japan and the United States suffered major recessions during the financial crisis and the coronavirus pandemic. In both countries, the recovery from the financial crisis was much slower than from previous recessions. The rate of economic growth in Japan and the United States is projected to recover in 2021, but then fall back below the long-term average rate of growth for the post-World War II period

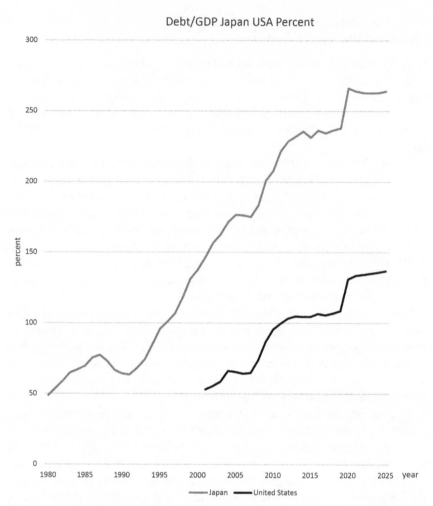

Figure 2.5 Debt/GDP Japan and the United States (percent). *Source*: International Monetary Fund (2020); World Economic Outlook Databases (October).

(International Monetary Fund 2020; Congressional Budget Office 2020a, 2020b, 2020c, 2020d, 2020e, 2021).

Many countries estimate debt sustainability using very long-term forecasts for the debt/GDP ratio. For example, the CBO's long-term forecast projects the debt/GDP ratio through 2051. The CBO estimates that the debt/GDP ratio will rise above 200 percent by the end of this period, comparable to the current debt/GDP ratio in Japan. However, it should be emphasized that this long-term forecast assumes current law. This is an unrealistic assumption, especially if the United States experiences fiscal stress with a higher risk of debt default. Thus, the long-term forecast by the CBO is not a prediction,

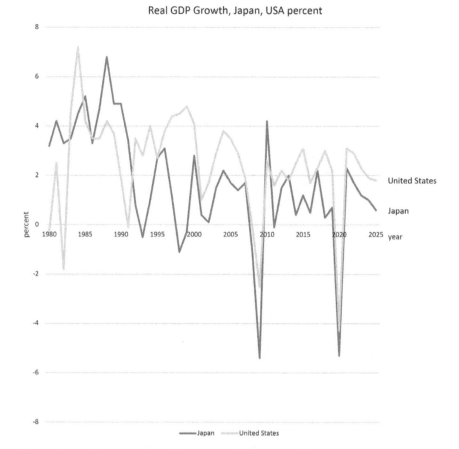

Real GDP Growth, Japan, USA percent

Figure 2.6   **Real GDP Growth Japan and the United States (percent).** *Source*: International Monetary Fund (2020); World Economic Outlook Databases (October).

but rather a pedagogical device, estimating an unsustainable debt trajectory (Congressional Budget Office 2021).

SUSTAINABLE DEBT TRAJECTORIES IN GERMANY, SWEDEN, AND SWITZERLAND

Estimates of a sustainable debt trajectory are shown in the following figures for Germany, Sweden, and Switzerland. In figure 2.7, there is an upward trend in the debt/GDP ratio for these countries in the 1990s. The ratio increased to 70 percent in Sweden, and 60 percent in Germany and Switzerland. The rise in the debt/GDP ratio during the 1991 recession was a wake-up call for these countries, especially in Sweden. Sweden experienced a sharp and prolonged

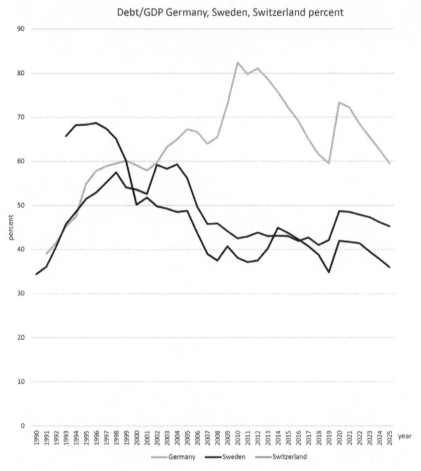

Figure 2.7   Debt/GDP Germany, Sweden, Switzerland (percent). *Source*: International Monetary Fund (2020); World Economic Outlook Databases (October).

recession accompanied by the depreciation of their currency. The perception in these countries, and especially in Sweden, was that the fiscal rules in place, including balanced budget provisions, were failing to adequately constrain deficits and debt accumulation. During the 1990s, these countries began to experiment with more stringent fiscal rules to constrain their debt growth. The most successful of the new fiscal rules was the debt brake enacted by Switzerland. Swiss-style debt brakes spread to other European countries, and eventually the European Union adopted one (International Monetary Fund 2020; Merrifield and Poulson 2016a, 2016b, 2017a, 2017b, 2018, 2020; Poulson et al. 2022).

The new fiscal rules enacted in Germany, Sweden, and Switzerland were effective in achieving a sustainable debt trajectory in the long term. Sweden and Switzerland reduced the debt/GDP ratio to close to 40 percent. What is surprising is that both countries were able to maintain the debt/GDP ratio close to that level even during the financial crisis and the coronavirus pandemic. The IMF forecasts that both countries will continue this sustainable debt trajectory in the coming years.

Germany's debt experience differs from that of Sweden and Switzerland over the period. The debt/GDP ratio in Germany continued to rise to more than 80 percent following the financial crisis. This was well above the debt limits set in EU rules. Although Germany enacted new fiscal rules like those enacted by Sweden and Switzerland, they circumvented the rules, allowing deficits and debt to exceed target levels. The sharp increase in the debt/GDP ratio that followed the financial crisis was a wake-up call for Germany to tighten their fiscal rules. Their fiscal reforms reduced the debt/GDP ratio to the target levels set in EU rules. The debt/GDP ratio again increased sharply during the coronavirus pandemic, but the IMF forecasts that the ratio will again fall to the 60 percent target over the forecast period (International Monetary Fund 2020; Merrifield and Poulson 2016a, 2016b, 2017a, 2017b, 2018, 2020; Poulson et al. 2022).

As shown in figure 2.8, improved economic growth in these countries reflects their ability to use improved fiscal rules to achieve a sustainable debt trajectory. After the sharp 1991 recession, these countries were able to restore rates of economic growth close to their long-term average in the post-World War II period. They experienced sharp contractions during the financial crisis and coronavirus pandemic, but growth rates are projected to recover in the coming years. As a result of their reforms, they avoided the long-term stagnation in economic growth experienced in Japan and the United States (International Monetary Fund 2020; Merrifield and Poulson 2016a, 2016b, 2017a, 2017b, 2018, 2020; Poulson et al. 2022).

THE CHALLENGE OF DEBT FATIGUE
IN THE UNITED STATES

Debt fatigue has put the United States on an unsustainable debt trajectory. Over the past two decades, major economic shocks have left the country with a greater debt burden and with a greatly expanded role for the federal government in the economy. The economic impact of the coronavirus pandemic has been comparable to a wartime economy; in responding to this recession, the federal government has incurred unprecedented amounts of debt and has all but abandoned rules-based fiscal and monetary policies.

The long-term forecast by the CBO is for a continuation of these trends over the next three decades. The fiscal policies pursued by the Biden

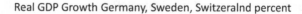

Real GDP Growth Germany, Sweden, Switzeralnd percent

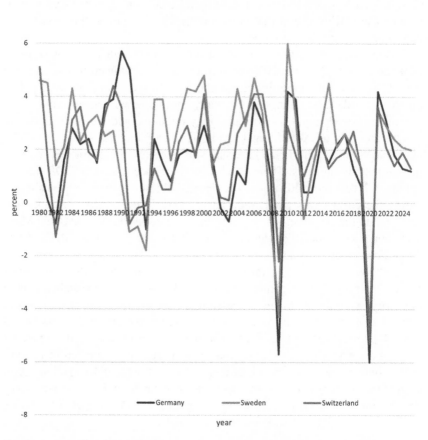

Figure 2.8   Real GDP Growth Germany, Sweden, Switzerland (percent). *Source*: International Monetary Fund (2020); World Economic Outlook Databases (October).

administration mean that the federal government will account for a greatly expanded share of GDP, and much of this expanded role for the federal government will be financed by debt.

The combination of debt fatigue and slowing in economic growth in Japan is the most likely path for the United States under current law. The question for the United States is whether there is an alternative path to the one projected in CBO long-term forecasts, and if so, how citizens can choose this alternative path. The experience in Germany, Sweden, and Switzerland reveals that an alternative path of sustainable debt is possible and that citizens in a democratic society are capable of choosing that path. In this book, we will explore the potential impact of Swiss-style fiscal rules on the U.S. budget and the economy over the next three decades. The dynamic simulation analysis reveals that with these fiscal rules in place, it is possible for the United States to stabilize and reduce debt to sustainable levels over the forecast period. With these fiscal rules in place downsizing the federal government, the United States can restore long-term economic growth. The empirical analysis also reveals how difficult this challenge will be, and why the United States is likely to continue to experience debt fatigue. The final section of the book explores issues of political economy in enacting Swiss-style fiscal rules in the United States.

NOTES

1. For a discussion of climacterics in economic growth, see Poulson and Dowling 1972.
2. See discussion in Debrun et al. 2019.
3. For a survey of the IMF literature on debt sustainability, see Debrun et al. 2019.
4. See discussion in Merrifield and Poulson 2020, and Poulson et al. 2022.
5. See discussion in "A New Generation of Zombie Enterprises" in this book.

REFERENCES

Abbas, S., A. Pienkowski, and K. Rogoff, 2019, *Sovereign Debt: A Guide for Economists and Practitioners*, Oxford, Oxford University Press.

Badia, M., P. Medas, P. Gupta, and Y. Xiang, 2020, "Debt is Not Free," IMF Working Paper WP/20/1, International Monetary Fund.

Bank for International Settlements, 2011, "The Real Effects of Debt," BIS Working Papers No. 352, September.

Congressional Budget Office, 2019, "The Effect of Government Debt on Interest Rates," Working Paper 2019-01, March, cbo.gov/publications/55018.

Congressional Budget Office, 2020a, *The Budget and Economic Outlook 2020-2030*, January 28, cbo.gov/publications/56020

Congressional Budget Office, 2020b, *Interim Economic Projection for 2020 and 2021*, May 19, cbo.gov/publications/56351

Congressional Budget Office, 2020c, *Federal Debt a Primer*, March, cbo.gov /publications/56165

Congressional Budget Office, 2020d, *An Update to the Economic Outlook: 2020 to 2030*, July, cbo.gov/publications/56442

Congressional Budget Office, 2020e, *CBO's Economic Forecast: Understanding the Slowdown of Productivity Growth*, NABE Foundation 17th Annual Economic Measurement Seminar. cbo.gov/publications/56531

Congressional Budget Office, 2022, *Long Term Budget Outlook*, July, cbo.gov /publications/57971.

Debrun, X., J. Ostry, T. Williams, and C. Wyless, 2019, "Public Debt Sustainability," in *Sovereign Debt: A Guide for Economists and Practitioners*, edited by S. Abbas,

A. Pienkowski, and K. Rogoff, International Monetary Fund, forthcoming, Oxford University Press.

Debrun, X., and L. Jonung, 2019, "Under Threat-Rules Based Fiscal Policy and How to Preserve it," *European Journal of Political Economy*, March, Vol. 57, 142–157.

Federal Reserve Bank of St. Louis, 2018, On the Supply and Demand for U.S. Treasury Debt, Economic Synopsis Number 5.

International Monetary Fund, 2022, *Staff Guidance Note on the Sovereign Risk and Debt Sustainability Framework for Market Access Countries*, August, http://www.imf.org/external/pp/ppindex.aspx.

International Monetary Fund, 2022, *World Economic Outlook Database*, April, imf.org/en/publications.

Merrifield, J., and B. Poulson, 2016a, *Can the Debt Growth be Stopped? Rules Based Policy Options for Addressing the Federal Fiscal Crisis*, Lexington Books, New York, NY.

Merrifield, J., and B. Poulson, 2016b, "The Swedish and Swiss Fiscal Rule Outcomes Contain Key Lessons for the U.S.," *Independent Review*, Vol. 21, No. 2, 251–275.

Merrifield, J., and B. Poulson, 2016c, "Stopping the National Debt Spiral: A Better Rules for Solving the Federal Fiscal Crisis," *Policy Brief*, The Heartland Institute.

Merrifield, J., and B. Poulson, 2017a, "New Constitutional Debt Brakes for Euroland Revisited," *Journal of Applied Business and Economics*, Vol. 19, No. 8, 110–132.

Merrifield, J., and B. Poulson, 2017b, *Restoring America's Fiscal Constitution*, Lexington Books, New York, NY.

Merrifield, J., and B. Poulson, 2018, "Fiscal Federalism and Dynamic Credence Capital in the U.S.," *ERN Institutional and Transition Economics Policy and Paper Series,* Vol. 10, No. 16, November 28.

Merrifield, J., and B. Poulson, 2020, *A Fiscal Cliff New Perspectives on the Federal Debt Crisis*, Cato Institute.

Organization for Economic Cooperation and Development, 2021, *Economic Outlook, Interim Report*, March, OECD Publishing, Paris.

Poulson, B., and M. Dowling, 1972, "The Climacteric in U.S. Economic Growth," *Oxford Economic Papers*, Vol. 25, No. 3, Nov. 420–434.

Poulson, B., J. Merrifield, and S. Hanke, 2021, *Debt Sustainability: International Perspectives*, Lexington Press, New York.

Reinhart, C., K. Rogoff, and M. Savastano, 2003, "Debt Intolerance," *Brookings Papers on Economic Activity*, Vol. 1(spring), 1–74.

Reinhart, C., and K. Rogoff, 2009, *This Time is Different: Eight Centuries of Financial Folly*, Princeton University Press.

Reinhart, C., and K. Rogoff, 2010, "Growth in a Time of Debt," *American Economic Review: Papers and Proceedings*, Vol. 100, No. 2, 573–578.

Reinhart, C., V. Reinhart, and K. Rogoff, 2012, "Public Debt Overhangs: Advanced Economy Episodes since 1800," *Journal of Economic Perspectives*, Vol. 26, No. 3, 69–86.

Turner, D., and F. Spinelli, 2012. "Interest Rate Growth Differentials and Government Debt Dynamics," *OECD Journal: Economic Studies*, Vol. 2012/1, 103–122.

Chapter 3

Debt Fatigue in the United States as a Failure of Macroeconomic Policy

EXPLAINING DEBT FATIGUE

Debrun et al. (2018) explore the causes for the growth of debt in high debtor developed countries, contrasting the experience of a high debtor country, Japan, with that of Germany, which has had more success in limiting the growth in debt. There are many parallels between the growth of debt in Japan and the United States; therefore, it is worth exploring the causes for debt growth Debrun et al. discuss in order to determine their relevance for the United States.

The authors suggest four possible explanations for why high debtor countries allow debt to grow at unsustainable rates:

> Implicit or explicit strategy of eventually defaulting. Confusion between trend and cycle: the authorities observe lower growth and adopt expansionary policies that fail to deliver the expected boost Conflict with the central bank that responds by raising interest rates. Lack of domestic support for fiscal discipline, which leads to destabilizing budgetary cycles when fiscal fatigue sets in. (Debrun et al. 2018, 16)

The first explanation can be ruled out for both Japan and the United States. For strategic reasons, it would be too costly for either country to default on debt. The best evidence for this in the United States is the extraordinary measures Treasury has taken to meet debt obligations in periods when actual debt approaches statutory debt limits.

The other explanations for debt fatigue involve failures in macroeconomic policy. For Debrun, an important question is whether monetary and fiscal rules in place have proven to be effective constraints on debt in the long run.

There is an extensive literature on this question for the United States, extending back to the seminal work of Milton Friedman.[1]

THE FAILURE OF MONETARY POLICY

The role of the central bank and monetary policy has emerged as crucial in determining the success or failure of fiscal policies designed to achieve sustainable debt. Milton Friedman made the famous statement that "Inflation is always and everywhere a monetary phenomenon" (Henderson 2021). Friedman's statement was based on his theoretical and empirical research. The relationship between money and prices is given in the quantity equation or the equation of exchange.[2] Empirical evidence for this direct relationship between money and prices was provided in the monumental work of Milton Friedman and Anna Schwartz (1963), "A Monetary History of the United States," tracing money history over several centuries. When Friedman was publishing these works, most economists were Keynesians and did not agree with him. But, during the stagflation of the 1970s, the evidence from the United States and other countries convinced most economists that Friedman was right (Henderson 2021).

The work of Friedman and other economists was the basis for rules-based monetary policy to replace the discretionary policies pursued by the Fed. In his seminal article, Taylor (1993) proposed a monetary rule, since referred to as the "Taylor Rule."[3] That rule would adjust the nominal interest rate in response to changes in inflation and output. He recommended a relatively high interest rate when inflation is above its target, or when output is above its full employment level, to reduce inflationary pressure. He recommended a relatively low interest rate in recessions to stimulate output and suggested that as a rule of thumb, when inflation rises by one percent, the nominal interest rate should increase by about 1.5 percent; if output falls by one percent, the interest rate should be decreased by about .5 percent. Since his original paper, Taylor and others have suggested numerous refinements to the Taylor Rule (Orphanides 2007; Davig and Leeper 2007; Taylor 2009, 2010, 2014).[4]

ABANDONING MONETARY RULES

Taylor (2010) follows in the positivist tradition of his mentor Milton Friedman by exploring the role of monetary policies during fluctuations in economic activity in the United States. He traces shifts in rules-based and discretionary monetary policy over several decades and finds a discontinuous shift in monetary policy beginning in the late 1970s and early 1980s when the Fed pursued an aggressive policy to reduce inflation. After decades of financial market repression, with short-term interest rates held below the real interest rate, Fed Chairman Paul Volcker introduced a policy controlling bank reserves directly. By slowing monetary growth, Volcker was able to reduce inflation rates from double digits to less than 4 percent by 1983. As shown in figure 3.1, the federal funds rate increased sharply, reaching a peak of almost 18 percent in 1980.

In the late 1980s and 1990s, Fed Chairman Alan Greenspan continued this Great Moderation in monetary policy. Taylor and others find evidence that during the late 1980s and 1990s, the Fed pursued monetary rules designed to stabilize inflation at a full employment level of output (Taylor 2010). While the Fed has never committed to an explicit monetary rule, Taylor maintains that monetary policy in the late 1980s and early 1990s followed a de facto Taylor Rule:

> It certainly appears that the changes in inflation and real GDP influenced the path of the federal funds rate. This evidence is especially important because monetary policy pursued during the period by the administrations of Ronald Reagan and George H. W. Bush are generally regarded as contributing to economic stability. (Taylor 1993, 203)

Taylor and other economists maintain that during this Great Moderation, growing confidence in Fed monetary policy led to expectations of low inflation (Taylor 2000, 2010; Eichenbaum 1997; Feldstein 2002, 2010). In this period, the federal funds rate approximated the "real rate" (see figure 3.1).

Taylor (2010) maintained that a shift back toward discretionary monetary policy occurred with the Fed's decision to hold the target rate of interest below the level implied by monetary rules during 2003–2005, and the interventions by the Fed during and after the financial crisis that began in 2008.

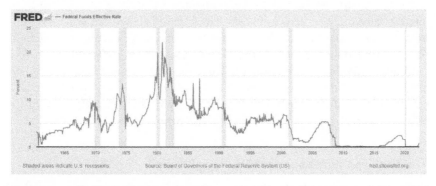

Figure 3.1 Effective Federal Funds Rate. *Source*: Board of Governors of the Federal Reserve System.

During the financial crisis, the Federal Reserve Board and Chairman Ben Bernanke introduced unconventional monetary policies (Bernanke 2008). This included lowering the federal funds rate to close to zero, engaging in large-scale asset purchases (credit allocation), and forward guidance. These policies were designed to encourage risk-taking and prop-up asset prices. The distinction between monetary and fiscal policies blurred, as the Fed purchased trillions of dollars in U.S. Treasuries and mortgage-backed securities.

One innovation in unconventional monetary policy introduced during the financial crisis would prove to be a fatal flaw. The Fed began to pay interest on excess reserves (IOER). This so-called "floor system" created incentives for banks to hold large excess reserve balances with the Fed. By increasing the demand for excess reserves, IOER broke the link between changes in the monetary base, the supply of money and credit, and nominal income. This innovation enabled the Fed to suppress interest rates without triggering monetary growth and inflation (Michel 2022).[5]

The floor system divorces the Fed's monetary policy from the size of its balance sheet. The Fed can purchase as many assets as it would like, while paying interest on any excess reserves created by those purchases. The fatal flaw in this floor system is that Congress now views the Fed as a free lunch. Congress can incur deficits financed by Fed purchases of Treasury securities, without triggering inflation. The explosion of debt since the financial crisis is not surprising as Congress has learned how to exploit this loophole in "unconventional" monetary policy. The Fed continues to pursue these unconventional monetary policies (Michel 2022). When the coronavirus hit in 2020, the economy collapsed. The Fed again pursued an unconventional monetary policy. The Fed reduced interest rates to close to zero and purchased more than $2 trillion in Treasury and mortgage-backed securities. In 2021, the Fed expanded its bond purchases to include corporate bonds and committed to maintaining the current pace of purchasing Treasury and mortgage-backed securities. Chairman Jerome Powell announced that the Fed plans to keep interest rates close to zero for years. He stated that "We are strongly committed to using our tools to do whatever we can and for as long as we can to provide some relief and stability" (*Wall Street Journal* 2020c, A1).

Chairman Powell's commitment to use the tools of monetary policy is a clear signal that the economic recovery from the coronavirus pandemic will be a long and difficult task. Until the recovery is complete, the Fed will in effect be monetizing government debt (*Wall Street Journal* 2020a).

The Lack of Consensus on Monetary Policy

In the second half of 2021, the U.S. inflation rate accelerated in excess of 5 percent, after a decade when the inflation rate fell consistently below 2 percent. In the September 2021 meeting of the Board of Governors, the consensus was to begin scaling back purchases of Treasuries and mortgage-backed securities. According to the minutes of that meeting, purchases would be reduced by $15 billion a month beginning in November, and purchases would conclude by July 2022 (*Wall Street Journal* 2021a, 2021b, 2021c).[6]

The decision of the Fed to conclude asset purchase suggests a return to "conventional" monetary policy. However, it is not clear that there is now a consensus in support of conventional monetary policy. For example, a research paper by a Fed staff economist takes issue with orthodox monetary theory that is the basis for conventional monetary policy. Jeremy Rudd (2021) presents a few equations and a few charts showing trends in inflation in the post-World War II period and reaches the startling conclusion that money doesn't matter for inflation. The hidden agenda for Rudd and other economists who reject conventional monetary policy is to justify the discretionary approach to monetary policy pursued by the Fed. The lack of consensus on conventional monetary policy suggests that the Fed will continue to pursue discretionary monetary policies as it has for the past two decades. "Mainstream economics is replete with ideas that everyone knows to be true, but that are actually arrant nonsense" (Rudd 2021, 1).

If the Fed continues to pursue discretionary monetary policy rather than rules-based monetary policy, we should expect those policies to reflect the biases of Fed Governors at any given point in time. The biases of the current Fed are clear; a high priority is placed on full employment, with price stability being a secondary concern.

Powell's aggressive monetary policy has been described as the "Powell Put," a reference to the monetary policies pursued by Fed Chairmen dating back to Alan Greenspan. After the 1987 stock market crash, Greenspan lowered interest rates and injected liquidity to prevent further deterioration in the market. This policy has been criticized as support for asset pricing that shifts the risk of investing from the private sector to the public sector (Miller et al. 2002).

There is a fundamental difference between the "Powell Put" and the "Greenspan Put." The aggressive monetary policy Greenspan pursued in 1987 was followed by more than a decade of conventional monetary policy, approximating the benchmarks set by the Taylor Rule. In his recent statements regarding monetary policy, Chairman Powell paid lip service to the Taylor Rule, stating that "Officials continued discussions about whether to tie their rate plans to certain economic outcomes, such as inflation returning to 2% and unemployment returning to its recent lows" (*Wall Street Journal* 2020c, A1).

The Fed is also considering imposing a cap on government bond yields (*Wall Street Journal* 2020b, B11). They would commit to purchase

Treasuries in whatever amounts are required to keep borrowing costs from exceeding a specific range. The Fed pursued this policy during World War II and in the postwar years to help the government finance war expenditures. The Fed commitment to this policy now would aid the government in financing increased expenditures in the wake of the coronavirus pandemic.

The unconventional monetary policies Chairman Powell pursues will diverge even further from the rules-based monetary policies pursued during the Great Moderation. During that era, the Fed increased the discount rate whenever unemployment fell to levels that economists believed would cause wages and prices to increase too much. Fed economists now reject this assumed tradeoff between unemployment and inflation. "Flattening" of the Phillips curve in recent years is used to justify the new approach to monetary policy. The 2 percent inflation target is now viewed as an average over the business cycle rather than a cap. The Fed now says that the discount rate will not be increased until inflation has reached 2 percent and is on track to exceed that target for some time, to make up for previous shortfalls. In February 2021, Chairman Powell stated that he does not expect inflation to reach such "troubling levels" and does not expect an increase in inflation to be large or persistent (*Wall Street Journal* 2021a, b, c). However, after inflation hit a forty-year high of 7.9 percent in February 2022, the Fed raised interest rates by a quarter percent and announced plans for six more quarter percent increases by year end (*Wall Street Journal* 2022a). Chairman Powell has since announced that they will raise interest rates by half percentage-point steps to levels high enough to slow the economy if such steps are warranted to bring down inflation (*Wall Street Journal* 2022b).

Chairman Powell has committed the Fed to pursue unconventional monetary policies until there is a significant improvement in labor markets. Fed economists have shifted the target for unemployment as well as inflation. They maintain that maximum strength in labor markets must take priority over controlling inflation. The target is not just measured unemployment, but also the millions of workers who are underemployed, and who have left the labor market (*Wall Street Journal* 2021a, b, c).

In 2021, Chairman Powell provided forward guidance that the Fed would maintain ultralow interest rates and continue to pursue unconventional monetary policies until "substantial further progress has been made." He also stated that those goals are "likely to take some time to achieve." The Powell Put sustained the increase in asset prices, a speculative mania reminiscent of the dot-com bubble. Speculation is evident not only in stocks but also across a broad cross-section of other assets, including real estate and commodities. The rise in asset prices reflects recovery of the economy from the coronavirus pandemic; but also, massive stimulus spending and unprecedented growth in money and credit (*Wall Street Journal* 2021a, 2021b, 2021c). The failure to commit to debt stabilization creates a fundamental conflict between monetary and fiscal policies; the Fed is now on the horns of a dilemma. If the Fed continues to accommodate expansionary fiscal policies this could boost employment in the short run, but this puts upward pressure on prices in the long run. If, on the other hand, the Fed fulfills the commitment to stabilize prices, this could result in higher levels of unemployment. Over the past two decades, the economy has experienced retardation in economic growth, with higher rates of unemployment. This means that the attempt by the Fed to accommodate the expansionary fiscal policies pursued by Congress is bound to fail.

Until 2021 the Fed was not forced to confront the horns of this dilemma. The unconventional operating monetary framework put into place in response to economic crises allowed the Fed to pursue accommodating monetary policy without triggering higher prices. But in 2021 the day of reckoning arrived. The new operating framework has fallen apart, and expansionary monetary and fiscal policies have triggered rates of inflation not seen since 1980. The inflation genie is out of the bottle, but the Fed continues to defend the unconventional monetary policies it has pursued over the past decade. In his semiannual address to Congress chairman Powell said that "We continue to expect inflation to decline over the course of the year as supply constraints ease and demand moderates because of the wandering effects of fiscal support and the removal of monetary accommodation" (*Wall Street Journal* 2022).

Some have argued that the Fed could normalize monetary policy by simply restoring a commitment to stable prices, as Fed chairman Paul Volker did in 1980 (*Wall Street Journal* 2022c). Paul Volker found that putting the genie back in the bottle was no easy task, but he did not face the horns of a dilemma confronting the Fed today. During the "Great Moderation" of the 1980s and 1990s, Congress fulfilled the commitment to stabilize debt. After two decades, in the 1990s expenditure was finally brought into balance with revenues, and the debt burdens were reduced. Current Fed chairman Jerome Powell, on the other hand, has committed the Fed to do whatever it takes to achieve the target levels of unemployment set by Congress. A failure to commit to price stability and debt sustainability means that the economy will most likely experience stagflation as it did during the 1960s and 1970s.

Today a strong case can be made for replacing the Federal Reserve Act with a charter establishing rules-based monetary policy. The charter should restore Fed independence and separate monetary and fiscal policies. It should replace discretionary monetary policy with rules-based monetary policy. There is controversy regarding the optimum design of a rules-based monetary policy. Some economists, in the tradition of Milton Friedman, argue for monetary rules designed to keep nominal GDP on a stable full employment path. A target rate of growth of the money supply would be set consistent with that rate of growth in nominal GDP. Other economists argue for the rules-based monetary policies first proposed in the pioneering work of John Taylor. These rules would rely on the traditional tools of monetary policy, adjusting the interest rates to achieve target levels of inflation and unemployment.

An alternative approach to monetary policy would eliminate the Fed and central bank control of the money supply entirely. Prior to the 1913 Federal Reserve Act, the United States had such a "free banking" system. In the free banking system private banks issue their own paper currency. These "banknotes" are then redeemable in underlying money, usually gold or silver. Some economists argue for a free banking system in which bank notes are redeemable in a standard bundle of diverse commodities. Milton Friedman argued for a free banking system in which bank notes are redeemable in a fiat currency fixed in supply.

Supporters of free banking argue that the commitment to stable prices is more credible in this monetary system than one which relies on fiat money and central bank control of the money supply. Given the commitments made by Chairman Powell, there is little likelihood that the Fed will be guided by the benchmarks set in the Taylor Rule and restore moderation in monetary policy, at least in the near future. If the Fed continues to pursue unconventional monetary policies as it has for two decades, it will have abandoned the rules-based monetary policies of the Great Moderation.

In his analysis of the Great Moderation, John Taylor poses a counterfactual hypothesis (Taylor 2000, 2009, 2010, 2014; Cogan et al. 2013a, 2013b). What if the rules-based approach to monetary policy that emerged in the late 1980s and 1990s had continued over the past two decades? He and his coauthors simulate the impact of a Taylor Rule on monetary policy and conclude that a Taylor Rule-based monetary policy could have avoided the destabilizing effects of the discretionary monetary policies pursued in this period.

Taylor and others argue that we can no longer rely on the Federal Reserve to pursue discretionary monetary policies to approximate a rules-based policy and that formal monetary rules, such as the Taylor Rule, should guide monetary policy. Subsequent research has explored different versions of the Taylor Rule as the basis for explaining monetary policy over business cycles in the United States (Orphanides 2008; Poulson and Baghestani 2012; Davig and Leeper 2007).

THE FAILURE OF FISCAL POLICY

Taylor recognized that commitment to a monetary policy rule such as the Taylor Rule was not a sufficient condition for price stability. If fiscal expectations are inconsistent with a stable price level, this could preclude price stability, even with a Taylor Rule in place.[7] He advocated a rules-based approach to fiscal policy as well (Taylor 1993, 2000). The Fiscal Taylor Rule (FTR) is a rule providing benchmarks to guide discretionary fiscal policy. The objective of the FTR is to promote economic stability over the business cycle, while maintaining debt sustainability in the long run.[8]

The FTR requires that a structural surplus is maintained over the business cycle. Application of the FTR means that fiscal policy is anchored in the sense that debt converges to a sustainable level in the long run. The nominal budget balance allows automatic stabilizers to support aggregate demand when actual output is below potential output, and for reductions in expenditures when actual output exceeds potential output. Taylor fits the FTR to U.S. fiscal data for 1960 to 1999 and finds that the FTR provides a good fit for the fiscal balance in the United States during the Great Moderation.

A number of studies have built upon the original Taylor design for an FTR. Debrun and Jonung (2018) recently generalized the Taylor FTR in a model that they also fit U.S. data.[9] Their model provides benchmarks for the nominal budget balance to provide for economic stabilization over the business cycle, and convergence of the debt/GDP ratio to a given target. They assume the 60 percent target for the debt/GDP ratio adopted by the European Union and the OECD. They fit the model to U.S. fiscal data for the period 1990 to 2017.

Debrun and Jonung (2018) find that in the United States, the actual budget balance in the 1990s exceeded the benchmark budget balance. In other words, the fiscal policies pursued during the Great Moderation were actually more prudent than that consistent with their FTR benchmarks.[10] However, over the past two decades, the actual budget balance was significantly below that consistent with the benchmarks. This suggests that over the past two decades fiscal policy no longer approximates the rules-based fiscal policy pursued during the Great Moderation.

Debrun and Jonung (2018) are somewhat sanguine regarding the prospects for a rules-based approach to fiscal policy in the United States. They argue that while the actual budget balance has been below the benchmark budget balance over the past two decades, there is evidence of convergence toward the benchmark after the financial crisis. They conclude that as the output gap closes, deficits will move back to levels consistent with long-term debt objectives. They seem to suggest that we should expect a return to a rules-based fiscal policy similar to that pursued during the Great Moderation.

Debrun and Jonung (2018) are also supportive of discretionary fiscal policy to stabilize the economy over the business cycle. The benchmarks in their FTR model provide for discretionary fiscal policy as well as automatic stabilizers. Taylor and other monetary economists are more skeptical of the effectiveness of discretionary fiscal policy in stabilizing the economy over the business cycle.

As Debrun and Jonung (2018) note, the simulation of FTRs that they and Taylor conducted is sensitive to data vintage, that is, the time period covered by their sample data. They have both chosen time periods that include the fiscal policies pursued during the Great Moderation. The Debrun and Jonung (2018) simulations end in 2017, prior to the impact of fiscal policies pursued by the Trump administration.

ABANDONING FISCAL RULES

We question the sanguine view that Debrun and Jonung have of the prospects for U.S fiscal policy. After the 2008 recession, the U.S. attempted to reduce deficits for several years but quickly abandoned these fiscal austerity measures, incurring trillion-dollar deficits, even in years of rapid economic growth.[11] The outcome is that for the past two decades, the United States has experienced debt fatigue, with debt increasing faster than GDP. The debt fatigue experienced in the United States stands in contrast to Germany and other countries in northern Europe that were successful in balancing their budgets and reducing debt burdens over the past two decades (Merrifield and Poulson 2016a, 2016b, 2016c, 2017a, 2018, 2020a; Poulson et al. 2022).

The long-term Congressional Budget Office (CBO) forecasts (2021) reveal that at least under current law the United States will incur greater deficits that will further deviate from benchmark budget balances required by an FTR. The debt/GDP level is projected to increase well above current levels and diverge even further from the 60 percent target for sustainable level. The United States does not appear to be returning to the rules-based fiscal policies pursued during the Great Moderation.

We conclude that over the past two decades, the United States has abandoned the rules-based fiscal policies pursued during the Great Moderation. If elected officials had continued to pursue those more prudent fiscal policies, the country could have avoided a debt crisis. If elected officials were guided by an FTR, we could stabilize the economy over the business cycle and reduce the debt/GDP ratio to a sustainable level. Because the United States has abandoned a rules-based fiscal policy, it will be even more difficult to solve the debt crisis.

There Is No Such Thing as a Free Lunch

President Biden submitted his 2022 budget to Congress and tweeted that it has a "zero price tag" and that "we are going to pay for everything that we spend" (*Washington Times* 2021). The president claimed that the proposed massive increase in spending would be paid for with higher taxes on corporations and the wealthy and that no new taxes would be imposed on anyone making less than $400,000.

President Biden's statements contradict analysis by the CBO and by his own Office of Management and Budget (Office of Management and Budget 2020). His budget proposed more than $5 trillion in new spending over the next decade, on top of the spending already projected in the CBO baseline budget. He proposed new taxes on businesses and individuals totaling $3.4 trillion. He also proposed cuts in defense and entitlement spending that would leave about $1.2 trillion to be financed with increased debt. Adding the interest cost on the new debt, his Office of Management and Budget estimated that the budget would add about $1.4 trillion to the total $28.4 trillion in debt over the next decade.

In March 2022, President Biden submitted his FY 2023 Budget. That budget assumes that his "Build Back Better" agenda to spend on climate change and social programs while lowering prescription drug costs and raising revenue is revenue neutral. The proposed budget includes substantial tax and spending increases. The Committee for a Responsible Federal Budget concludes that "It is impossible to understand the true impact of his budget or agenda without knowing how these tax and spending changes fit into it."

> Failure to make our entitlement programs sustainable and put debt on a clear path over the long run will ultimately slow economic growth, increase the cost of living, reduce the nation's flexibility to address future needy, leave benefit levels of important support programs in jeopardy, increase the ultimate risk of a fiscal crisis, and leave us vulnerable to future economic and geographical emergencies. (Committee for a Responsible Federal Budget 2022c)

A Broken Budget Process

The reconciliation framework used by Congress is a special budget process created as part of the Budget Act of 1974 (Committee for a Responsible Federal Budget 2021a). Reconciliation instructions are part of the concurrent budget resolution adopted by Congress. The instructions set cost or savings targets for Congressional Committees. The Congressional Committees then identify specific policies to meet these goals. The reconciliation bill can then be enacted on a fast-track basis. A reconciliation bill is privileged in limiting debate time. Most importantly, a non-debatable motion to proceed means that a reconciliation bill cannot be filibustered in the Senate—allowing the Senate to pass the bill by a simple majority vote rather than needing sixty votes to end debate. In the current Congress, this means that Democrats with a majority, and with the vice president able to cast a tiebreaking vote, can pass a reconciliation bill without a single Republican vote.

A reconciliation bill is allowed to either decrease or increase the deficit over the period covered by the resolution, that is, ten years. Provisions in a reconciliation bill that increase the deficit beyond ten years are subject to a sixty-vote point of order under the "Byrd Rule," unless the costs are offset by savings from other provisions in the same reconciliation bill.

Both the House and the Senate have advanced budget resolutions using the reconciliation framework (Committee for a Responsible Federal Budget 2021a, 2021b). In March 2022, Congress approved a fiscal year omnibus appropriations bill providing $1.5 trillion of budget authority, a 6 percent increase over FY 2021 levels. CFRFB (2022a) estimates that this increase in discretionary spending will boost the debt/GDP ratio from 107.5 percent to 109.0 percent in 2031. These budget bills are not constrained by any spending caps. CFRFB (2022b) argues that the spending caps in place in prior years should be restored to constrain both discretionary and mandatory spending.

Perhaps the most controversial part of these reconciliation bills is the claim by President Biden and some policy makers that the expenditures package will be fully paid for, without any increase in debt (Committee for a Responsible Federal Budget 2021a, 2021b, 2022a, 2022b). They claim that in addition to increased revenue from taxes and spending cuts, $600 billion in revenue will be generated from the dynamic feedback from higher rates of economic growth over the next decade. In fact, there is no basis for this claim. The Committee for a Responsible Budget estimates that to generate $600 billion in increased revenue the legislation would have to boost output by 3.5 percent by 2031. The CBO long-term forecast is for the rate of economic growth to fall back to about 2 percent over this period. In other words, this claim is true only if the legislation more than doubles the growth rate projected by the CBO and by other forecasters (Poulson et al. 2022).

The CBO has not scored the reconciliation bills in its long-term forecast. However, unofficial scoring of the reconciliation bills by independent think tanks challenged the assumption that the legislation will generate more revenue from dynamic feedback effects from higher rates of economic growth. The Penn Wharton Budget Model (PWBM) has been used to estimate the macroeconomic impact of the 2021 Senate Reconciliation package (Penn Wharton Model 2021). Because the PWBM dynamic scoring follows closely that used in CBO studies, it provides the closest thing to an official estimate of the macroeconomic impact of this legislation. PWBM is used to simulate the macroeconomic impact of this legislation using two different scenarios.

The first scenario assumes that non-health-related discretionary spending provisions expire at the end of the ten-year budget window to conform to the "Byrd Rule." In this scenario, GDP is reduced by 2.4 percent in 2031 and by 4.0 percent in 2050. Government debt is increased by 8.4 percent in 2031 and by 8.9 percent in 2050.

In the second scenario, the provisions of the Senate reconciliation bill are extended indefinitely beyond the ten-year budget window. In this scenario, GDP is reduced by 2.5 percent in 2031 and by 4.8 percent in 2050. Government debt is increased by 8.4 percent in 2031 and by 16.4 percent in 2050.

Under realistic assumptions regarding economic growth, the new reconciliation bills will add trillions of dollars in debt in the long term relative to that forecast in CBO baseline long-term forecasts (Antoni et al. 2021).

It is not surprising that legislators are using gimmicks to hide the true impact of reconciliation bills on debt to satisfy the "Bird Rule" (Tax Foundation 2021). One gimmick is to count increased tax revenues over ten years, but increased spending over a shorter period. For example, lawmakers are counting extension of the childcare tax credit for only one year. Expansion of health care coverage policies under the Affordable Care Act is counted for three years. If these measures are made permanent rather than temporary, they would boost spending by $1.2 trillion over the next decade.

Can the United States Restore Rules-Based Monetary and Fiscal Policy?

The debt crisis now confronting the United States is the culmination of decades of failed macroeconomic policies. Elected officials have virtually abandoned the prudent macroeconomic policies pursued during the Great Moderation. While the rules-based monetary and fiscal policies used during the Great Moderation were not perfect, they allowed the government to balance the budget, reduce debt burdens, and achieve price stability. These macroeconomic policies were accompanied by rapid growth in output and employment. All citizens, including low-income families, benefited from the increased economic opportunities and upward mobility that accompanied this rapid economic growth.

Rules-based macroeconomic policies have been replaced by discretionary policies. The reconciliation bill passed in 2022 is not constrained by the spending caps enacted in the Budget Control Act (BCA). Abandonment of the spending caps in BCA means that fiscal policies are now discretionary rather than rules-based, and these discretionary policies are biased toward deficits and debt accumulation. The legislature is about to pass the largest increase in spending, and the sharpest increase in taxes in decades. These fiscal decisions are made in the absence of transparency and accountability that was historically part of the budget process. Reconciliation bills reflect the outcome of a broken budget process. Monetary policies are now dominated by these expansionary fiscal policies. Citizens cannot rely on discretionary fiscal and monetary policies to achieve budget stabilization and debt sustainability. The monetary and fiscal rules enacted during the Great Moderation have proven to be ineffective in addressing the debt crisis. Citizens must now look to the new fiscal rules enacted in other countries that have proven to be effective in addressing their debt crises.

In the final sections of this book, we explore issues of political economy in enacting debt brakes, balanced budget amendments, and other fiscal rules. Debrun et al. (2018) conclude that the explanation for unconstrained growth of debt in high debtor developed countries is the lack of domestic support for fiscal discipline. Why do citizens in countries such as Switzerland support fiscal discipline, while citizens in countries such as Japan and the United States abandon it?

Feld and Kirchgassner (2001, 2008), Kirchgassner (2013a, 2013b, 2015), and Blankert (2000, 2011, 2015) explore Swiss debt brakes and provide a nuanced explanation for Swiss citizens' support for fiscal discipline using the concept of "dynamic credence capital."

The path Switzerland chose can be traced to a crucial court decision in 1998. In that year, the municipality of Leukerbad could not service its debt and turned to the canton of Wallis for a bailout. The court ruled that the canton was not liable for the debt incurred by the municipality, leaving Credit Suisse First Boston and other creditors to absorb the loss.

In his work, Blankert argues that this "no-bailout" rule has been the key to the success of fiscal rules in constraining debt at all levels of government in Switzerland. Each level of government perceives that it is autonomous and independent in their fiscal affairs, and it cannot depend on other governments for a bailout. To avoid default on their debt, municipal and cantonal governments enacted debt brakes, fiscal rules limiting the ability of elected officials to spend and incur debt. A debt brake was then enacted at the federal level through a referendum, with overwhelming support from Swiss citizens. Blankert maintains that the fiscal discipline imposed by these debt brakes has resulted in growing dynamic credence capital. Over time, Swiss citizens have gained greater confidence in the ability of their elected officials to pursue prudent fiscal policies within the framework of these fiscal rules.

Debrun and Jonung (2019) and Merrifield and Poulson (2016b, 2017a, 2018, 2020b; and Poulson et al. 2022) explore whether the fiscal rules enacted in Switzerland and other European nations can be effective in the United States. The question is why domestic support for fiscal discipline has deteriorated in the United States in recent decades. The public choice literature identifies deficit bias of elected officials, combined with erosion in fiscal rules constraining rent-seeking behavior as the source of deficits and unsustainable debt. The ability to finance expenditures with debt has increased the fiscal commons and created more incentives to engage in rent-seeking (Krogstrup et al. 2010; Wagner 2012).

Surveys reveal that the majority of U.S. citizens support rules that would balance the budget and set constraints on government expenditures (Guldens-huh 2021). Yet Congress has consistently rejected resolutions calling for a balanced budget amendment to the constitution. As in Switzerland, the path to enacting new fiscal rules may require citizens to exercise the powers of direct democracy provided under the constitution. In Switzerland, citizens were able to use the initiative provided in their constitution to enact debt brakes. While the U.S. Constitution does not provide for initiative or referendum, Article V gives citizens the power to propose amendments to the constitution through an amendment convention. Citizens have now passed resolutions in twenty-eight states calling for a balanced budget amendment convention. Given the failure of Congress to propose a balanced budget amendment, citizens acting through their state legislatures may be the path to a balanced budget amendment to the constitution.

NOTES

1. For a survey of this literature, see Merrifield and Poulson (2016a, 2017b).

2. The quantity equation or equation of exchange is MV = Py. In this equation, M is the supply of money, V is the velocity of money (which is inversely related to the demand for money), P is the price level, and y is real gross domestic product. If V and y are constant, then an increase in M must cause an increase in P.

3. On his personal website, Taylor provides the following equation for the rule he proposed. $R = 2 + \pi + 0.5 (\pi - 2) + 0.5Y$. Where R is the federal funds rate, π is the inflation rate, and Y is the GDP gap.

4. Some economists advocate nominal GDP targeting as an alternative to the Taylor rule (Sumner 2011, 2012; Hendrickson 2012a, 2012b). Koenig (2012) argues that nominal GDP targeting is just a special case of the Taylor rule.

5. Kurt Couchman points out limitations in the Fed's ability to use the new operating framework. For example, a limiting factor in the use of interest on excess reserves is the extent to which financial institutions believe that they can achieve higher risk adjusted returns in markets than they can get for (allegedly) risk-free return from the Fed (Couchman 2022).

6. A true measure the government's fiscal position would also include the risks associated with direct loans and loan guarantees (Couchman 2022).

7. As Sargent and Wallace argued, there might be inconsistency between monetary and fiscal policies, and this outcome is most likely to exist when the government pursues a discretionary fiscal policy (Sargent and Wallace 1975).

8. For a survey of this literature on rules-based approaches to fiscal policy, see Debrun and Jonung 2018; and Reicher 2009.

9. Debrun and Jonung (2018) generalizes the FTR in the following model:

$$bt = bt^* + \beta yt$$

where

bt is the nominal budget balance

$$bt^* = -ł^*t \ d^*FTR$$

1+ ø*t is a long-term objective defined as the nominal balance ensuring the convergence of the public debt to GDP ratio to a given number if the output gap is always zero ø*t is the ten year moving average of nominal GDP growth.

β is the deficit allowance for cyclical stabilization.

yt is the output gap.

10. Kurt Couchman points out that throughout the period of Great Moderation, the United States befitted from a stable and then radically improved security environment. The outbreak of war in the Ukraine has greatly increased economic uncertainty and the difficulty in normalizing monetary and fiscal policies (Couchman 2022).

11. Kurt Couchman views the post financial crisis from 2011 to 2014 as a huge, missed opportunity when the government could have implemented a rules-based approach to fiscal policy. He argues that this failure was the result partly due to the poorly crafted fiscal rules in place, and to a divided Congress.

REFERENCES

Antoni, E., V. Ginn, and S. Moore, 2021, "Reversing the Recovery: How President Biden's "Build Back Better" Plan Raises Taxes, Kills Jobs, and Punishes the Middle Class," Texas Public Policy Foundation, October.

Bank for International Settlements, 2011, "The Real Effects of Debt," BIS Working Papers No. 352, September.

Bernanke, B., 2008, *The Economic Outlook*, Testimony before the Committee on the Budget, U. S. House of Representatives, January.

Blankart, C., 2000, "The Process of Government Centralization: A Constitutional View," *Constitutional Political Economy* 11(1): 27–39.

Blankart, C., 2011, *An Economic Theory of Switzerland*, CESifo DICE Report 3/2011.

Blankart, C., 2015, "What the Eurozone Could Learn from Switzerland," *CESfio FORUM* 16(2): 39–42.

Board of Governors of the Federal Reserve System, 2021, "Federal Funds Effective Rate," FRED.

Cogan, J., J. Taylor, V. Weiland, and M. Wolters, 2013a, "Fiscal Consolidation Strategy," *Journal of Economic Dynamics and Control* 37(2): 404–421.

Cogan, J., J. Taylor, V. Weiland, and M. Wolters, 2013b, "Fiscal Consolidation Strategy: An Update for the Budget Reform Proposal of March 2013," Mimeo.

Committee for a Responsible Federal Budget, 2021a, "BBB Expirations Could Hide $1 to $2 Trillion of True Costs," October 21.

Committee for a Responsible Federal Budget, 2021b, "Reconciliation 101," August 13.

Committee for a Responsible Federal Budget, 2021c, "Reconciliation Unlikely to Produce $600 Billion in Dynamic Revenue," September 22.

Committee for a Responsible Federal Budget, 2022a, "What's in the FY 2022 Omnibus Bill," March 15.

Committee for a Responsible Federal Budget, 2022b, "The Case for Restoring Discretionary Spending Caps," January 27.

Committee for a Responsible Federal Budget, 2022c, "Analysis of the President's FY 2023 Budget," March 28.

Congressional Budget Office, 2021, "Long Term Budget Outlook."

Couchman, K., 2022, Comments on *Restoring Sustainable Macroeconomic Policies in the United States*, Mimeo.

Davig, T., and E. Leeper, 2007, "Generalizing the Taylor Principle," *American Economic Review* 97(3): 607–635.

Debrun, X., J. Ostry, T. Williams, and C. Wyless, 2018, "Public Debt Sustainability," in *Sovereign Debt: A Guide for Economists and Practitioners,* IMF Conference, edited by S. Abbas, A. Pienkowski, and K. Rogoff, International Monetary Fund, forthcoming, Oxford University Press.

Debrun, X., and L. Jonung, 2019, "Under Threat-Rules Based Fiscal Policy and How to Preserve it," *European Journal of Political Economy* March, 57: 142–157.

Eichenbaum, M., 1997, "Some Thoughts on Practical Stabilization Policy," *American Economic Review* 87(2): 236–239.

Feld, L., and G. Kirchgassner, 2001, Does Direct Democracy Reduce Public Debt? Evidence from Swiss Municipalities. *Public Choice* 109: 347–370.

Feld, L., and G. Kirchgassner, 2006, "On the Effectiveness of Debt Brakes: The Swiss Experience," Center for Research in Economics Management and the Arts, Working Paper No. 2006–21.

Feld, L., and G. Kirchgassner, 2008, "On the Effectiveness of Debt Brakes? The Swiss Experience," in *Sustainability of Public Debt*, edited by J.E. Sturm and R Neck, MIT Press, Cambridge, MA, pp. 223–255.

Feldstein, M., 2002, "The Role for Discretionary Fiscal Policy in a Low Interest Environment," National Bureau of Economic Research Working Paper No 9203.

Feldstein, M., 2010, "Preventing a National Debt Explosion," National Bureau of Economic Research Working Paper No 16451.

Friedman, M., and A. Schwartz, 1963, *A Monetary History of the United States, 1867–1960*, Princeton University Press, Princeton.

Goff, B., 1993, "Evaluating Alternative Explanations of Post War Federal Deficits," *Public Choice* 75: 247–261.

Guldenshuh, D., 2017, *Article V Convention Legislative Progress Report*, The Heartland Institute.

Henderson, D., 2021, "Inflation: True or False, Defining Ideas," Hoover Institution, May 20.

Hendrikson, J., 2012a, "An Overhaul of Federal Reserve Doctrine: Nominal Income and the Great Moderation," *Journal of Macroeconomics* 34(2): 304–317.

Hendrikson, J., 2012b, "Nominal Income Targeting and Monetary Stability," in *Boom and Bust Banking: The Causes and Cures of the Great Recession*, edited by David Beckwith, Independent Institute, Oakland, CA.

Kirchgaessner, G., 2013a, "Fiscal Institutions at the Cantonal Level in Switzerland," *Swiss Journal of Economics and Statistics* 149(2): 139–166.

Kirchgaessner, G., 2013b, "On the Political Economy of Public Deficits and Debt," *German Economic Review* 15(1): 116–130.

Kirchgaessner, G., 2015, "Direct Democracy: Chances and Challenges," CESifo Working Paper No. 5376, May.

Koenig, E., 2012, "All in the Family: The Close Connection Between Nominal GDP Targeting and the Taylor Rule," *Staff Papers* No. 17, Federal Reserve Bank of Dallas.

Krogstrup, S., and C. Wyplosz, 2010, "A Common Pool Theory of Supranational Deficit Ceilings," *European Economic Review* 54(2): 273–281.

Merrifield, J., and B. Poulson, 2016a, *Can the Debt Growth be Stopped? Rules Based Policy Options for Addressing the Federal Fiscal Crisis*, Lexington Books, New York, NY.

Merrifield, J., and B. Poulson, 2016b, "The Swedish and Swiss Fiscal Rule Outcomes Contain Key Lessons for the U.S.," *Independent Review* 21(2): 251–275.

Merrifield, J., and B. Poulson, 2016c, "Stopping the National Debt Spiral: A Better Rules for Solving the Federal Fiscal Crisis," Policy Brief, The Heartland Institute.

Merrifield, J., and B. Poulson, 2017a, "New Constitutional Debt Brakes for Euroland Revisited," *Journal of Applied Business and Economics* 19(8): 110–132.

Merrifield J., and B. Poulson, 2017b, *Restoring America's Fiscal Constitution*, Lexington Books: New York, NY.

Merrifield, J., and B. Poulson, 2018, "Fiscal Federalism and Dynamic Credence Capital in the U.S.," ERN *Institutional and Transition Economics Policy and Paper Series* 10(16). November 28.

Merrifield, J., and B. Poulson, 2020a, *A Fiscal Cliff: New Perspectives on the U.S. Federal Debt Crisis*, Cato Institute.

Michel, N., 2022, "Monetary Policy and the Worsening U.S. Debt Crisis," in *Public Debt Sustain Ability: International Perspectives*, edited by Poulson et al., Lexington Press, forthcoming.

Miller, M., P. Weller, and C. Zhuang, 2002, "Moral Hazard and the U.S. Stock Market: Analyzing the 'Greenspan Put,'" *The Economic Journal* 112(478): C171–C186.

Office of Management and Budget, 2020, "President's Fiscal Year (FY) 2021 Budget, Economic and Budget Analysis,"

Organization for Economic Cooperation and Development, 2013, "General Government Fiscal Balance" in *Government at a Glance* 2013, OECD Publishing, Paris.

Orphanides, A., 2007, "Taylor Rules," *The New Palgrave Dictionary of Economics*, 2nd Edition v. 8: 2000–2004.

Penn Wharton Budget Model, 2021, "The Macroeconomic Effects of the August 2021 Senate Budget Reconciliation Package," August 9.

Poulson, B., and H. Baghestani, 2012, "Federal Reserve Forecasts of Nonfarm Pay-roll Employment across Different Political Regimes," *Journal of Economic Studies* 39(3): 280–289.

Poulson, B., J. Merrifield, and S. Hanke, 2022, *Debt Sustainability: International Perspectives,* Lexington Books, forthcoming.

Reicher, C., 2009, "Fiscal Taylor Rules in the Postwar United States," Kiel Working Papers. No. 1509.

Rudd, J., 2021, "Why Do We Think That Inflation Expectations Matter for Inflation? (and Should We?)," Finance Economic Discussion Series 2021-062, Division of Research and Statistics and Monetary Affairs, Federal Reserve Board, Washington DC.

Sargent, T., and N. Wallace, 1975, "Rational Expectations, the Optimal Monetary Instrument, and the Optimal Money Supply Rule," *Journal of Political Economy* 83: 241–254.

Schaechter, A., T. Kinda, N. Budina, and A. Weber, 2012, "Fiscal Rules in Response to the Crisis- toward the Next Generation Fiscal Rules, a New Dataset," International Monetary Fund, Working Papers WP/12/187, July.

Sumner, S., 2011, "Re-targeting the Fed," *National Affairs*, No. 9: 79–96.

Sumner, S., 2012, "The Case for Nominal GDP Targeting," Mercatus Center at George Mason University, Arlington, VA.

Tax Foundation, 2021, "Build Back Better Act: Details & Analysis of the $3.5 Trillion Budget Reconciliation Bill," September.

Taylor, J., 1993, "Discretion versus Policy Rules in Practice," *Carnegie Rochester Conference Series on Public Policy* 39: 195–214.

Taylor, J., 2000, "Reassessing Discretionary Fiscal Policy," *The Journal of Economic Perspectives* 14(3): 21–36.

Taylor, J., 2009, *Getting off Track: How Government Actions and Interventions Caused, Prolonged, and Worsened the Financial Crisis,* Hoover Institution Press, Stanford.

Taylor, J., 2010, "Swings in the Rules-discretion Balance," Conference on the Occasion of the 40th Anniversary of Microeconomic Foundations of Employment and Inflation Theory. Columbia University Press, New York.

Taylor, J., 2014, "The Fed Needs to Return to Monetary Rules," *Wall Street Journal* (June 27. A13).

Wagner, R., 2012, "Rationality, Political Economy, and Fiscal Responsibility: Wrestling with Tragedy in the Fiscal Commons," *Constitutional Political Economy* 23: 261–277.

Washington Times, 2021, "President Biden Says Spending Bill will Have a 'Zero Price Tag," Friday, September 24.

Wall Street Journal, 2020a, "Federal Reserve Says It's Launching New Corporate Bond-buying Program," Tuesday June 16, 8A.

Wall Street Journal, 2020b, "Fed Looks to Put Cap on Treasury Yields," Friday June 12, B11.

Wall Street Journal, 2020c, "Fed Vows Low Rate for Years," Thursday June 11, A1–A2.

Wall Street Journal, 2021a, "Haggling to Resume on Package," Monday October 18, A4.

Wall Street Journal, 2021b, "How the Fed Finances U.S. Debt," Thursday October 14, A19.

Wall Street Journal, 2021c, "Inflation Orthodoxy Questioned Inside the Fed," Thursday October 14, A2.

Wall Street Journal, 2021d, "Minutes Show More Consensus on Taper," Thursday October 14, A2.

Wall Street Journal, 2022a, "Let's Start Getting Interest Rates Up," Tuesday March 15, A19.

Wall Street Journal, 2022b, "Powell Says Fed Will Consider More-Aggressive Interest Rate Increases to Reduce Inflation," March 21.

Wall Street Journal, 2022c, "Inflation, Deficits and Paul Volcker," March 3.

Woodford, M., 2001, "Fiscal Requirements for Price Stability," *Journal of Money Credit and Banking* 33(3): 669–728.

Chapter 4

The Zombies Are Coming

DEBT FATIGUE, AN INTERNATIONAL PHENOMENON

In the post-World War II period, virtually every country has at some point experienced debt fatigue, allowing debt to increase more rapidly than gross domestic product (GDP). By definition, a country's debt cannot exceed the present value of future surpluses (net of interest). In the long term, countries that experience debt fatigue must pursue more prudent policies to reduce debt to sustainable levels, but imposing limits on debt has proven to be very controversial in recent years. Some countries have pursued fiscal consolidation policies stabilizing and reducing the ratio of debt to GDP. These countries have been able to respond to economic shocks without great fiscal stress, while sustaining economic growth. Other countries that have failed to pursue policies of fiscal consolidation have encountered fiscal stress and slowing economic growth as the ratio of debt to GDP increased. These differences reflect each country's unique experience in responding to major shocks—the financial crisis of 2008 and the coronavirus pandemic in 2020.

Legislators across the globe have responded to these economic shocks by authorizing massive fiscal stimulus policies. Central banks have followed the lead of the U.S. Federal Reserve Bank in pursuing nonconventional monetary policies, cutting interest rates and buying securities in the open market. These macroeconomic policies were designed to shore up the financial system and stabilize their economies. But much of the money created by global governments in response to the coronavirus pandemic has now leaked into asset prices. The appetite for risk and irrational exuberance is evident across a wide range of asset classes. The speculative bubble includes stocks, real estate, commodities, and esoteric assets such as bitcoin. Investors have poured unprecedented amounts of money into mutual and exchange-traded funds tracking global stocks' values in Europe and Asia, as well as the United States have hit all-time highs. Even in Japan where stocks have been depressed for decades, the Nikkei index increased above 3,000 for the first time in 30 years.

Despite the massive stimulus programs launched in the United States in response to the financial crisis and the coronavirus pandemic, the United States continues to experience slowing economic growth. A new policy framework has allowed the Fed to provide substantial monetary stimulus through low federal funds rates, large-scale asset purchases, and other refinancing operations. But the Fed has not been able to achieve target levels for inflation and unemployment. The post-stimulus U.S. economy is projected to continue to experience slowing in productivity change and economic growth.

The underperformance of the U.S. economy appears increasingly like Japan's lost decades. For three decades, Japan has experienced slowing economic growth. The Japan government has incurred deficits over this entire period, leaving it with the highest debt levels in the world. The Bank of Japan has pursued nonconventional monetary policies, purchased massive quantities of public and private securities, and pushed interest rates well into negative territory. These macroeconomic policies have failed to jump-start the Japanese economy, and the Bank of Japan (BOJ) appears to have reached the limit in pursuing nonconventional monetary policy. BOJ economists are not likely to push interest rates even further into negative territory, and they have given up any hope of hitting the 2 percent target rate of inflation in the near term. The BOJ is now undertaking a major review of monetary policy, recognizing that a major shift is now required. But it is not clear what that new policy might be (*Wall Street Journal* 2021, March 10 B12).

The United States and Japan are not unique in experiencing retardation in economic growth; these trends are evident in European countries and other developed countries as well.

ZOMBIE ENTERPRISES, A SYMPTOM OF DEBT FATIGUE

The term "zombification" was first used by Caballero et al. (2008) in their analysis of Japan's lost decade of the 1990s. Different criteria have been used to identify zombie enterprises. For instance, Banaerjee and Hofmann (2018) define zombie firms as ones that are unable to cover debt servicing costs from current profits over an extended period of time. Another criterion in this literature is whether a firm is receiving subsidized credit at rates below that of the most creditworthy firms (Cabballro et al. 2008; Acharya et al. 2018). Banerjee and Hofmann (2018, 2020) argue that a firm may receive subsidized credit for reasons other than insolvency.

A simple definition of a zombie enterprise is one that is insolvent, that is, unable to meet financial obligations in full and on time. Zombie enterprises are kept afloat only due to federal bailouts; and as a result, new, more efficient firms do not enter. This misallocation of resources is causing slowed productivity and economic growth. Solving the debt crisis is more difficult because of the higher levels of debt and slower economic growth.

Zombie lending is defined as the extension of cheap credit to weak firms by weakly capitalized banks. Zombification results when nonviable firms are kept afloat. There is growing evidence that zombification contributes to a "climacteric" or deceleration in economic growth (Caballro et al. 2008; Giannetti and Simonov 2013; Acharya et al. 2019; Borio and Hofman 2017; and Poulson et al. 2022).

There is some confusion between zombification and secular stagnation. The term secular stagnation refers to the Neo-Keynesian argument that private markets are not able to sustain aggregate demand at full employment levels of output. Keynesians argue that fiscal and monetary stimulus is required to offset inadequate demand and achieve full employment levels of output. The literature on zombification suggests that, at least in recent years, the expansionary fiscal and monetary responses to economic shocks are the source of retardation in productivity change and economic growth. Zombification is a result of failed macroeconomic policies, not a private market failure.

Interest in zombie enterprises has increased due to the rising number of such firms since the late 1980s. Recent studies find an upward trend in the incidence of zombie enterprises linked to economic downturns that are not fully reversed in subsequent recoveries (McGowen et al. 2017; Banerjee and Hofmann 2018, 2020; *Financial Times* 2021; Gagnon 2020; Kalemli-Ozcan et al. 2019). These studies find a discontinuous increase in zombie firms in advanced economies following the financial crisis in 2008. Preliminary data for several countries, including the United States, suggest that the coronavirus pandemic has been accompanied by a similar discontinuous rise in zombie firms (Jorda et al. 2020).

A number of studies explore the causes for zombie firms. Financial repression, which holds interest rates low over long periods of time, may cause corporate zombification (Sharam 2019; Taylor 2019; and Armstrong 2020). These studies find that weak banks have an incentive to roll over loans to nonviable firms rather than absorbing losses when they default on their loans (Story et al. 2017; Schivardi et al. 2017). Other studies point to the drop in interest rates after each business cycle, which reduces the pressure on zombie firms to restructure or exit the industry (Borio and Hofmann 2017; Banerjee and Hofmann 2018, 2020). Finally, when bankruptcy laws inhibit corporate restructuring, countries have a higher prevalence of zombie firms (Andrew and Petroukis 2017).

In the empirical literature on zombie enterprises, the extension of zombie credit impacts firms in several ways. These studies compare industries with high versus low percentages of zombie enterprises. With zombie credit, some weaker firms that would have exited remain in the industry, while some entrant firms choose not to enter. The existence of zombie credit causes a reduction in firm markups, prices, value added, and productivity. Following the extension of zombie credit, there is an increase in the number of active firms, firm input costs, and aggregate sales.

The economic impact of zombie firms at the micro level has been explored in several studies. Banerjee and Hofmann (2018, 2020) find evidence that the survival of zombie firms tends to crowd out entry and investment by healthy firms. They find that in the years before they become zombies, these firms experience falling profitability, productivity, employment, and investment. They also find that these firms are highly leveraged and are able to stay afloat by receiving subsidized credit and disposing of assets. The zombie firms have a high probability of exiting the market through bankruptcy and takeover.

The link between zombie firms and retardation in productivity and economic growth is identified in several studies. Zombie firms are less efficient, and a higher share of zombie firms in an industry tends to reduce aggregate productivity (Caballro et al. 2008; Mcgowen et al. 2017; Banerjee and Hofmann 2018, 2020). The zombie firms crowd out more productive firms by locking in resources (so-called congestion effects). They do so by depressing the price of the firm's products and by competing for resources, which increases wages and funding costs. In recent years, because of the increased reliance on unconventional monetary policy, the rising trend of zombie firms has contributed to deflation. Acharya et al. (2000) find a number of links between zombie firms and deceleration in productivity and economic growth, due in part to the spillover effects of zombie firms to non-zombie firms. They find that industries with a large share of zombie firms (1) have more active firms, (2) have lower firm exit and entry rates, (3) have lower average markups, (4) have high average material costs, (5) experience higher average sales growth, and (6) have lower value added. It is clear that zombification significantly misallocates capital and labor resources. Industries with a large share of zombie firms tend to have excess capacity, and lower average net investment and labor productivity. These industries experience retardation in the rate of growth in output and productivity.

ZOMBIFICATION IN JAPAN

There is an extensive literature exploring how unconventional monetary policies create zombie enterprises, and the impact of this zombification on economic activity. Japan was the first country to enact unconventional monetary policies resulting in zombification. The so-called "lost decades" in Japan extend back to the early 1990s, and the BOJ introduced the first quantitative easing policy in 2000. Most central banks, including the Federal Reserve Bank, did not pursue such unconventional monetary policies until the financial crisis in 2008. The BOJ has continued to pursue unconventional monetary policy down to the present, including negative interest rate policies, large-scale assets purchases, yield curve control, and forward guidance.

The impact of unconventional monetary policies in creating zombie enterprises was first documented in Japan (Hoshi 2006; Caballero et al. 2008). More recent studies have explored the transmission mechanism from unconventional monetary policies to zombie firms in Japan (Gagnon 2020; Lubik and Schwartzman 2020; and Hong et al. 2021). These studies show how unproductive firms are kept afloat by unconventional monetary policy.

A prevalence of zombie enterprises results in low investment, slower productivity advance, and slowing in the rate of growth in output and employment. The Japanese government has encouraged the continued financing or "evergreening" of loans to insolvent firms by banks. Some studies show how the preservation of inefficient and unprofitable firms negatively impacts aggregate productivity advance in Japan. The productivity loss from subsidized lending to zombie enterprises in Japan was estimated at about 1 percent annually in the 1990s (Lam and Shin 2012; Kwon et al. 2015; Hong et al. 2021). The negative impact of unconventional monetary policy on Japanese financial markets is explored in Ugai 2007; Oda and Ueda 2007; Kimura and Small 2006; Lam 2011; and Ueda 2011; and Oda and Kazuo 2007.

An important factor contributing to zombification in Japan is a generous public credit guarantee scheme. Most Japanese firms rely on a long-term bank-firm relationship for financing. During the financial crisis and more recently during the coronavirus pandemic, about 1.5 million companies received credit guarantees through the Small and Medium Size Credit Assurance Act. This law shifts the risk of bank loans to the government (Fukuda 2001; Ono and Vesugi 2014; Colacelli and Hong 2019; Hong et al. 2020).

ZOMBIFICATION COMES TO THE UNITED STATES

McGowan et al. (2017) found evidence for an increase in the share of zombie firms (the zombie share) across a broad cross-section of developed countries following the financial crisis. More recently, Banaerjee and Hoffman's studies (2018, 2020) show a ratcheting up of the zombie share of firms in the wake of economic downturns in developed countries over several decades extending back to the 1980s.

Favara et al. (2021) define zombie firms as those that are highly leveraged and unprofitable. In contrast to other studies, they require that zombie firms not only have limited debt capacity but also have bleak prospects. Figure 4.1 shows their estimate of the share of zombie firms in the United States. They find that the share of zombie firms fluctuates in a narrow range and closely tracks business cycles and industry dynamics. They find a lower share of zombie firms than that reported in the financial press and in other academic studies.

The Leuthold Group defines zombie firms as "Companies where profits are less than interest paid on their debt for at least three years" (*Financial Times* 2021). They find that during the Great Moderation of the 1990s, the zombie share was less than 10 percent, and by the end of that decade, it had fallen to 6 percent. The share of zombie firms peaked at17 percent during the dotcom bubble in 2000. In the years following the dotcom bubble, the zombie share fell below 10 percent. During the financial crisis in 2008, the zombie shares again increased to 10 percent and remained at about that level for the next decade. In the years prior to the coronavirus pandemic, the zombie shares increased and during the pandemic increased to levels comparable to that during the dotcom bubble.

The link between zombification and macroeconomic policy is clear. The Great Moderation of the 1990s was a period of normalization in

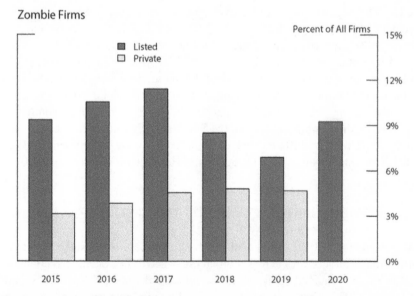

Figure 4.1   Share of Zombie Firms. *Source*: Giovanni Favara, Camelia Minou, and Ander Perez-Orive, "U.S. Zombie Firms: How Many and How Consequential?" Feds Notes, Federal Reserve Board, July 30, 2021.

macroeconomic policy. Orthodox monetary policy kept interest rates close to the long-term real-market interest rate. The Fed did not attempt to bail out financial firms or corporations during the recession in 1991. The prudent monetary policies constrained corporate borrowing. Corporations had an incentive to borrow only when borrowing costs could be covered by profits. By the end of that decade, a relatively small share of corporations could be classified as zombies.

The sharp rise and fall of zombie enterprises during the dotcom bubble is not surprising. Speculative borrowing and investing by technology firms during those years is now well documented.

What is unique is the growth of zombie firms over the past two decades. Zombification of firms in this period is linked to the failure to normalize macroeconomic policy. Nonorthodox monetary policy designed to support fiscal stimulus has created an environment conducive to zombification. When interest rates are held artificially below long-term real-market interest rates, firms have an incentive to borrow even when borrowing costs cannot be covered by profits (Acharya et al. 2018; Jorda et al. 2020).

The market intervention by the Fed in response to the coronavirus pandemic reduced borrowing costs to zombie firms to unprecedented levels. The Fed announcement in March 2020 that it would purchase corporate bonds and exchange traded funds (ETFs) triggered a huge rally in corporate bonds, including those issued by zombie firms. Corporate bonds issued by zombie firms in 2020 hit an all-time high of almost $2 trillion (Bloomberg News 2021). Bloomberg analysis estimates that zombies now account for nearly a quarter of the 3,000 largest publicly traded U.S. corporations.

The distortion of credit markets resulting from Fed policies is most evident in the market for junk bonds, that is, bonds rated (CCC). In February 2021, the average yield on the S&P U. S. high yield index was below 4 percent. This index includes some of the firms in retailing and energy that have been hardest hit by the coronavirus pandemic. That yield is less than 300 basis points above the 10-year Treasury yield. In January and early February 2021, companies issued $139 billion of bonds and loans below investment grade. More than $13 billion of that debt had junk bond rating (CCC) (S&P Global Market Intelligence 2021).

Becker and Benmelech (2021) find that bond issuance was more than twice as high in the COVD-19 period as in previous years. This sharp increase in bond issuance was primarily in investment grade issues rather than high yield issues, as shown in figure 4.2.

The strong demand for junk bonds has allowed weaker companies to refinance debt and, in some cases, avoid default. Some of these companies are able to pay interest in bonds rather than cash. These deals are evidence of an overheated market; they contributed to the financial crisis in 2008 (*Wall*

Panel A: Number of IG issues

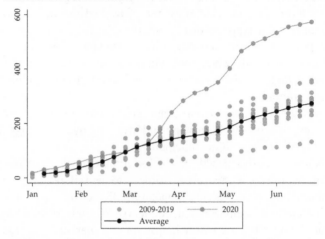

Panel B: Number of HY issues

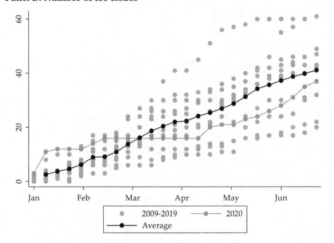

Figure 4.2   Flow of Bond Issue in 2020 by Credit Quality. *Source*: Bo Becker and Efraim Benmelech, "The Resilience of the U.S. Corporate Bond Market During Financial Crises," National Bureau of Economic Research, Working Paper 28868, May 2021.

Street Journal 2021). Another benchmark of an overheated market is the ratio of debt to earnings. Regulators caution against extending debt to companies with debt exceeding six times earnings. In January 2021, more than half of the mergers and acquisitions paid for with junk bonds exceeded that benchmark (*Wall Street Journal* 2021e).

The growth in junk bond issues has created a new generation of zombie firms, including enterprises that would most likely have defaulted on their bonds in the absence of the federal bailout. For example, Carnival, one of the largest cruise ship operators, has been kept afloat by the Fed bailout (Richter 2021). It was able to issue $900 million in bonds with deep junk bond rating, CCC, at a yield of 10 percent. With no operating income, Carnival is burning its way through this debt. Carnival is clearly insolvent and at some point, it will have to restructure this debt through bankruptcy or exit the industry. Meanwhile, instead of restructuring, Carnival and other cruise operators continue to take on debt backed by the Fed.

HOW THE FAILURE TO NORMALIZE MONETARY POLICY CREATES ZOMBIE ENTERPRISES

Recent studies explore the causes for zombie enterprises in a broad cross-section of countries. In recent years, the failure to normalize monetary policy and the pursuit of unconventional monetary policy have been major factors in this zombification. By lowering interest rates and purchasing bonds directly, central banks reduce the pressure on zombie firms to restructure or exit the industry (Borio and Hofmann 2017; Borio et al. 2017; Banerjee and Hofmann 2018a, 2018b). Weak banks have an incentive to keep zombie firms from defaulting on their loans, by rolling over the loans (Storz et al. 2017; Schivardi et al. 2017).

Some studies find evidence of a negative impact from unconventional monetary policies that remain in place for long periods of time. Financial market repression, holding interest rates low, has a negative impact on bank profitability (Claessens et al. 2018). Low interest rates also result in deterioration in corporate balance sheets (Banerjee and Hofmann 2018; Hong et al. 2021). In the long term, when low interest rates result in debt overhang, this has a negative impact on investment (Caballero et al. 2008; Kalemi-Ozcan 2019; Cloyne et al. 2019; Acharya and Plantim 2019; Hong et al. 2021).

Zombification in the United States is linked to failed monetary policy. As the Fed shifted from conventional to nonconventional monetary policy over the past decade, the new policy framework allowed the Fed to provide monetary stimulus through low federal funds rates, large-scale asset purchases, direct extension of credit, and other refinancing operations.

During the Great Moderation, the Fed pursued conventional monetary policies designed to bring inflation under control. The primary objective was to reduce inflation from the double-digit rates of the 1970s. The Fed implemented this monetary policy mainly through open-market operations, that is, buying and selling short-term Treasury securities. By conducting open-market operations, the Fed controlled the amount of money in the banking system, thereby increasing or decreasing the amount of credit that banks could extend.

In this conventional monetary policy, banks regularly lent and borrowed reserves in the federal funds market to satisfy their legal reserve requirements. The interest rate in the federal funds market was a market-determined rate depending on the supply and demand for excess reserves. While the Fed did not determine the federal funds rate, it set a target for that rate depending on macroeconomic conditions. Targeting the federal funds rate is a key part of a rules-based or conventional monetary policy. Taylor rules provide for adjustments in the target federal funds rate based on the rate of inflation and unemployment (Taylor 1993, 2000, 2009, 2010).

Normalization of monetary policy during the Great Moderation is clear in figure 4.3. Prior to the Great Moderation, the inflation rate exhibits an upward trend peaking at 14 percent in 1980. During the 1970s, the inflation rate fluctuated widely, between 3 percent and 14 percent. The federal funds rate also exhibits an upward trend peaking at 19 percent in 1980. The federal funds rate is also volatile in the 1970s, fluctuating between 4 percent and 14 percent.

The conventional monetary policies pursued in the 1980s and 1990s were effective in taming inflation. Inflation was reduced to less than 2 percent by the end of the period. Volatility in inflation was also significantly reduced. This normalization of monetary policy was accompanied by a sharp reduction in the federal funds rate. During the 1990s, the federal funds rate fluctuated between 3 percent and 6 percent. Taylor argues that the normalization of monetary policy was abandoned in the following decade, when the federal funds rate varied between 1 percent and 5 percent (Taylor 1993, 2000, 2009, 2010, 2014, 2017; Poulson and Baghestani 2012).

The major break with conventional monetary policy occurred during the financial crisis that began in 2008. The Fed introduced the first quantitative easing program, purchasing large quantities of long-term financial assets. Soon after, the Fed began allocating credit directly to certain firms to keep them afloat. These unconventional monetary policies significantly increased

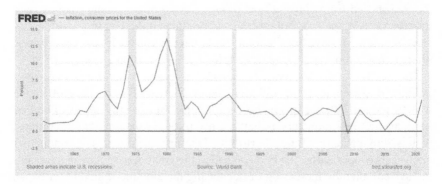

Figure 4.3   Inflation. *Source*: World Bank, fred.stlouisfed.org.

liquidity and reserves in the banking system. To maintain control over the federal funds rate and the money supply, the Fed sterilized its liquidity operations by selling short-term treasuries from its portfolio. By selling Treasury securities, the Fed took reserves out of the banking system at the same time that it was injecting reserves into the system (Kroeger et al. 2017; Michel 2014, 2021).

During the financial crisis, the Fed set a target for the federal funds rate at 2 percent, but this interest targeting approach was falling apart. The Fed was running out of short-term treasuries to sell, exhausting its ability to sterilize emergency lending. By 2010, the federal funds rate had been reduced to close to zero. The Fed had no choice but to lower its target federal funds rate (Bernanke 2015). At that point, the Fed introduced a new unconventional monetary policy. For the first time, the Fed began to pay interest on reserves, including interest on excess bank reserves (IOER). The goal was to sterilize the large quantity of excess reserves created by the lending operations. The Fed accomplished this goal by setting the interest rate on excess reserves higher than the banks could earn lending the reserves in the federal funds market. Initially, the IOER rate was below the target federal funds rate, but by early 2008 the IOER exceeded the target federal funds rate, a practice that continues to this day (Bernanke 2015).

By setting an attractive interest rate on reserves, the Fed can induce banks to hold excess reserves rather than make new loans. This aspect of the new operating framework has had far-reaching consequences for monetary and fiscal policy. When the Fed purchases assets, this no longer automatically translates into expansionary monetary policy. In effect, the Fed can purchase as many assets as it likes regardless of monetary policy objectives, by paying firms to hold the money as excess reserves. The new policy framework breaks the nexus between purchasing assets and the inflationary process. The enormous buildup of reserves during the 2008 financial crisis eventually caused the interbank lending markets to break down and contributed to the Fed abandoning its traditional operating procedures. The Fed adopted a new operating procedure that relies on bureaucratically administered interest rates rather than the traditional approach that depended on market forces and targeting a market rate. This new framework divorces the Fed's monetary policy from the size of its balance sheet (Dutkowsky and VanHoose 2017, 2018; Dorn 2020).

More important than this break in operating procedures was a more fundamental change in monetary policy. During the Great Moderation, the primary objective of monetary policy was price stabilization. The Fed was able to accomplish this objective, while fulfilling its other mandate to achieve and maintain full employment.

In the aftermath of the 2008 financial crisis, a shift occurred in monetary policy that would become explicit in later years. During the financial crisis, the inflation rate fell below zero for the first time in half a century. In 2010, the inflation rate recovered above the inflation ceiling of 2 percent set in Fed policy. Disinflation then set in, with the inflation rate falling to zero again in 2015. The unemployment rate hit a peak at about 10 percent in 2009. With slow economic recovery, the unemployment rate remained high for several years, and full employment was not reached again until 2016 (Kroeger et al. 2017).

Normalization of monetary policy was not pursued until 2016. For half a decade after the financial crisis, the Fed used its new operating framework to pursue expansionary monetary policy. The Fed balance sheet increased from $870 billion in 2007 to $4.5 trillion in 2015. The federal funds rate remained below.5 percent until 2016. In its open-market committee meeting in 2016, the Fed committed to formally adopt "policy normalization." Over the next few years, the Fed balance sheet fell to $3.8 trillion, and the federal funds rate rose to 2.4 percent. But, before this policy normalization could be fully implemented, the coronavirus pandemic brought a new economic shock (Kroeger et al. 2017).

In contrast to monetary policy during the Great Moderation, monetary policy in the post-financial crisis era places a lower priority on price stabilization—and a high priority on achieving full employment. This shift in monetary policy would become explicit under the chairmanship of Jerome Powell. The new monetary framework was in place when the coronavirus hit in 2020. The Fed responded with a more vigorous policy of monetary easing than that pursued during the financial crisis. In 2020, the Fed increased total assets on the balance sheet to more than $7 trillion. The federal funds rate was again reduced to close to zero (Powell 2020; Clarida 2021).

The Fed tweaked the policy framework by shifting from an inflation ceiling of 2 percent to an average inflation rate of 2 percent over the business cycle. While it is not clear how much inflation over 2 percent will be tolerated or for how long, price stabilization now has a significantly lower priority. During the Great Moderation, the Fed increased the target federal funds rate whenever unemployment fell to levels that economists believed would cause wages and prices to rise too much. In the new framework, the Fed will not increase the target federal funds rate until inflation exceeds 2 percent and is on track to exceed that target for some time to offset previous shortfalls. Chairman Powell stated that "the kind of troubling inflation that people like me grew up with seems far away and unlikely" (*Wall Street Journal* 2021c, 2021d).

Chairman Powell underscored his determination to achieve full employment. The Fed further tweaked the policy framework by redefining full employment to reflect underemployment and the large numbers of workers who have left the labor force. Chairman Powell stated that the Fed will not begin to tighten easy monetary policies until it sees much more improvement in labor markets. Chairman Powell stated that "We've shown that we can get to low levels of unemployment, and that the benefits to society, including particularly lower and moderate income people—are very substantial" (*Wall Street Journal* 2021a, 2021b).

The COVID-19 pandemic required unprecedented coordination of monetary and fiscal policies. Unconventional monetary policies were pursued to provide the fiscal space required to respond to the pandemic. The challenge now is to normalize monetary and fiscal policies and restore macroeconomic stability. This requires a commitment to stable prices and debt levels, but the credibility of these two commitments is now called into question.

Debt fatigue has put the country on an unsustainable debt trajectory. Major economic shocks have left the country with an unsustainable debt burden, and an expanded role for the federal government in the economy. The current administration has further expanded the demands on fiscal policy, including investing in infrastructure, decarbonizing the economy, and redistributing income and wealth. To fulfill the commitment to stabilize debt, Congress must close the fiscal gap and bring expenditures into balance with revenues in the long term, but there is no indication that Congress will meet this commitment.

In the absence of sustainable debt, it will be impossible for the Fed to fulfill the commitment to stable prices. The unconventional monetary policies pursued by the Fed have created the impression of a free lunch. The traditional boundaries between monetary and fiscal policies have blurred, and political actors now have a greater incentive to exploit the Fed for political purposes.

The failure to commit to debt stabilization creates a fundamental conflict between monetary and fiscal policies; the Fed is now on the horns of a dilemma. If the Fed continues to accommodate expansionary fiscal policies this could boost employment in the short run, but this puts upward pressure on prices in the long run. If, on the other hand, the Fed fulfills the commitment to stabilize prices, this could result in higher levels of unemployment. Over the past two decades, the economy has experienced retardation in economic growth, with higher rates of unemployment. This means that the attempt by the Fed to accommodate the expansionary fiscal policies pursued by Congress is bound to fail.

Until 2021, the Fed was not forced to confront the horns of this dilemma. The unconventional operating monetary framework put into place in response to economic crises allowed the Fed to pursue accommodating monetary policy without triggering higher prices. But in 2021 the day of reckoning has arrived. The new operating framework has fallen apart, and expansionary monetary and fiscal policies have triggered rates of inflation not seen since 1980. The inflation genie is out of the bottle.

Some have argued that the Fed could normalize monetary policy by simply restoring a commitment to stable prices, as Fed chairman Paul Volker did in 1980. Paul Volker found that putting the genie back in the bottle was no easy task, but he did not face the horns of a dilemma confronting the Fed today. During the Great Moderation of the 1980s and 1990s, Congress fulfilled the commitment to stabilize debt. After two decades, in the 1990s expenditures were finally brought into balance with revenues, and the debt burdens were reduced. Current Fed chairman, Jerome Powell, on the other hand, has committed the Fed to do whatever it takes to achieve the target levels of unemployment set by Congress. A failure to commit to price stability and debt sustainability means that the economy will most likely experience stagflation as it did during the 1960s and 1970s.

Today a strong case can be made for replacing the Federal Reserve Act with a charter establishing rules-based monetary policy. The charter should restore Fed independence and separate monetary and fiscal policies. It should replace discretionary monetary policy with rules-based monetary policy. There is controversy regarding the optimum design of a rules-based monetary policy. Some economists, in the tradition of Milton Friedman, argue for monetary rules designed to keep nominal GDP on a stable full employment path. A target rate of growth of the money supply would be set consistent with that rate of growth in nominal GDP. Other economists argue for the rule-based monetary policies first proposed in the pioneering work of John Taylor. These rules would rely on the traditional tools of monetary policy, adjusting the interest rates to achieve target levels of inflation and unemployment.

An alternative approach to monetary policy would eliminate the Fed and central bank control of the money supply entirely. Prior to the 1913 Federal Reserve Act, the United States had such a "free banking" system. In free banking system, private banks issue their own paper currency. These "banknotes" are then redeemable in underlying money, usually gold or silver. Some economists argue for a free banking system in which bank notes are redeemable in a standard bundle of diverse commodities.

Milton Friedman argued for a free banking system in which bank notes are redeemable in a fiat currency fixed in supply. Supporters of free banking argue that the commitment to stable prices is more credible in this monetary system than one which relies on fiat money and central bank control of the money supply.

At the end of the day, the question is whether any monetary system can fulfill the commitment to stable prices when the government fails to commit to sustainable debt. The experience in high debtor countries is that in the long run, a failure to commit to sustainable debt levels exposes the country to devaluation of the currency and debt default. The United States is not immune to these risks despite the fact that it prints a reserve currency.

The macroeconomic performance of the U.S. economy appears increasingly like Japan's "lost decades." Both countries experienced deflationary pressures characterized by low interest rates and "zombie lending," that is, the extension of credit to weaker firms, often by banks that are weakly capitalized. The United States and Japan are not unique in this regard. Those trends are also evident in European countries over the past decade. These countries exhibit similar macroeconomic trends, that is, a persistent low interest rate environment that sets the stage for zombie lending. Zombification refers to the outcome when this type of lending keeps nonviable firms afloat (Caballero et al. 2008; Acharya et al. 2020; Borio and Hofmann 2017).

HOW THE FAILURE TO NORMALIZE FISCAL POLICY CREATES ZOMBIE ENTERPRISES?

Another cause for zombie enterprises is the failure to normalize fiscal policy. During the Great Moderation in the United States, government bailouts of private enterprises were limited by effective budget constraints. However, over the past two decades, massive government bailouts set the stage for a new generation of zombie enterprises, comparable to that in Japan. Accelerated zombification in the United States was linked to the financial crisis in 2008 and the coronavirus pandemic in 2020.

The Bush administration responded to the 2008 financial crisis by enacting the Emergency Economic Stabilization Act. That act was the basis for the Troubled Asset Relief Program (TARP) that authorized up to $700 billion in subsidies to bail out financial institutions (Congressional Budget Office 2012). That amount was later reduced to $475 billion, and actual disbursements from the fund were estimated at $431 billion.

TARP was designed to purchase toxic assets and equity from financial institutions to strengthen the financial sector. The Fed used the funds to bail out selected financial institutions. Some favored financial institutions considered "too big to fail," such as AIG, Citigroup, Bank of America, JP Morgan Chase, Wells Fargo, Goldman Sachs, and Morgan Stanley, were rescued; other institutions, such as Bear Stearns, were allowed to go into bankruptcy (Congressional Budget Office 2012).

The Bush bailout of financial institutions was followed in 2009 by a more ambitious bailout under the Obama administration, the $830 billion American Recovery and Reinvestment Act (ARRA) (Congressional Budget Office 2009). The act targeted subsidies to two auto firms, Chrysler and General Motors. The government then forced financial institutions that had received TARP funding to purchase the stock of these auto firms, in effect nationalizing the firms. Federal government mandates on the auto industry, and other industries have continued since then. The Congressional Budget Office (2009) estimated that the ARRA would increase deficits by $185 billion in 2009, $399 billion in 2010, and $134 billion in 2011, or $787 billion over the 2009–2011 period.

The actual deficits incurred by the Obama administration were as-yet unprecedented. In Obama's first year in office, deficits tripled from about half a trillion dollars to almost one and a half trillion dollars. Deficits remained above a trillion dollars per year while these bailout programs were in effect, and then decreased to about half a trillion dollars when they ended. To support fiscal stimulus, the Fed expanded the money supply, pushing interest rates close to zero. Through quantitative easing, the Fed purchased billions in government bonds and mortgage-backed securities to shore up the financial system. These monetary policies were designed to support the expansionary fiscal policies pursued by the Obama administration, a policy shift that compromised the independence of the Fed from both the executive and legislative branches of government (Taylor 2009, 2010, 2014).

In 2019, the Fed made a commitment to normalize monetary policy. After years of financial market repression, the Fed made a commitment to restore interest rates to something closer to real interest rates, planning "to undertake open market operations as necessary to maintain the federal funds rate in a tight range of 1-3/4 to 2 percent" (Federal Reserve Board 2019). But before the Fed made much progress in normalizing monetary policy, the coronavirus pandemic triggered a new era of fiscal stimulus and monetary easing.

The onset of the coronavirus in 2020 led to new, massive bailouts by the federal government, first in the Consolidated Appropriations/Response Relief Act. The Committee for a Responsible Federal Budget (CRFB) (2021a) estimated the various relief measures that have been enacted by Congress total more than $5.0 trillion (Committee for a Responsible Federal Budget 2021b).

Congress also enacted legislation that greatly expands the role for the Federal Reserve in providing relief through emergency lending, asset purchases, and other liquidity actions. The CRFB (2021a) estimates the total relief funds initially allocated to the Fed at $7.3 trillion, which was subsequently reduced to $5.7 trillion. In an unprecedented relief measure, the Treasury set aside $195 billion as a backstop for the Fed to lend directly to private firms. This backstop for the Fed allowed for $1.95 trillion in direct lending and liquidity operations. This program was terminated in 2020, after the Fed provided only $42 billion through direct lending operations.

The macro-policy response to the financial crisis in 2008 and the coronavirus pandemic in 2020 have made it more difficult to address the debt crisis in several ways. Fiscal stimulus has ratcheted up spending in the years following each crisis. The new monetary framework created by the Fed is designed to support fiscal stimulus, low interest rates and asset purchases are pursued long after the crisis. In short, over the past two decades, the federal government has failed to normalize fiscal and monetary policies, and there is little evidence that it will do so in the near term. These macro-policy failures set the stage for a new generation of zombie enterprises.

AN ALTERNATIVE PATH

In 2021 the United States has virtually abandoned rules-based monetary and fiscal policies. The discretionary monetary and fiscal policies pursued in response to the coronavirus pandemic are unprecedented. The question is how to restore rules-based monetary and fiscal policies when the economy has recovered from the pandemic.

There are now two competing approaches to addressing the debt crisis in the United States. Debrun and Jonung (2019) argue that the United States should return to the indicative Fiscal Taylor Rules (FTR) that proved to be effective during the Great Moderation of the 1980s and 1990s. These are referred to as indicative fiscal rules because they simply set benchmarks or objectives against which to measure the effectiveness of fiscal policies. This approach does not rely on formal fiscal rules or objectives that require sanctions and enforceability when the objectives are not met.

Debrun and Jonung (2019) maintain that this indicative fiscal rule approach is a more viable alternative than the formal fiscal rules enacted in many countries in recent decades. The fact that many countries have evaded or abandoned formal fiscal rules suggests that lack of enforceability is undermining the credibility and public support for rules-based fiscal policy. They conclude that indicative fiscal rules, such as FTRs, combined with institutional reforms to provide greater transparency and accountability may be the only viable way to restore rules-based fiscal policy in the long run. Further they argue that institutional innovations such as Fiscal Responsibility Councils may be required to boost reputational effects as well as provide for greater transparency and accountability.

There are several reasons why this indicative fiscal rule approach may fail in addressing the debt crisis in the United States. The FTR that were effective in the 1980s and 1990s may prove to be ineffective in the twenty-first century. During the Great Moderation, the United States experienced high rates of economic growth, with modest recessions.

We conclude that the pursuit of indicative fiscal rules will fail in the United States for the same reason that they have failed in Japan. For three decades, Japan has set benchmarks for inflation that it has failed to achieve. Inflation rates have remained stubbornly well below the 2 percent target rate over most of this period. Japan has also experienced retardation in the rate of growth in output and employment. Japan has failed to achieve benchmarks despite aggressive monetary and fiscal policies. The BOJ has kept interest rates at or below 0 percent. The Japanese government has pursued a series of fiscal stimulus packages over these years, with the BOJ monetizing the debt. The outcome is the highest debt/GDP ratio among advanced economies. The combination of debt fatigue and slowing in economic growth in Japan is the most likely path for the United States under current law.

The question for the United States is whether there is an alternative path to the one projected in Congressional Budget Office long-term forecasts, and if so, how citizens can choose this alternative path. The experience in Switzerland and other European countries reveals that there is an alternative path and that citizens in a democratic society are capable of choosing that path. In the book, we explore the potential impact of Swiss-style fiscal rules on the budget and the economy over the next three decades. Dynamic simulation analysis reveals that with these fiscal rules in place, it is possible for the United States to stabilize and reduce debt to sustainable levels over the forecast period. With these fiscal rules in place downsizing the federal government, the United States can restore long-term economic growth. The empirical analysis also reveals how difficult this challenge will be, and why the United States is likely to continue to experience debt fatigue. The book also explores issues of political economy in enacting Swiss-style fiscal rules in the United States.

REFERENCES

Acharya, V., T. Eisert, C. Eufinger, and C. Hirsh. 2018. "The Real Effects of the Sovereign Debt Crisis in Europe: Evidence from Syndicated Loans," mimeo July.

Acharya, V., and G. Plantin. 2019. "Monetary Easing, Leveraged Payouts and Lack of Investment," NBER Working Paper No. 26471.

Acharya, V., M. Crosignani, T. Eisert, and C. Eufinger. 2020. "Zombie Credit and (Dis-) Inflation: Evidence from Europe," Federal Reserve Bank of New York, Staff Report No. 955, December.

Andrews, D. and F. Petroulakis. 2017. "Breaking the Shackles: Weak Banks and Depressed Restructuring in Europe," OECD Economics Department Working Papers, no 1433.

Banerjee, R., and B. Hofmann. 2018a. "The Rise of Zombie Firms: Causes and Consequences," BIS Quarterly Review, September 23.

Banerjee, R., and B. Hofmann. 2018b. "Corporate Zombies: Life Cycle and Anatomy," Bank for International Settlements, mimeo.

Banerjee, R., and B. Hofmann. 2020. "Corporate Zombies: Anatomy and Life Cycle," BIS Working Papers No. 882, September 2.

Bank for International Settlements. 2018. "Annual Economic Report 2018," Box II.A, June.

Becker, B., and E. Benmelech. 2021. "The Resilience of the U.S. Corporate Bond Market During Financial Crises," Working Paper 28868, National Bureau of Economic Research, May.

Bernanke, B. 2015. *The Courage to Act: A Memoir of a Crisis and Its Aftermath,* W.W. Norton & Company, New York, p. 144.

Bloomberg News. 2021. "America's Zombie Companies Rack up $2 Trillion of Debt," December 16.

Board of Governors of the Federal Reserve. 2021. "Inflation, Income. Prices, for the United States," Fred.

Borio, C., L. Gambacorta, and B. Hofmann. 2017. "The Influence of Monetary Policy on Bank Profitability," *International Finance* 20(1): 48–63. Also available as BIS Working Papers, no 514, October 2015.

Borio, C., and B. Hofmann. 2017. "Is Monetary Policy Less Effective When Interest Rates are Persistently Low?," BIS Working Papers, no 628, April.

Caballero, R., T. Hoshi, and A. Kashyap. 2008. "Zombie Lending and Depressed Restructuring in Japan," *American Economic Review* 98(5): 1943–1977.

Claessens, S., N. Coleman, and M. Donnelly. 2018. "Low-for-Long Interest Rates and Banks' Interest Margins and Profitability: Cross Country Evidence, Journal of Financial Intermediation, Vol. 35, Part A, July 1–16.

Clarida, R. 2021. "U.S. Outlook and Monetary Policy," Remarks at the C. Peter McColough Series on International Economics Council on Foreign Relations, January 8, bis.org/review/r210512e.htm

Colacelli, M., and G. Hong. 2019. "Productivity Drag from Small and Medium-Sized Enterprises in Japan," IMF Working Paper No. 19/13739.

Committee for a Responsible Federal Budget. 2021a. "Breaking Down $3.4 Trillion in COVID Relief," Jan. 7.

Committee for a Responsible Federal Budget. 2021b. "Biden to Unveil 1.9Trillion Response Plan," Jan. 14.

Congressional Budget Office. 2009. *Budgetary Impact of ARRA*, Washington D.C., February.

Congressional Budget Office. 2012. *Report on the Troubled Asset Relief Program*, October.

Debrun, X., and L. Jonung. 2019. "Under Threat-Rules Based Fiscal Policy and How to Preserve it," *European Journal of Political Economy* 57: 142–157.

Dorn, J. 2020. "Maintaining Distance Between Monetary and Fiscal Policy," Cato Institute, November 18.

Dutkowsky, D., and D. VanHoose. 2017. "Interest on Reserves, Regime Shifts, And Bank Behavior," *Journal of Economics and Business* 91(2017): 1–15.

Favara, G., C. Miniou, and A. Perez-Orive. 2021. "U.S. Zombie Firms: How Many and How Consequential?," Feds Notes, Federal Reserve Board, July 30.

Federal Reserve Board. 2019. "Statement Regarding Monetary Policy Implementation," FOMC Communications Related to Policy Normalization, October 11.

Financial Times. 2021. "Pandemic Debt Binge Creates New Generation of Zombie Companies," January 15.

Fukuda, S., and J. Nakamura. 2011. "Why Did 'Zombie' Firms Recover in Japan?" *The World Economy* 34(7): 1124–1137.

Gagnon, J. 2020. "Who's Afraid of Zombie Firms?" Real-Time Economic Issues Watch, Peterson Institute for International Economics, October 22.

Hong, G., A. Ito, Y. Saito, and A. Nguyen. 2020. "Structural Changes in Japanese Firms: Business Dynamism in an Aging Society," IMF Working Paper No. 20/182.

Hong, G., D. Igan, and D. Lee. 2021. "Zombies on the Brink: Evidence from Japan on the Reversal of Monetary Policy Effectiveness," IMF Working Paper WP/21/44.

Hoshi, T. 2006. "Economics of the Living Dead," *Japanese Economic Review* 57(1): 30–49.

Jorda, O., M. Kornejew, M. Schularick, and A. Taylor. 2020. "Zombies at Large? Corporate Debt Overhang and the Macroeconomy," Federal Reserve Bank of New York Staff Reports, No. 951, December.

Kalemli-Ozcan, S., L. Laeven, and D. Moreno. 2019. "Debt Overhang, Rollover Risk, and Corporate Investment: Evidence from the European Crisis," ECB Working Paper No.2241.

Kimura, T., and D. Small. 2006. "Quantitative Monetary Easing and Risk in Financial Asset Markets," *The B.E. Journal of Macroeconomics* 6(1): 1–54.

Kroeger, A., J. McGowan, and A. Sarkar. 2017. "The Pre-Crisis onetary Policy Implementation Framework," Federal Reserve of New York Staff Report No. 809, March 2017, 15.

Kwon, H., F. Narita, and M. Narita. 2015. "Resource Reallocation and Zombie Lending in Japan in the 1990s," *Review of Economic Dynamics* 18(4): 709–732.

Lam, W. 2011. "Bank of Japan's Monetary Easing Measures: Are They Powerful and Comprehensive?" IMF Working Paper No. 11/264.

Lam, W., and J. Shin. 2012. "What Role Can Financial Policies Play in Revitalizing SMEs in Japan?" IMF Working Paper No. 12/291.

Lubik, T., and F. Schwartzman. 2020. "Public and Private Debt after the Pandemic and Policy Normalization," Economic Brief No. 20-06, Federal Reserve Bank of Richmond.

McGowan, A., M. D. Andrews, and V. Millot. 2017. "The Walking Dead: Zombie Firms and Productivity Performance in OECD Countries," OECD Economics Department Working Papers, no 1372.

Michel, N. 2014. "The Fed at 100: A Primer on Monetary Policy," Heritage Foundation Backgrounder No. 2876, January 29.

Michel, N. 2021. "Monetary Policy and the Worsening U.S. Debt Crisis," in *Public Debt Sustainability: International Perspectives*, B. Poulson, J. Merrifield, and S. Hanke, editors, Lexington Books, New York, 219–241.

Oda, N., and U. Kazuo. 2007. "The Effects of the Bank of Japan's Zero Interest Rate Commitment and Quantitative Monetary Easing on the Yield Curve: A Macro-Finance Approach," *Japanese Economic Review* 58(3): 303–328.

Ono, A., and I. Uesugi. 2014. "SME Financing in Japan during the Global Financial Crisis: Evidence from Firm Surveys," HIT-REFINED Working Paper Series 6, Institute of Economic Research, Hitotsubashi University, Tokyo.

Powell, J. 2020. "Statement before the Committee on Banking, Housing, and Urban Affairs U.S. Senate," Dec. 1.

Poulson, B., and H. Baghestani. 2012. Federal Reserve Forecasts of Nonfarm Payroll Employment across Different Political Regimes," *Journal of Economic Studies* 39(3): 280–289.

Poulson, B., J. Merrifield, and S. Hanke. 2022. *Debt Sustainability: International Perspectives*, Lexington Press.

Richter, W. 2021. "The Zombie Companies are Coming," *Wolf Street*, August 26.

Schivardi, F., E. Sette, and G. Tabellini. 2017. "Credit Misallocation during the European Financial Crisis," BIS Working Papers, no 669, December, 410.

S&P Global Market Intelligence. 2021. "U.S. Corporate Bond Issuance, Triple-C Rated or Lower," Feb. 10.

Storz, M., M. Koetter, R. Setzer, and A. Westphal. 2017. "Do We Want these Two to Tango? On Zombie Firms and Stressed Banks in Europe," ECB Working Papers, no 2104.

Taylor, J. 1993. "Discretion Versus Policy Rules in Practice," *Carnegie Rochester Conference Series on Public Policy* 39: 195–214.

Taylor, J. 2000. "Reassessing Discretionary Fiscal Policy," *The Journal of Economic Perspectives* 14(3): 21–36.

Taylor, J. 2009. *Getting Off Track: How Government Actions and Interventions Caused, Prolonged, and Worsened the Financial Crisis*, Hoover Institution Press, Stanford.

Taylor, J. 2010. "Swings in the Rules-discretion Balance," *Conference on the Occasion of the 40th Anniversary of Microeconomic Foundations of Employment and Inflation Theory*, Columbia University Press, New York.

Taylor, J. 2014. "The Fed Needs to Return to Monetary Rules," *Wall Street Journal* (June 27. A13).

Taylor, J. 2017. "Reserve Balances and the Fed's Balance Sheet in the Future," *Economics One*, June 24. https://economicsone.com/2017/06/24/reserve-balances-and -thefedsbalance-sheet-in-the-future/

Ueda, K. 2011. "The Effectiveness of Non-Traditional Monetary Policy Measures: The Case of the Bank of Japan," CARF Working Paper, CARF-F-252.

Ugai, H. 2007. "Effects of the Quantitative Easing Policy: A Survey of Empirical Analyses," *Monetary and Economic Studies* 25(1): 1–48.

Wall Street Journal. 2021a. "Fed Chief Vows Support for Labor Market," February 25, A2.

Wall Street Journal. 2021b. "The Money Boom is Already Here," February 22, A17.

Wall Street Journal. 2021c. "Questions for Chairman Powell," February 23, A14.

Wall Street Journal. 2021d. "Powell Says Full Ease Ahead," February 25, A16.

Wall Street Journal. 2021e. "Borrowing Binge Reaches Riskiest Companies," Feb. 15.

Chapter 5

A Look Back at the New
Era of Fiscal Rules

INTRODUCTION

The 1980s and 1990s launched a new era of rules-based fiscal and monetary policy.[1] The consensus that new fiscal and monetary rules were needed was grounded in the public choice perspective of macroeconomic policy. It was clear that the rapid and sustained accumulation of debt could not be explained by orthodox principles of public finance. The public choice literature was the starting point for the new rules-based approach to fiscal policy. In a democratic society elected officials, motivated by their private interests, pursue fiscal policies biased toward deficits and debt. They perceive that debt-financed current expenditures generate more support, while tax-financed expenditures yielding benefits in the long term generate less support. Time inconsistency leads elected officials to renege on commitments to debt sustainability. As a result, traditional fiscal rules, such as annually balanced budget requirements, are often honored in the breach and fail to fulfill the commitment to sustainable debt.[2]

Solving the debt crisis required a commitment to stable prices and sustainable debt, which in turn required coordination of monetary and fiscal policies. The consensus was that commitment to stable prices is best achieved by an independent monetary authority pursuing rules-based monetary policy. John Taylor, and others, formalized the benchmarks for such a rule-based monetary policy. The rules-based monetary policy could be implemented using orthodox monetary policies targeting interest rates. If output and employment fell below potential or full employment output, the monetary rules called for lower interest rates and a more expansionary monetary policy. A period of rapid economic growth in which actual output exceeded potential output called for higher interest rates and tighter monetary policy.

The commitment to sustainable debt also required new rules-based fiscal policies. The new fiscal reforms enacted in the European countries and other countries reflected a broad consensus on the need for more effective fiscal rules. Many of these countries experienced a major recession with a sharp increase in deficits and debt. The debt/GDP ratio in many of these countries increased at rates that economists considered unsustainable. Policy makers recognized that traditional fiscal rules such as annually balanced budget requirements were not enforced and were ineffective in constraining the growth in deficits and debt. Capital markets in these countries also signaled those fiscal policies were on an unsustainable path, as revealed by a sharp increase in interest rates accompanied by devaluation of their currency.

By the 1990s, citizens in some European countries perceived that the fiscal rules in place were ineffective in constraining deficits and allowed debt to increase at unsustainable rates. The fiscal stress experienced in these countries led them to begin experimenting with new fiscal rules, often referred to as debt brakes. The origin of these fiscal rules can be traced to sharp recessions experienced in Switzerland and Sweden in the late1980s and early 1990s.[3] A debt brake was first enacted at the cantonal level and then at the federal level in Switzerland. Beginning in Switzerland, and then extending to other European countries, citizens began to experiment with new fiscal rules referred to as debt brakes (Schaechter et al. 2012; Siegenthaler 2013; Wyplosz 2005, 2012). Debt brakes are formal fiscal rules incorporated in constitutional and statutory law that impose constraints on discretionary fiscal policy. The rules set targets for debt and require that expenditures be brought into line with revenues in the near term. The rules set caps on expenditures and require that deficits be offset by surplus revenue. By the early 2000s, the debt brakes enacted in some countries were effectively constraining deficits and debt, and this led to the enactment of new fiscal rules at both the national and supranational level in Europe (Andrle et al. 2015; Eyraud et al. 2018; Eyraud and Wu 2014; Gaspar, and Amaglobeli 2019; Bauer 2013; Bedna 2009; Beljeab and Geier 2013).

The effectiveness of these new fiscal rules in constraining debt varied considerably, especially during the financial crisis that began in 2008.[4] The rules did not prevent heavily indebted countries, such as Italy, from continuing to pursue unsustainable fiscal policies. Critics questioned whether the new rules were a credible commitment to fiscal stabilization in Europe, and the default, or threatened default, in several countries reinforced this view. Following the Great Recession in 2008 a "second generation" of fiscal rules was enacted in some European countries to improve their effectiveness in constraining debt while responding to the economic instability. Some countries, such as Germany, modified their rules to make them more effective constraints on deficits and debt. Some countries, such as Sweden, introduced new fiscal institutions, such as Fiscal Responsibility Councils, to provide more transparency and accountability in the budget process. This second generation of fiscal rules proved to be more effective in addressing the debt crisis.[5] Over the past two decades, debt brakes have proven to be more effective in northern European countries than in the southern tier of countries.

The debt brakes enacted in European countries required fundamental reforms in their fiscal institutions and budget processes. The transition from discretionary fiscal policies to rules-based policies required that elected officials relinquish some of their powers to independent fiscal agencies, such as Fiscal Stabilization Councils. The increased transparency and accountability created by the rules allowed the citizen to monitor whether elected officials were meeting the targets and guidelines set by the rules, and to hold them accountable.

In this new era of fiscal rules, the United States is decidedly an underachiever. After the breakdown of the Bretton Woods Agreement in 1971, the United States, like the European countries, began to incur deficits and accumulated debt. The Congressional Budget Act (BCA) enacted in 1974 mandated that budget resolutions set maximum levels for spending and a floor for revenue. But the act provided no enforcement mechanisms and proved to be ineffective in constraining budget decisions.

In the 1980s and 1990s, the United States also perceived that the growth in debt was not sustainable. In those years, during the Great Moderation, the United States enacted new statutory fiscal rules designed to eliminate deficits and restore sustainable debt levels. The Balanced Budget and Emergency Deficit Control Act 1985/1987 (referred to as Gramm-Rudman-Hollings) mandated that Congress balance the budget in the near term. The Budget Enforcement Act of 1990 amended BCA, providing enforcement through Statutory Pay-As You-Go. In contrast to the European countries, the United States experienced more rapid economic growth. By the late 1990s, the United States was able to balance the budget and stabilize the debt as a share of GDP. Debt sustainability was achieved primarily due to rapid economic growth, rather than the constraints imposed on fiscal policy by the new statutory fiscal rules. At the end of the 1990s, Congress chose not to renew the statutory fiscal rules then in place.

In 2011, Congress attempted to revive Gramm-Rudman-Hollings, enacting the Budget Control Act (BCA). BCA capped discretionary spending for FY 2013–2021. The act also attempted to revive Statutory Pay-As-You-Go to enforce spending caps. The budget process rules are based on the 1974 Congressional Budget Act, which requires Congress to agree on a budget resolution as the framework for tax and expenditure bills. As amended, the act requires Congress to set a revenue floor and an expenditure ceiling. The spending caps are enforced through sequestration. If Congress and the president can't agree on a budget consistent with these rules, sequestration requires across-the-board cuts in spending. The act also requires Congress to determine debt levels as part of the budget resolution, in conformity to debt limits.

Over the past two decades, the consensus in support of rules-based macro-economic policy in the United States has virtually disappeared. The United States has emerged as one of the most heavily indebted nations in the world. There is in fact widespread agreement that the statutory fiscal rules enacted in the United States have failed and that the budget process is broken. For a number of years, Congress has failed to agree on a budget resolution and has found many ways to circumvent the constraints imposed by fiscal rules. Congress suspends the spending caps and then sets higher spending limits to sanction increased spending. Congress also routinely suspends the debt ceiling and increases the ceiling to sanction more debt. The outcome in recent years is unconstrained growth in spending accompanied by trillion-dollar deficits. Debt is projected to continue to increase at unsustainable rates in the coming decades. With expiration of the BCA spending caps in 2022 Congress is no longer constrained by these statutory fiscal rules.[6]

The failure of fiscal rules and breakdown of the budget process has not prevented Congress from passing budgets. In the absence of effective fiscal rules, there is no budget constraint, so it is more accurate to refer to these as spending or appropriation bills than budgets. Each year elected officials congratulate themselves on restoring what they refer to as "regular order." Appropriation bills are advanced in both the House and the Senate, and most of the spending bills pass on the floor in each chamber. Congress relies on continuing resolutions, and spending bills are often passed in an ad hoc manner. An omnibus spending bill is then passed late in the year without much input from Congress as a whole. But Congress passes these appropriation bills without agreeing on a budget resolution, and every appropriation bill calls for a significant increase in spending. It is easy to reach bipartisan agreement on spending when there is no budget constraint.

In 2016, the House Budget Committee chaired by Republican Tom Price provided an assessment of the new era of fiscal rules and the challenges facing the United States. The recommendations of that Committee were very clearly focused on solving the debt crisis in the long run. In addition to strengthening existing fiscal rules, the Committee recommended consideration of new fiscal rules that have proven to be successful in addressing the debt crisis at both the state and national level. In particular, the Committee noted the success of new fiscal rules adopted in the European Union. In those countries, a debt target is set at a sustainable level. An expenditure limit is then imposed to achieve that debt target within a medium-term time frame. Annual budgets are adjusted based on the expenditures limit and the debt target. Guardrails are imposed in the form of deficit and debt brakes; when deficits or debt approach tolerance levels a more stringent spending limit is imposed.

The Price Committee noted the success of European countries, such as Switzerland, that have imposed the new fiscal rules for several decades. These countries reduced debt levels significantly. This has given them more flexibility to pursue a discretionary fiscal policy in response to recessions and financial crises. The Swiss rules require a cyclically balanced budget with deficits in periods of recession offset by surplus revenue in periods of expansion. An emergency fund allows them to exceed the spending limit in response to unforeseen events. The Committee noted that over this time period, the United States has incurred higher levels of debt, which will make it more difficult to impose these fiscal rules. The Committee concluded that failure to address the debt crisis with current fiscal rules underscores the need for the United States to consider new fiscal rules that have proven to be successful in other countries. As the United States emerges from the economic shock of the coronavirus pandemic with an even greater debt burden, the questions posed by the Price Committee are even more relevant.

- "Will the United States, like heavily indebted countries in Europe, continue to pursue unsustainable fiscal policies accompanied by retardation and stagnation in economic growth? If the United States now has limited fiscal space to respond to economic shocks, will the next recession result in even greater economic instability?
- The United States is clearly behind the learning curve compared to other countries that have enacted the second generation of fiscal rules. If current fiscal rules have failed, what reforms and policies are required to solve the debt crisis? Should the United States enact our own debt brake to address the crisis?
- What reforms in financial markets are required to put effective fiscal rules in place? Do we need supporting institutions in the form of insolvency laws and no-bailout rules? Could budget process reforms provide better transparency and accountability in fiscal decisions? Should the United States introduce new budget institutions, such as a Fiscal Responsibility Council?
- What political reforms are required for effective fiscal rules? Do we need stronger fiscal federalism with inter-jurisdictional competition and tax and spending autonomy? Do we need to strengthen institutions of direct democracy, relying more on the initiative and referendum in tax and spending decisions?
- If Congress fails to enact more effective fiscal rules, should citizens do so through an Article V constitutional convention? Would such a convention energize public support for effective fiscal rules in this country, as it did

in Switzerland?"(Committee on the Budget 2016a, 2016b, 2016c, 2016d, 2016e)

A colloquium of scholars has begun to explore these questions, providing new insights into rules-based fiscal policy. In this study, we attempt to answer these questions by exploring what we have learned about the new era of fiscal rules.

CHALLENGING RULES-BASED FISCAL POLICY AND THE GREAT MODERATION IN MACROECONOMIC POLICY

Challenges to rules-based fiscal policy can be traced back to Keynes and his disciples in the United States. Alvin Hansen argued that during the Great Depression the United States was experiencing secular stagnation, with aggregate demand insufficient to sustain output at full employment levels. Hansen argued that secular stagnation is due to the excess of savings over investment. He defined secular stagnation as "sick resources that die in their infancy, and depressions that feed on themselves" (Hansen 1941).

Neo-Keynesian argues that the United States is experiencing a new era of secular stagnation (Blanchard and Summers 2019, 2020; Blanchard and Toshiro 2019; Summers 2015). Indeed, they argue that economic shocks in the modern era provide even more justification for Keynesian fiscal stimulus. Comparing the Great Depression to the financial crisis in 2008, they maintain that the turning point in the recovery from the financial crisis occurred much earlier than that following the Great Depression due to fiscal stimulus and expansionary monetary policy. However, they argue that recovery following the financial crisis has not been as strong as recovery from the Great Depression. In this Neo-Keynesian literature, there are two sources of secular stagnation. One source of low output growth is low productivity growth and/ or low working-age population growth. Another source of low output growth is some combination of high private savings and low private investment.

Neo-Keynesians provide a new rationale for Keynesian policies to stimulate aggregate demand. In the current economic environment in the United States, inflation as measured by the consumer price index (CPI) has been running about 1 percent below the 2 percent target set by the Fed. If the expected rate of inflation is equal to the target rate of inflation, this suggests that there is a negative output gap. If the expected inflation rate is below the target rate, but close to the actual inflation rate, this suggests that there is no output gap. But in either case, the implication from a Neo-Keynesian perspective is expansionary fiscal policy. Fiscal stimulus can increase demand and eliminate the output gap. It can also lead to a positive output gap, increasing inflation to match the target rate of inflation (Auerbach 2019).

Neo-Keynesians argue that in the current environment of low interest rates, the cost of deficit financed fiscal stimulus is low (Elmendorff and Sheiner 2016; Blanchard 2019a, 2019b; Blanchard and Toshiro 2019). The government can increase debt, never raise taxes, and the debt/GDP ratio will never explode, but rather decrease slowly over time. Olivier Blanchard (Blanchard 2019a) in his presidential address to the American Economic Association argued that the prevalence and persistence of low interest rates in recent years should lead us to question the conventional wisdom regarding the costs of deficits and debt. He stated that "the issuance of debt without a later increase in taxes, may well be feasible." Blanchard argued that traditional analysis of debt dynamics assumes that the interest rate exceeds the growth rate. Under this assumption to avoid a debt explosion, an increase in debt must be offset by larger primary surpluses in the long run, in the form of higher taxes or lower spending. But when the interest rate is lower than the growth rate, this conclusion does not follow. In that case, the government can run a primary deficit forever while keeping the debt-to-GDP ratio constant. Neo-Keynesians have used this argument to justify primary deficits, even in high debtor countries such as Japan and the United States. Because of weak aggregate demand, they maintain that these countries need a combination of low interest rates and budget deficits to maintain aggregate demand at full employment levels of output (Blanchard 2019b; Blanchard and Pisani-Ferry 2019; Blanchard and Summers 2020; Blanchard and Summers (eds) 2019; Blanchard and Tashiro 2019; Blanchard et al. 2018).

Some economists have interpreted this Neo-Keynesian view to mean that higher debt may have no fiscal costs. Blanchard (Blanchard 2019b, 2019c) is careful to point out that this is not the case.

> The higher the level of debt, the greater the crowding out of capital, the higher the marginal product of capital, and, ceteris paribus, the higher all interest rates, including the rate on government bonds. For some high enough level of debt, the rate on government bonds will exceed the growth rate and the intertemporal budget constraint will bind. At this stage the government will need to run a primary surplus to avoid a debt explosion. (Blanchard 2019b)

A number of economists have argued that the low interest rates in the United States provides the fiscal space to pursue Keynesian fiscal stimulus policies and to postpone the fiscal tightening required to stabilize or reduce the debt/GDP ratio (Mauro and Zhou 2019). Modern Monetarist theorists maintain that in this low interest rate environment a debt crisis is inconceivable because the United States issues its own currency. Further, they argue that when most public debt is held domestically this decreases the risk of default on the debt.

It is certainly true that low interest rates reduce the cost of debt and that this has allowed countries such as the United States to issue massive amounts of debt without increasing interest costs on debt as a share of GDP. But that does not necessarily imply that the United States has the fiscal space to pursue Keynesian fiscal stimulus policies. Nor is it true that a negative interest rate growth differential guarantees against a debt crisis. The empirical evidence shows that interest rates in a country can rise abruptly and unpredictably relative to interest rates in world markets for a number of reasons (Mauro and Zelinsky 2016). The rise in interest rates can occur even when a country is experiencing recession or secular stagnation. Debt tolerance ultimately depends upon investor's perceptions of debt sustainability in a country, and those expectations can change abruptly.

Empirical studies also show that the current interest rate growth differential is not that unusual. In advanced countries, the interest rate growth differential has been negative most of the time. Research by the IMF shows that the most important predictor of financial cries is the presence of a high debt/GDP ratio and that rising interest rates cause total government borrowing costs—and thus the deficit—to increase (Mauro and Zhou 2019; Moreno-Badia et al. 2020). As larger deficits are incurred, the debt/GDP ratio in subsequent years rises. Increased risk of default leads investors to demand even higher interest rates before purchasing new debt. The relationship between higher debt/GDP ratios and higher interest rates is nonlinear. A shock may cause interest rates to rise abruptly, shifting the country from a good equilibrium with stable debt and low interest rates to a bad equilibrium with rising debt/GDP ratios and high interest rates, potentially ending in a financial crisis and default. In the empirical literature, there are numerous examples of financial crises brought about by increased interest rates, often accompanied by declines in economic growth. This includes large developed and emerging counties that issue their own currency.

The current low interest rate environment has actually increased the importance of fiscal rules and prudent fiscal policies. As countries encounter an effective lower bound on policy rates, the ability to use monetary policy to achieve price stability and economic stabilization is increasingly limited. The role of fiscal policy in business cycle stabilization becomes more important, and that is best achieved through enhanced automatic stabilizers. In countries where the debt/GDP ratio has increased to levels that risk default, the best way to reduce the chance of a debt crisis is to impose fiscal rules mandating a gradual but sustained fiscal adjustment through expenditure cuts. The expenditure rules must be designed to achieve sustainable debt/GDP levels, while allowing flexibility to respond to the business cycle and economic shocks. A consensus in support of effective expenditure rules is reflected in a growing number of countries that enact expenditure rules each year. The expenditure rules must be complemented by other fiscal rules to deliver the debt anchor.

NEW FRONTIERS IN RULES-BASED FISCAL POLICY

Using Public Sector Balance Sheets to Improve Transparency and Accountability

Over the past three decades, a number of innovations have improved the effectiveness of rules-based fiscal policies. One of the most important of those innovations is the use of Public Sector Balance Sheets (PSBS). As a complement to the system of fiscal rules focusing on deficits and debt, the PSBS can provide new data on a wide range of issues in macroeconomics. A PSBS measures the sum of assets and liabilities for a government, similar to the balance sheets used to measure corporate assets and liabilities. Net worth is calculated as the government's total assets minus liabilities, similar to the calculation of corporate net worth. Net worth is an alternative way to measure solvency to traditional measures based on government deficits and debt. We can think of PSBS as a snapshot of the government's solvency based on total assets and liabilities, complementing measures of solvency based on the flow of revenues and expenses that generate deficits and debt accumulation (Detter and Fölster 2015; Gaspar and Amaglobeli 2019; Gonguet and hellwig 2019; Hughes et al. 2019; Mauro and Zilinsky 2016).

Empirical evidence reveals important differences in the trend of overall balance among the developed countries (Eichengreen and O'Rourke 2010; IMF 2018, 2020). Tables 5.1 and 5.2 show the public sector balance sheet data for advanced countries compiled by the International Monetary Fund (IMF 2021, 59–65).

Some European countries emerged from the financial crisis with significant negative balances, including Greece, Ireland, Lithuania, Portugal, and Spain. Japan and the United States also emerged from the financial crisis with negative balances comparable to these European countries. What is surprising is that over the past decade the European countries all made significant progress in reducing their negative balances. Ireland, for example, is an incredible success story. In 2011, Ireland had the highest negative balance of all the developed countries. By 2021, Ireland had virtually eliminated the negative balance. At the other end of the spectrum are countries with positive overall balances, including Norway and Singapore.

The trend in the overall balance for Japan diverged significantly from that of the United States. After the financial crisis both countries emerged with high negative balances. But over the last decade, Japan reduced the negative balance well below the average for all developed countries. The United

Chapter 5

Table 5.1 Advanced Economies General Government Overall Balance, 2012–2026 (percent of GDP)

	2012	2013	2014	2015	2016	2017	2018	2019	2020	2021	2022	2023	2024	2025	2026
Average	-5.5	-3.7	-3.1	-2.6	-2.7	-2.4	-2.5	-2.9	-11.7	-10.4	-4.6	-3.2	-3.0	-3.0	-2.8
Euro Area	-3.7	-3.0	-2.5	-2.0	-1.5	-0.9	-0.5	-0.6	-7.6	-6.7	-3.3	-2.3	-1.8	-1.6	-1.6
G7	-6.5	-4.3	-3.6	-3.0	-3.3	-3.3	-3.4	-3.7	-13.2	-11.9	-5.0	-3.5	-3.4	-3.5	-3.3
G20 Advanced	-6.1	-4.1	-3.5	-2.9	-3.1	-3.0	-3.1	-3.6	-12.7	-11.5	-5.0	-3.5	-3.3	-3.4	-3.2
Australia	-3.5	-2.8	-2.9	-2.8	-2.4	-1.7	-1.2	-3.8	-9.9	-10.4	-6.8	-4.9	-3.8	-3.1	-2.7
Austria	-2.2	-2.0	-2.7	-1.0	-1.6	-0.7	0.2	0.7	-9.6	-6.5	-3.6	-2.2	-1.4	-1.0	-0.9
Belgium	-4.3	-3.1	-3.1	-2.4	-2.4	-0.7	-0.8	-1.9	-10.2	-7.3	-5.0	-4.9	-5.0	-4.9	-4.9
Canada	-2.5	-1.5	0.2	-0.1	-0.5	-0.1	0.3	0.5	-7.8	-3.9	-1.3	-0.2	0.1	0.2	
								-10.7							
Cyprus[1]	-5.6	-5.2	-0.2	0.2	0.2	2.0	-3.5	1.5	-5.0	-3.2	-0.8	-0.4	0.0	0.6	0.8
Czech Republic	-3.9	-1.2	-2.1	-0.6	0.7	1.5	0.9	0.3	-5.9	-7.8	-6.3	-5.6	-5.1	-4.5	-4.0
Denmark	-3.5	-1.2	1.1	-1.3	-0.1	1.8	0.7	3.8	-3.5	-1.8	-1.8	-1.2	-0.8	0.0	0.0
Estonia	-0.3	-0.2	0.7	0.1	-0.3	-0.4	-0.5	0.0	-5.4	-7.1	-6.3	-5.2	-4.4	-3.6	-3.0
Finland	-2.2	-2.5	-3.0	-2.4	-1.7	-0.7	-0.9	-1.0	-4.8	-4.3	-3.0	-2.2	-2.0	-1.8	-1.6
France	-5.0	-4.1	-3.9	-3.6	-3.6	-2.9	-2.3	-3.0	-9.9	-7.2	-4.4	-3.8	-3.6	-3.5	-3.5
Germany	0.0	0.0	0.6	1.0	1.2	1.4	1.8	1.5	-4.2	-5.5	-0.4	0.4	0.5	0.6	0.6
Greece	-6.7	-3.6	-4.1	-2.8	0.6	1.1	0.9	0.6	-9.9	-8.9	-2.6	-2.0	-1.8	-1.7	-1.5
Hong Kong SAR	3.1	1.0	3.6	0.6	4.4	5.5	2.3	-0.6	-10.0	-4.7	-0.1	-0.1	-0.1	-0.1	-0.1
Iceland	-2.6	-1.2	0.3	-0.4	12.5	1.0	0.9	-1.5	-7.3	-10.2	-8.9	-6.9	-4.1	-3.1	-3.2
Ireland[1]	-8.1	-6.2	-3.6	-2.0	-0.7	-0.3	0.1	0.5	-5.3	-5.5	-2.8	-1.4	-1.0	-0.4	-0.3
Israel	-4.4	-4.1	-2.4	-1.1	-1.4	-1.1	-3.6	-3.9	-11.8	-8.9	-4.4	-4.1	-3.9	-3.8	-3.7
Italy	-2.9	-2.9	-3.0	-2.6	-2.4	-2.4	-2.2	-1.6	-9.5	-8.8	-5.5	-3.8	-2.2	-2.0	-1.8
Japan	-8.5	-7.9	-5.9	-3.9	-3.8	-3.3	-2.7	-3.1	-12.6	-9.4	-3.8	-2.5	-2.3	-2.3	-2.4
Korea	1.5	0.6	0.4	0.5	1.6	2.2	2.6	0.4	-2.8	-2.9	-2.4	-2.5	-2.4	-2.3	-2.0
Latvia	0.2	-0.6	-1.7	-1.5	-0.4	-0.8	-0.7	-0.4	-3.9	-6.7	-1.8	-0.9	-0.5	-0.6	-0.5
Lithuania	-3.1	-2.6	-0.7	-0.2	0.3	0.5	0.6	0.3	-8.0	-6.1	-1.8	-0.8	-0.4	0.0	0.4
Luxembourg	0.5	0.9	1.4	1.3	1.9	1.3	3.1	2.4	-3.8	-1.5	-0.5	-0.1	0.0	0.0	0.0

Malta	-3.4	-2.3	-1.7	-1.0	0.9	3.2	2.0	0.5	-9.0	-5.7	-3.1	-2.5	-2.0	-1.5	-0.9
The Netherlands	-3.9	-2.9	-2.2	-2.0	0.0	1.3	1.4	2.5	-5.6	-4.3	-2.5	-1.6	-0.9	-0.3	-0.1
New Zealand	-2.2	-1.3	-0.4	0.3	1.0	1.3	1.1	-2.3	-5.7	-5.1	-3.9	-2.7	-1.7	-0.7	-0.2
Norway	13.8	10.7	8.6	6.0	4.1	5.0	6.9	5.6	-7.0	-0.2	1.4	2.9	3.9	4.5	4.3
Portugal	-6.2	-5.1	-7.3	-4.4	-1.9	-3.0	-0.3	0.1	-6.1	-5.0	-1.9	-1.4	0.5	0.3	0.3
Singapore	7.3	6.0	4.6	2.9	3.7	5.3	3.7	3.8	-8.9	-0.2	3.1	3.1	3.1	2.5	2.6
Slovak Republic	-4.4	-2.9	-3.1	-2.7	-2.6	-0.9	-1.0	-1.4	-7.3	-7.1	-4.9	-4.4	-3.9	-3.6	-3.3
Slovenia	-4.0	-14.6	-5.5	-2.8	-1.9	-0.1	0.7	0.5	-8.5	-6.2	-4.2	-3.4	-2.8	-2.2	-2.0
Spain[1]	-10.7	-7.0	-5.9	-5.2	-4.3	-3.0	-2.5	-2.9	-11.5	-9.0	-5.8	-4.9	-4.3	-4.3	-4.3
Sweden	-1.0	-1.4	-1.5	0.0	1.0	1.4	0.8	0.5	-4.0	-3.9	-1.8	-0.2	0.1	0.3	0.3
Switzerland	0.2	-0.4	-0.2	0.5	0.2	1.1	1.3	1.4	-2.6	-3.4	-0.7	-0.1	-0.1	0.0	0.0
United Kingdom[2]	-7.6	-5.5	-5.5	-4.5	-3.3	-2.4	-2.2	-2.3	-13.4	-11.8	-6.2	-4.0	-3.4	-3.3	-3.3
United States[2]	-8.0	-4.6	-4.1	-3.5	-4.3	-4.6	-5.4	-5.7	-15.8	-15.0	-6.1	-4.6	-4.7	-5.0	-4.7

Source: IMF staff estimates and projections. Projections are based on staff assessments of current policies (see "Fiscal Policy Assumptions" in text). *Note:* For country-specific details, see "Data and Conventions" in text, and Table B.

[1]Data include financial sector support. For Cyprus, 2014 and 2015 balances exclude financial sector support.

[2]For cross-economy comparison, the expenditures and fiscal balances of the United States are adjusted to exclude the imputed interest on unfunded pension liabilities and the imputed compensation of employees, which are counted as expenditures under the 2008 System of National Accounts (2008 SNA) adopted by the United States, but not in economies that have not yet adopted the 2008 SNA. Data for the United States in this table may thus differ from data published by the US Bureau of Economic Analysis.

Table 5.2 Advanced Economies: General Government Gross Debt, 2012–26 (percent of GDP)

	2012	2013	2014	2015	2016	2017	2018	2019	2020	2021	2022	2023	2024	2025	2026
Average	105.6	104.2	103.6	103.0	105.5	103.1	102.5	103.8	120.1	122.5	121.6	121.8	121.5	121.4	121.1
Euro Area	90.7	92.6	92.8	90.9	90.1	87.7	85.8	84.0	96.9	98.2	96.5	95.6	94.4	93.1	91.9
G7	120.9	118.6	117.5	116.2	119.3	117.2	116.8	118.0	136.7	139.5	138.1	138.2	138.1	138.1	138.0
G20	114.1	112.2	111.4	110.7	113.7	111.4	111.2	112.7	130.8	133.7	132.8	133.1	133.0	133.1	133.0
Advanced Australia[1]	27.5	30.5	34.0	37.7	40.5	41.1	41.7	47.5	63.1	72.1	77.0	78.0	77.2	76.0	75.0
Austria	81.7	81.0	83.8	84.4	82.5	78.6	74.0	70.5	85.2	87.2	85.7	84.6	82.7	80.1	78.0
Belgium	104.8	105.5	107.0	105.2	105.0	102.0	99.8	98.1	115.0	115.9	116.2	117.4	118.9	120.6	122.2
Canada[1]	85.4	86.1	85.6	91.2	91.7	88.8	88.8	86.8	117.8	116.3	112.8	109.3	105.7	102.0	98.1
Cyprus	79.4	102.9	109.1	107.2	103.1	93.5	99.2	94.0	118.2	113.0	105.4	102.3	95.1	91.4	85.7
Czech Republic	44.2	44.4	41.9	39.7	36.6	34.2	32.1	30.2	37.6	44.0	48.0	51.4	53.9	56.1	55.0
Denmark	44.9	44.0	44.3	39.8	37.2	35.5	33.8	33.0	43.4	41.6	42.9	43.8	44.2	44.3	44.3
Estonia	9.8	10.2	10.6	10.0	9.9	9.1	8.2	8.4	18.5	25.1	30.3	34.4	37.3	39.5	40.8
Finland	53.6	56.2	59.8	63.6	63.2	61.2	59.6	59.3	67.1	68.8	69.2	69.9	70.6	70.9	71.2
France	90.6	93.4	94.9	95.6	98.0	98.3	98.0	98.1	113.5	115.2	114.3	115.2	115.9	116.3	116.9
Germany	81.1	78.7	75.6	72.3	69.3	65.1	61.8	59.6	68.9	70.3	67.3	64.8	62.2	59.6	57.1
Greece	162.0	179.0	181.5	179.0	183.4	182.4	189.9	184.9	213.1	210.1	200.5	193.1	189.1	184.8	179.6
Hong Kong SAR[1]	0.5	0.5	0.1	0.1	0.1	0.1	0.1	0.3	0.3	0.9	0.9	0.8	0.6	0.5	0.3
Iceland	133.9	122.0	115.2	97.2	79.9	69.4	61.1	68.3	79.9	82.5	86.1	88.7	88.5	86.9	77.5
Ireland	119.9	120.0	104.4	76.6	74.2	67.3	62.9	57.4	59.8	63.2	63.2	61.4	59.7	57.7	54.4
Israel	68.5	67.1	65.7	63.8	62.1	60.6	60.9	60.0	73.0	78.3	78.8	79.3	79.7	80.2	80.7
Italy	126.5	132.5	135.4	135.3	134.8	134.1	134.4	134.6	155.6	157.1	155.5	155.1	153.7	152.0	151.0
Japan	226.1	229.6	233.5	228.4	232.5	231.4	232.5	234.9	256.2	256.5	253.6	252.9	253.4	254.0	254.7
Korea	35.0	37.7	39.7	40.8	41.2	40.1	40.0	42.2	48.7	53.2	57.2	61.0	64.4	67.3	69.7
Latvia	41.6	39.2	40.9	36.5	39.8	40.1	36.4	37.0	45.5	47.2	45.3	43.6	42.2	40.7	39.2
Lithuania	39.7	38.7	40.5	42.7	39.9	39.3	33.7	35.9	47.0	49.5	47.7	45.6	43.2	40.7	38.1

Luxembourg	22.0	23.7	22.7	22.0	20.1	22.3	21.0	22.0	25.5	26.8	27.3	27.4	27.2	27.1	27.0
Malta	65.9	65.8	61.6	55.9	54.3	48.5	44.8	42.0	55.4	57.9	56.6	55.5	53.1	50.3	47.2
The Netherlands	66.4	67.8	68.0	64.6	61.9	56.9	52.4	47.6	54.0	56.1	56.1	55.9	55.0	53.5	51.8
New Zealand	35.7	34.6	34.2	34.2	33.4	31.1	28.1	32.1	41.3	46.4	50.5	52.8	53.7	52.5	50.4
Norway	31.1	31.6	29.9	34.5	38.1	38.6	39.7	40.9	41.4	41.6	41.3	41.0	40.7	40.4	40.2
Portugal	129.0	131.4	132.9	131.2	131.5	126.1	121.5	116.8	131.6	131.4	125.6	122.0	117.6	113.9	110.6
Singapore	106.7	98.2	97.8	102.2	106.5	107.8	109.8	129.0	128.4	129.5	130.7	131.9	133.1	134.3	135.5
Slovak Republic	51.8	54.7	53.6	51.9	52.4	51.7	49.9	48.5	60.7	64.0	64.3	63.3	63.4	64.0	64.5
Slovenia	53.6	70.0	80.3	82.6	78.5	74.1	70.3	65.6	81.5	80.5	78.2	77.7	76.7	75.5	74.2
Spain	86.3	95.8	100.7	99.3	99.2	98.6	97.4	95.5	117.1	118.4	117.3	117.3	116.8	117.7	118.4
Sweden	37.5	40.2	44.9	43.7	42.3	40.7	38.9	35.1	38.5	40.4	40.2	38.8	37.3	35.7	34.0
Switzerland	42.2	41.6	41.6	41.7	40.5	41.2	39.2	39.8	42.9	44.8	44.1	43.4	42.3	41.5	40.4
United Kingdom	83.2	84.2	86.1	86.7	86.8	86.3	85.8	85.2	103.7	107.1	109.1	110.7	111.4	112.2	113.0
United States[1]	103.4	104.8	104.6	104.7	106.6	105.6	106.6	108.2	127.1	132.8	132.1	132.4	133.0	133.9	134.5

Source: IMF staff estimates and projections. Projections are based on staff assessments of current policies (see "Fiscal Policy Assumptions" in text). Note: For economy specific details, see "Data and Conventions" in text, and Table B.

[1] For cross-economy comparison, gross debt levels reported by national statistical agencies for economies that have adopted the 2008 System of National Accounts (Australia, Canada, Hong Kong SAR, and United States) are adjusted to exclude unfunded pension liabilities of government employees' defined benefit pension plans.

States, on the other hand, made little progress; and during the coronavirus pandemic in 2020 the balance was a negative 15.8 percent, the highest negative balance recorded for a developed country in the past decade.

The IMF projects that advanced economies will make significant progress in improving their overall balance over the next decade. Most European countries are projected to eliminate their negative balance. Japan is projected to make progress, reducing the balance to −2.4 percent of GDP by 2026. The United States is projected to reduce the negative balance from the high levels incurred during the coronavirus pandemic. But, at the end of the period the United States will still have the highest negative balance among advanced economies −4.7 percent. From this PSBS perspective, the United States has the highest debt burden among advanced countries, exceeding even that of Japan.

The empirical evidence reveals that balance sheet strength is an important determinant of debt stabilization (Akitoby and Stratmann 2008; Ardagna et al. 2007; Dell'Erba et al. 2013). Balance sheet strength influences the yield on government bonds. Financial markets pay attention to the government's asset position as well as total debt in determining borrowing costs. Financial markets also distinguish between debt reduction through asset accumulation or reduction, versus a primary balance surplus (Jaramillo and Weber 2013; Gruber and Kamin 2012).

Empirical studies also reveal that a country's balance sheet strength impacts the fiscal space to respond to business cycles and economic shocks (Bernardini and Forni 2017; International Monetary Fund 2016). Countries with strong balance sheets experience shallower and shorter recessions compared to countries with weaker balance sheets; they are better able to respond with countercyclical fiscal policy. The research shows that countries with strong balance sheets recover economic growth more quickly after recessions, complementing the work of Rinehart and Rogoff (2010).

Research on balance sheets helps to explain the poor performance of the U.S. economy over the past decade. The financial crisis had a greater impact on the United States than most developed countries; the recession was deeper and more prolonged. The countercyclical policies pursued by the United States in response to the financial crisis were accompanied by a sharp discontinuous increase in debt.[7] In contrast, the European countries with strong balance sheets had more fiscal space to respond to the recession and were able to pursue countercyclical policy with relatively stable debt/GDP ratios. In those countries, the recession was shallower, and they were able to recover economic growth more quickly. It is not a coincidence that the European countries with the strongest balance sheets enacted the most effective fiscal rules (Yousefi 2019).

Balance sheet strength is an alternative to the debt/GDP ratio in measuring debt stability. Closing the fiscal gap means that a country is able to stabilize or reduce the debt/GDP ratio. The IMF measures the ratio of gross debt to GDP over this period. The IMF projects that after reaching a high of 98 percent in 2021, the European region as a whole will close the fiscal gap over the forecast period. With few exceptions, the European countries are projected to stabilize or reduce the debt/GDP ratio in the coming years. Even the most heavily indebted nations, Greece and Italy, are projected to close the fiscal gap.

Japan has the highest debt/GDP ratio among the advanced nations. However, Japan is also projected to close the fiscal gap in the coming years. In the United States, on the other hand, the debt/GDP ratio is projected to increase to 135 percent in 2026. By 2026, the United States will be the fourth most indebted of the advanced nations, after Japan, Greece, Italy, and Singapore. The CBO projects that the gross debt/GDP ratio will continue rising in the coming decades, reaching more than 250 percent by midcentury. The United States is one of the few advanced countries not able to close the fiscal gap.

The PSBS approach is relatively new and shows promise in helping address a wide range of macroeconomic issues. The treatment of public investment has been problematic in addressing the debt crisis. Countries practicing the Golden Rule of public finance have found that this loophole makes it difficult to enforce fiscal rules. The PSBS provides a more accurate picture of the public finance impact of public investment. This is especially important for a country such as the United States that is about to embark on a major new infrastructure investment program. The PSBS approach provides support for prefunding major infrastructure projects such as the interstate highway system. The highway trust fund is projected to be exhausted in the coming years. PSBS analysis shows why that trust fund should be restored and similar trust funds created for other infrastructure projects. The PSBS is especially important in assessing alternative energy projects. The new agenda for the United States calls for a greatly expanded role for public enterprises, public private partnerships, federal loans, and loan guarantees to private corporations. These public and quasipublic ventures should be audited the same way that private ventures are audited, based on the strength of their balance sheets. In the energy sector, where public ventures compete with private ventures, balance sheet strength can help determine whether public ventures are competitive. That can help identify inefficiencies and misallocation of public investments. PSBS analysis could help to identify and prevent boondoggles such as the Synfuels Corporation that was allocated $30 billion to develop alternative energy during the energy crisis in the 1970s, and shut down in 1986. Despite that failure, we continue to waste public investments in failed energy projects. Solyndra, a solar energy project funded with $536 million in government backed loans, went bankrupt in 2011. Crescent Dunes is another solar energy project, funded with $737 million in government loan guarantees. The company has not produced any power in the last two years. PSBS can help determine when these public venture fail to compete with private energy firms and identify inefficiencies and misallocation of public investments. Termination and privatization of failed public sector venture can reallocate resources more efficiently.

Another issue that can benefit from the PSBS approach is the impact of population dynamics on public finance. The PSBS approach captures the impact of population aging on unfunded liabilities in social security and health care programs. The analysis provides a rationale for prefunding these entitlement programs. For a country such as the United States, where the trust funds for entitlement programs are about to be exhausted, the PSBS approach is especially important.

An issue that will be of greater importance in the coming years is climate change policy. The PSBS approach can provide essential information on the impact of climate change policies on public sector assets and liabilities, and debt sustainability.

Fiscal Responsibility Councils

Deficit and debt sustainability problems can undermine both economic stability and economic growth, and in the worst cases lead to economic and financial crises. A number of institutional reforms have been proposed to create incentives for policy makers to use discretionary fiscal policy responsibly, reduce deficit bias, and improve macroeconomic policy. These proposals reflect the need to constrain discretionary fiscal policy, impose fiscal discipline, and avoid excessive borrowing and debt accumulation.

Among the most important of these institutional reforms are independent fiscal agencies. These institutions are usually proposed as a complement to fiscal responsibility laws and fiscal rules (Calmfors 2003; Calmfors and Wren-Lewis 2011; Debrun and Kumar 2008; Debrun et al. 2009, 2011; Debrun et al. 2013; Debrun and Kinda 2014; Fabrizio and Mody 2006; International Monetary Fund 2015b; Wyplosz 2005, 2011).

There is a major distinction between the two types of independent fiscal agencies (IMF 2013, 2014). Independent Fiscal Councils (IFC) are institutional arrangements in which some fiscal policies are delegated to an independent authority, replacing discretionary fiscal policy of the legislative branch. An IFC is comparable to an independent monetary authority, such as the Federal Reserve Board. An IFC is charged with setting short-term fiscal balance targets based on fiscal rules designed to achieve budget stabilization and debt sustainability. The literature provides a strong analytical basis for IFCs, but to date no country has enacted this institutional reform. An IFC raises questions of democratic accountability beyond those encountered by other independent monetary authorities. Not surprisingly no legislative body has been willing to surrender their control over fiscal policy to an IFC. This controversy is especially relevant in the European Union where an IFC has been proposed to complement the monetary union.

An Advisory Fiscal Council (AFC) does not require a significant delegation of fiscal power from the legislative body. However, AFCs can play a significant role in implementing rules-based fiscal policy. AFCs were established in European countries to implement the new fiscal rules enacted at the national level over the past three decades. To be effective the new fiscal rules required greater transparency and accountability for fiscal rules and fiscal policies. These AFCs often play a crucial role in the budget process. They are quasi-independent authorities appointed by the head of government, with approval from the legislative body. They work closely with government ministries in drafting the budget. They are responsible for monitoring fiscal policy to assure that it is consistent with the fiscal rules. They make normative judgments regarding the appropriateness of fiscal policy in a given macroeconomic environment. That role may include reporting on the effectiveness of fiscal policy in meeting the targets set in a medium-term fiscal framework and recommending corrective actions when fiscal policy deviates from the targets. In addition, AFCs often have a broad mandate to assess macroeconomic conditions. The AFC may also be charged with the analysis of the long-term fiscal impact of demographic change, entitlements, environmental impacts of climate change, and other factors influencing fiscal sustainability.[8]

The FRC created by Sweden as part of the new National Medium Term Budgetary Framework has become a model for this type of IFC (Swedish Fiscal Policy Council 2019). The experience in Sweden shows that an IFC can play a crucial role in implementing rules-based fiscal policy. As a quasi-independent fiscal authority, it can guide the budget process toward fiscal sustainability. The role of the IFC is not just in providing greater transparency, but also in enforcement and accountability. The Swedish FRC does not have enforcement powers per se, but its publications and recommendations have an important impact on parliament. When elected officials choose to deviate from the fiscal rules, they must explain why and propose remedial fiscal policies. When elected officials violate the fiscal rules this can have important reputational effects.

Fiscal Federalism

Fiscal Federalism has emerged as a major challenge for many countries in addressing the debt crisis. When subnational governments can issue debt, the fiscal rules of the game may bias them to issue debt that increases the risk of default for all levels of government (Berger et al. 2018; Eyraud et al. 2017).

Orthodox public finance explores the concept of optimum fiscal federalist systems based on assumptions that may not be fulfilled in the real world (McKinnon 1963; Mundell 1961; Musgrave 1959; Oates 1972). The assumption is that each subnational unit of government exercises autonomy in tax and expenditure decisions. It is further assumed that subnational governments face a hard budget constraint and a no bail-out rule imposing fiscal discipline. The reality is that there is often strong fiscal interdependence, with subnational governments dependent on transfers from the central government (Eichengreen 1991; Bordo et al. 2011). Weak fiscal rules at the state and local levels create incentives for elected officials to increase expenditures financed by debt and shift the cost of that debt to other units of governments. The national government may not fully commit to a no bail-out rule, increasing incentives for profligate fiscal policies at the state and local levels. In this literature, Argentina stands out as a country in which the debt crisis reflects a failed system of fiscal federalism (Sturzenegger and Werneck 2006; Tommasi 2002; DellaPaolera et al. 1999). Over the past half-century, all levels of government in Argentina have incurred unsustainable levels of debt. The debts incurred at the provincial level have been a major source of financial and macroeconomic instability. The provinces account for a major share of total debt, financed largely by loans and transfers from the central government. The provinces also borrow from provincial banks who then discount the debt at the central bank, shifting the cost of that debt to the central government. In periods of financial crisis, the central government issues treasury bonds to finance loans to the provinces (Saiegh and Tommasi 1999).

The increasing risk on Argentine debt is reflected in higher interest rates, especially on the debt issued by the provinces (Bordo and Vegh 2002). Over this period Argentina has experienced a series of economic shocks in which it was forced to default on debt. Despite many attempts at reforms designed to impose fiscal discipline, the failed federalist system in Argentina remains a source of macroeconomic instability.

Fiscal federalism in Germany exhibits many of the flaws encountered in the Argentine system (Ziblatt 2004; Hefeker 2001). The West German Constitution, the Basic Law, divided responsibilities between the federal government and the Lander. While the Lander are responsible for the provisions of many government services, their power to tax is quite limited. Because most taxing power and revenues are at the federal level, the German system relies on an extensive system of government transfers. The Lander have the discretion to issue debt with few constraints from the federal government. The incentive for elected officials in the Lander is to increase expenditures financed by debt and then shift the debt burden to the federal government.

During the financial crisis the debt/GDP ratio in Germany increased well above the debt limits imposed by their national fiscal rules, and also debt limits set by the EU (Berger et al. 2018).

The German Parliament responded to that debt crisis by enacting more effective fiscal rules similar to the Swiss debt brake. The new rules require both the Lander and the federal government to balance their budgets, with no new debt except under special circumstances. An extended transition period was provided for the Lander and the federal government to comply with the new fiscal rules. The more heavily indebted Lander were given a time frame within which to bring their budgets into balance, and transition assistance was extended to several highly indebted Lander. A Fiscal Responsibility Council (FRC) was created consisting of the finance ministers of the Lander and the economic and finance ministers of the federation. The success of the new fiscal rules is reflected in the decrease in the debt/GDP ratio below the 60 percent debt limit over the past decade. While the debt/GDP ratio has again increased above that debt limit during the coronavirus pandemic, projections are for the debt to again fall below the debt limit in the coming years.

A PATH FORWARD

As we look back on the new era of fiscal rules it is clear that the United States has chosen the wrong path. The path not taken is that chosen by Sweden, Germany, Switzerland, and other countries pursuing new rules-based fiscal policies. The new fiscal rules have required institutional innovations such as a public sector balance sheet (PSBC), fiscal responsibility Councils (FRC), and strengthened fiscal federalism. These countries are pursuing fiscal policies consistent with budget stabilization and debt sustainability. The United States enacted statutory fiscal rules that are easily suspended and evaded and failed to introduce institutional reforms needed to make fiscal rules more effective. The United States is on a path of unsustainable fiscal policies in which each major economic shock is accompanied by a sharp discontinuous increase in debt. The unsustainable debt trajectory is accompanied by secular retardation in economic growth. It is unreasonable to assume that in the current economic environment, Congress will voluntarily restore the Great Moderation in macroeconomic policy.

The question explored in the remaining chapters of this book is whether the United States could follow this alternative path, replacing discretionary fiscal policies with formal fiscal rules. A debt brake is designed for the United States, patterned after the Swiss debt brake. The macroeconomic impact of the debt brake is estimated using a dynamic simulation model. The debt brake is simulated using historical data extending back to the 1990s,

and over the next three decades. As we would expect, it is much more difficult to use a debt brake to solve the debt crisis today than it would have been
if the rules were enacted in the 1990s. Nonetheless, the simulation analysis
reveals that the United States could use a debt brake to begin to address the
debt crisis and follow the path chosen by Switzerland and other European
counties.

Enacting a debt brake in the United States would require fundamental
reform in fiscal institutions just as it did in Europe. Given the virtual abandonment of fiscal rules in the United States over the past few decades, it will
be more difficult to impose these fiscal rules. The budget process must be
reformed to provide transparency and accountability in fiscal policy. Independent fiscal authorities must be introduced without conflicting with constitutional provisions limiting the delegation of fiscal powers from Congress. In
the final sections of the book, we explore these reforms in fiscal institutions
and budget processes.

The authors of this study view the debt crisis as a challenge. We think
that the United States will emerge from the coronavirus pandemic with a
debt crisis and a zombie economy that is unprecedented. After the euphoric
response to this fiscal and monetary blowout, reality will set in, as elected
officials are forced to confront the failures of these monetary and fiscal
policies. This occurred in the 1970s in an era of stagflation, when elected
officials were forced to recognize the failures of Keynesian fiscal policy.
We think that the same paradigm shift will occur in the 2020s as elected
officials cope with the impact of unsustainable growth in debt, that is,
increased macroeconomic instability and secular retardation in economic
growth.

The authors have created the Friedman Project as an antidote to outdated
Keynesian ideas. The project is named for the founder of rules-based fiscal
and monetary policy, Milton Friedman. Friedman proposed these ideas at a
time when the Keynesian paradigm dominated the economics profession.
His view was that eventually policy makers learn that rules-based fiscal
and monetary policies are a prerequisite for budget stabilization and debt
sustainability.

The authors have created what is in effect a shadow fiscal responsibility
council (FRC). This shadow FRC is composed of economists and policy
experts who support rules-based monetary and fiscal policy in the Friedman
tradition. These scholars and policy experts meet informally at professional
meetings and other venues where these ideas are discussed and debated.
Some of the papers are published as white papers or in book publications
and are posted on the website vetfiscalrules.net. The Friedman Project has
received support from the Koch Foundation, R Street Institute, the American
Legislative Exchange Council, and other private contributors.

NOTES

1. For surveys of fiscal rules see Luc Eyraud et al. 2018, "Second-Generation Fiscal Rules: Balancing Simplicity, Flexibility, and Enforceability," IMF Staff Discussion Note no. 18/04, April 2018; see also Alberto Alesina and Allan Drazen, "Why are Stabilizations Delayed?," *American Economic Review* 81, no. 5 (1991): 1170–1188; Torsten Persson and Guido Tabelini, *Political Economics: Explaining Economic Policy* (Cambridge, MA: The MIT Press, 2000); Jürgen von Hagen, "A Note on the Empirical Effectiveness of Formal Fiscal Restraints," *Journal of Public Economics* 44 (March 1991): 199–210.

2. For a discussion of the deficit bias in the European Monetary Union, see Organization for Economic Cooperation and Development (2003).

3. John D. Merrifield and Barry W. Poulson, "Swedish and Swiss Fiscal-Rule Outcomes Contain Key Lessons for the United States," *The Independent Review*, 2016; John D. Merrifield and Barry W. Poulson, "New Constitutional Debt Brakes for Euroland Revisited," *Journal of Applied Business and Economics* 19(8), November 1, 2017.

4. Victor Lledó et al., "Second-Generation Fiscal Rules: Balancing Simplicity, Flexibility, and Enforceability," IMF Discussion Note SDN/18/04, International Monetary Fund, April 2018; John D. Merrifield and Barry W. Poulson, *Can the Debt Growth be Stopped? Rules Based Policy: Options for Addressing the Federal Fiscal Crisis* (New York: Lexington Books, 2016); John D. Merrifield and Barry W. Poulson, *Restoring America's Fiscal Constitution* (New York: Lexington Books, 2017).

5. Luc Eyraud et al. 2018, "Second-Generation Fiscal Rules: Balancing Simplicity, Flexibility, and Enforceability," IMF Staff Discussion Note no. 18/04, April 2018.

6. There is some evidence that voters reward fiscal responsibility, but on balance the bias of elected officials is toward deficits. For a discussion of the deficit bias in the European Monetary Union (EMU), see Organization for economic Cooperation and Development (2003).

7. Higher debt levels in the United States also reflect the expanded role for federal programs in health, housing, financial markets, and so on.

8. It is argued that the Congressional Budget Office (CBO) and General Accounting Office (GAO) combined approximate and Advisory Fiscal Council in the United States. In the final chapter of this book, we critically evaluate the role of the CBO and the rationale for a new Fiscal Responsibility Council (FRC) similar to that in Sweden and other European countries.

REFERENCES

Akitoby, B., and T. Stratmann. 2008. "Fiscal Policy and Financial Markets," *Economic Journal* 118: 1971–1985.

Alesina, A., and A. Drazen. 1991. "Why Are Stabilizations Delayed?" *American Economic Review* 81: 1170–1188.

Andrle, M., J. Bluedorn, L. Eyraud, T. Kinda, P. Koeva Brooks, G. Schwartz, and A. Weber. 2015. "Reforming Fiscal Governance in the European Union," IMF Staff Discussion Note 15/09.

Ardagna, S., F. Caselli, and T. Lane. 2007. "Fiscal Discipline and the Cost of Public Debt Service: Some Estimates for OECD Countries," *The B.E. Journal of Macroeconomics* 7(1): 1–35.

Auerbach, A. 2019. "The Future of Fiscal Policy," Keynote Address, Fourth ECB Biennial Conference on Fiscal Policy and EMU Governance.

Baur, M., P. Bruchez, and B. Schlaffer. 2013. "Institutions for Crisis Prevention: the Case of Switzerland," *Global Policy* 4, Supplement 1, July.

Bednar, J. 2009. *The Robust Federation: Principles of Design*, Cambridge University Press.

Berger, H., G. Dell'Ariccia, and M. Obstfeld. 2018. "Revisiting the Case for a Fiscal Union in the Euro Area." Departmental Paper, IMF Research Department, International Monetary Fund, Washington, DC.

Bernardini, M., and L. Forni. 2017. "Private and Public Debt: Are Emerging Markets at Risk?" IMF Working Paper 17/61 International Monetary Fund Washington, DC.

Blanchard, O. 2019a. "Public Debt and Low Interest Rates," *American Economic Review* 109(4): 1197–1229.

Blanchard, O. 2019b. "Revisiting the EU Fiscal Framework in an Era of Low interest Rates," Presentation to the Peterson Institute for International Economics, Frankfort, December.

Blanchard, O., and J. Pisani-Ferry. 2019. "The Euro Area Is Not (Yet) Ready for Helicopter Money," Peterson Institute for International Economics, https://www.piie.com/blogs/realtime-economic-issues-watch/euro-area-not-ready-helicopter-money.

Blanchard, O., and L. Summers. 2020. "Automatic Stabilizers in a Low-Rate Environment," Peterson Institute for International Economics, Policy Brief 20–2, February.

Blanchard, O., and L. Summers (eds). 2019. *Evolution or Revolution? Rethinking Macroeconomic Policy after the Great Recession*, MIT Press.

Blanchard, O., and T. Tashiro. 2019. "Fiscal Policy Options for Japan," Peterson Institute for International Economics, Policy Brief 19-27.

Blanchard, O., Á. Leandro, S. Merler, and J. Zettelmeyer. 2018. "Impact of Italy's Draft Budget on Growth and Fiscal Solvency," Peterson Institute for International Economics, Policy Brief 18-24.

Blankart, C. 2000. "The Process of Government Centralization: A Constitutional View," *Constitutional Political Economy* 11(1): 27–39.

Blankart, C. 2011. *An Economic Theory of Switzerland*, CESifo DICE Report 3/2011.

Blankart, C. 2015. "What the Eurozone Could Learn from Switzerland," *CESfio FORUM* 16(2): 39–42.

Blankart, C., E. Fasten, and A. Klaiber. 2006. "Foderalismus ohne insolvenz?" *Wirtschaftsdienst* 86(9): 567–571.

Bordo, M., et al. 2011. "A Fiscal Union for the Euro: Some Lessons From History," Working Paper 17380 National Bureau of Economic Research.

Bordo, M., and C. Vegh. 2002. "If Only Alexander Hamilton had been Argentinean: A Comparison of the Early Monetary Experience of Argentina and the United States," *Journal of Monetary Economics* 49(3): 459–494.

Calmfors, L. 2003. "Fiscal Policy to Stabilize the Domestic Economy in the EMU," *CESifo Economic Studies* 49(3): 319–353.

Calmfors, L., and S. Wren-Lewis. 2011. "What Should Fiscal Councils Do?," CESifo Working Paper No. 3382.

Canada, B. 2003. "Federal Grants to State and Local Governments: A Brief History," *Congressional Research Services RL-30705*, Feb. 19.

Committee on the Budget. 2016a. *Reclaiming Constitutional Authority through the Power of the Purse*, U.S. House of Representatives, Washington DC.

Committee on the Budget. 2016b. *Making Budget Enforcement More Effective*, U.S. House of Representatives, Washington DC.

Committee on the Budget. 2016c. *The Need for Fiscal Goals*, U.S. House of Representatives, Washington DC.

Committee on the Budget. 2016d. *Growing Risks to the Budget and the Economy*, U.S. House of Representatives, Washington DC.

Committee on the Budget. 2016e. *The Need to Control Automatic Spending and Unauthorized Programs*, U.S. House of Representatives, Washington DC.

Congressional Budget Office. 2009. *Budgetary Impact of ARRA*, Washington DC. February.

Congressional Budget Office. 2012. *Report on the Troubled Asset Relief Program*, Washington DC. October.

Congressional Budget Office. 2016a. *Statutory Limits on Total Spending as a Method of Budget Control*, Washington DC.

Congressional Budget Office. 2016b. *Legislative Procedures for Adjusting the Public Debt Limit: A Brief Overview*, Washington DC.

Congressional Budget Office. 2021a. "History," cbo.gov/about/history.

Congressional Budget Office. 2021b. *The Budget and Economic Outlook*, Washington DC (January).

Debrun, Xavier. 2011. "The Theory of Independent Fiscal Agencies: Where Are We? And Where Do We Go from There?" *Economic Policy Papers (Wirtschaftspolitische Blätter)*, 1–2011: 559–570. Also available as IMF Working Paper No 11/173.

Debrun, Xavier, David Hauner, and Manmohan S. Kumar. 2009. "Independent Fiscal Agencies," *Journal of Economic Surveys* 23: 44–81.

Debrun, Xavier, and Tidiane Kinda. 2014. "Strengthening Post-Crisis Fiscal Credibility—Fiscal Councils on the Rise. A New Dataset," IMF Working Paper No 14/58, International Monetary Fund, Washington, DC.

Debrun, Xavier, Tidiane Kinda, Teresa Curristine, Luc Eyraud, Jason Harris, and Johann Seiwald. 2013. "The Functions and Impact of Fiscal Councils," IMF Policy Paper, available at http://www.imf.org/external/np/fad/council/.

Dell'Erba, S., R. Hausmann, and U. Panizza. 2013. "Debt Levels, Debt Composition, and Sovereign Spreads in Emerging and Advanced Economies," *Oxford Review of Economic Policy* 29(3): 518–547.

Detter, D., and S. Fölster. 2015. *The Public Wealth of Nations How Management of Public Assets Can Boost or Bust Economic Growth*, Palgrave MacMillan Publishing.

Eichengreen, B. 1991. "Is Europe an Optimum Currency Area?" NBER Working Paper no. 3579.

Eichengreen, B., and K. O'Rourke. 2010. "What Do the New Data Tell Us?," voxeu .org.

Elmendorf, D., and S. Sheiner. 2016. "Federal Budget Policy with an Aging Population and Persistently Low Interest Rates," Working Paper 18, Hutchins Canter on Fiscal and Monetary Policy. Brookings Institution, Washington.

Eyraud, L., X. Debrun, A. Hodge, V. Lledo, and C. Pattillo. 2018. "Second-Generation Fiscal Rules: Balancing Simplicity, Flexibility, and Enforceability," IMF Discussion Note SDN/18/04, April.

Eyraud, L., V. Gaspar, and T. Poghosyan. 2017. "Fiscal Politics in the Euro Area," in *Fiscal Politics*, edited by V. Gaspar, S. Gupta, and C. Mulas-Granados, 439–76, IMF, Washington, DC.

Eyraud, L., X. Debrun, A. Hodge, V. Lledó, and C. Pattillo. 2018. "Second-Generation Fiscal Rules: Balancing Simplicity, Flexibility, and Enforceability," IMF Staff Discussion Note 18/04.

Eyraud, L., and T. Wu. 2014. "Playing by the Rules: Reforming Fiscal Governance in Europe," IMF Working Paper 15/67.

Fisher R., and R. Wassmer. 2014. "The Issuance of State and Local Debt During the United States Great Recession," *National Tax Journal* March 67(1): 113–150.

Gaspar, V., and D. Amaglobeli. 2019. "Fiscal Rules," SUERF Policy Note, Issue No 60.

Gonguet, F. and K. Hellwig. 2019. Public Wealth in the United States, International Monetary Fund, IMF Working Paper, 2019(19).

Gruber, J. W., and S. B. Kamin. 2012. "Fiscal Positions and Government Bond Yields in OECD Countries," *Journal of Money, Credit, and Banking* 44(8): 1563–1587.

Hansen, A. 1941. *Fiscal Policy and Business Cycles*, W.W. Norton, New York.

Hefeker, C. 2001. "The Agony of Central Power: Fiscal Federalism in the German Reich," *European Review of Economic History* 5: 119–142.

Hughes, R., J. Leslie, C. Pacitti, and J. Smith. 2019. "Totally (net) Worth It: The Next Generation of UK Fiscal Rules," Resolution Foundation.

IMF. 2013. "The Functions and Impact of Fiscal Councils," IMF Policy Paper 2013.

IMF. 2014. "Fiscal Governance in the Euro Area: Progress and Challenges," Euro Area Policies, Selected Issues, IMF Country Report No. 14/199.

IMF. 2015a. "Fiscal Rules Dataset," available at: http://www.imf.org/external/datamapper/FiscalRules/map/map.htm.

IMF. 2015b. "Fiscal Councils Dataset," available at: http://www.imf.org/external/np /fad/council/.

IMF. 2016. "Fiscal Monitor: Debt – Use It Wisely," Washington, DC.

IMF. 2018. "Managing Public Wealth," Fiscal Monitor, October 2018.

IMF. 2020. "Fiscal Policy: Look Beyond Deficit & Debt to the Balance Sheet," IMF Intranet article.

IMF. 2021. "Strengthening the Credibility of Public Finance," Fiscal Monitor, October, 59–65.

Jaramillo, L., and A. Weber. 2013. "Bond Yields in Emerging Economies: It Matter What State You Are In," *Emerging Markets Review* 17: 169–185.

Kopits, G. 2001. "Fiscal Rules: Useful Policy Framework or Unnecessary Ornament?" IMF Working Paper 01/145, International Monetary Fund, Washington, DC.

Kopits, G., and S. Symansky. 1998. "Fiscal Policy Rules," IMF Occasional Paper 162, International Monetary Fund, Washington, DC.

Lledó, V., S. Yoon, X. Fang, S. Mbaye, and Y. Kim. 2017. "Fiscal Rules at a Glance," 2015 IMF Fiscal Rules Database Background Note, International Monetary Fund, Washington, DC. http://www.imf.org/external/datamapper/FiscalRules/map/map.htm.

Mauro, M., and J. Zilinsky. 2016. "Reducing Government Debt Ratios in an Era of Low Growth," Peterson Institute for International Economics Policy Brief 16-10.

Mauro, P., and J. Zhou. 2019. "r − g < 0: Can We Sleep More Soundly?," draft paper presented at the 20th Annual Research Conference, November 7–8, 2019.

McKinnon, R. 1963. "Optimum Currency Areas," *American Economic Review* 53: 717–724.

Merrifield, J., and B. Poulson. 2016a. "The Swedish and Swiss Fiscal Rule Outcomes Contain Key Lessons for the U.S.," *Independent Review* 21(2) Fall 251–274.

Merrifield, J., and B. Poulson. 2016b. *Can the Debt Growth be Stopped? Rules Based Policy Options for Addressing the Federal Fiscal Crisis*, Lexington Books, New York.

Merrifield, J., and B. Poulson. 2017a. *Restoring America's Fiscal Constitution*, Lexington Books, New York.

Merrifield, J., and B. Poulson. 2017b. "New Constitutional Debt Brakes for Euroland Revisited," *Journal of Applied Business and Economics* 19(8): 110–132.

Moreno-Badia, M., P. Medas, P. Gupta, and Y. Xiang. 2020. "Debt is Not Free," IMF Working Paper 20/1.

Mundell, R. 1961. "A Theory of Optimum Currency Areas," *American Economic Review* 51: 509–517.

Nadler, D., and S. Hong. 2011. "Political and Institutional Determinants of Tax-Exempt Bond Yields," Harvard Kennedy School Report No. 11-04.

NBER. 2011. "Fiscal Fatigue, Fiscal Space and Debt Sustainability in Advanced Economies," Working Paper 16782, Cambridge, MA, February.

Oates, W. 2005. "Toward a Second Generation Theory of Federalism," *International Tax and Public Finance* 12(4): 349–373.

Organization for Economic Cooperation and Development. 2003. "Discretionary Fiscal Policy and Elections: The Experience of the Early Years of the EMU," OECD Economics working papers, no. 351.

Persson, T., and G. Tabellini. 2000. *Political Economics: Explaining Economic Policy*. The MIT Press, Cambridge, MA.

Paolera, D., and A. Taylor. 1999. "Economic Recovery from the Argentine Great Depression: Institutions, Expectations and the Change of Macroeconomic Regime," *Journal of Economic History* 59: 567.

Reinhart, Carmen M., and Kenneth S. Rogoff. 2010. "Growth in a Time of Debt," *American Economic Review* 100(2): 573–578.

Rodden, J. 2003. "Reviving Leviathan: Fiscal Federalism and the Growth of Government," *International Organization* 57: 695–729.

Rodden, J., G. Eskeland, and J. Livtak (eds.). 2003. *Fiscal Decentralization and the Challenge of Hard Budget Constraints*, MIT Press, Cambridge, MA.

Rodden, J. 2006. *Hamilton's Paradox. The Promise and Peril of Fiscal Federalism*, Cambridge University Press, New York.

Saiegh, S., and M. Tommasi. 1999. "Why is Argentina's Fiscal Federalism So Inefficient? Entering the Labyrinth," *Journal of Applied Economics* 2: 169–209.

Schaechter, A., T. Kinda, N. Budina, and A. Weber. 2012. "Fiscal Rules in Response to the Crisis – Toward the 'Next-Generation' Rules. A New Dataset," IMF Working Paper 12/187, International Monetary Fund, Washington, DC.

Schick, A. 2010. "Post-Crisis Fiscal Rules: Stabilizing Public Finance while Responding to Economic Aftershocks." *OECD Journal on Budgeting* 2010(2): 1–17.

Scorsone, E. 2014. "Municipal Fiscal Emergency Laws Background and Guide to State-Based Approaches," Working Paper No. 14-21, Mercatus Center George Mason University, July.

Shah, A. 1995. "Intergovernmental Fiscal Relations in Canada: An Overview," in *Macroeconomic Management and Fiscal Decentralization*, edited R. Jayanta, EDI seminar series, The World Bank, Washington, D.C.

Siegenthaler, P. 2013. "Lessons from the History and Challenges for the Future of the Swiss Debt Brake: A Note," *Swiss Journal of Economics and Statistics* 149(2): 137–138.

Studenski, P., and H. Kroos. 1963. *Financial History of the United States*, McGaw Hill, New York.

Sturzenegger, F., and R. Werneck. 2006. "Fiscal Federalism and Pro-cyclical Spending: The Cases of Argentina and Brazil," *Económica* 52: 151–194.

Summers, L. 2015. "Have We Entered an Age of Secular Stagnation?" *IMF Economic Review* 63: 277–328.

Swedish Fiscal Policy Council. 2019. "Fiscal Policy Council Report 2019," Stockholm.

Von Hagen, J. 1991. "A Note on the Empirical Effectiveness of Formal Fiscal Restraints," *Journal of Public Economics* 44: 199–210.

Von Hagen, J., and I. J. Harden. 1995. "Budget Processes and Commitment to Fiscal Discipline," *European Economic Review* 39: 771–779.

Wassman, R., and R. Fisher. 2011. "State and Local Government Debt 1992–2008," State Tax Notes, 427, Aug 15.

Weingast, B. 2009. "Second Generation Fiscal Federalism: The Implications of Fiscal Incentives," *Journal of Urban Economics* 65: 279–293.

Weingast, B. 2014. "Second Generation Fiscal Federalism: Political Aspects of Decentralization and Economic Development," *World Development* 53: 14–25.

Wildasin, D. 2004. "The Institutions of Federalism: Toward and Analytical Framework," *National Tax Journal* 57: 247–272.

Wyplosz, C. 2005. "Fiscal Policy: Institutions versus Rules. National Institute," *Economic Review* 191: 70–84.

Wyplosz, C. 2012. "Fiscal Rules: Theoretical Issues and Historical Experiences," National Bureau of Economic Research. Working Paper No. 17884. (March).

Wyplosz, C. 2013. "Fiscal Rules: Theoretical Issues and Historical Experience," in *Fiscal Policy after the Financial Crisis*, edited by A. Alesina and F. Giavazzi, University of Chicago Press, Chicago.

Wyplosz, Charles. 2011. "Fiscal Discipline: Rules Rather than Institutions," *National Institute Economic Review* 217: R19–R30, National Institute of Economic and Social Research.

Yousefi, S. 2019. "Public Sector Balance Sheet Strength and the Macro-Economy," IMF Working Paper WP/19/170, August.

Ziblatt, D. 2004. "Rethinking the Origins of Federalism. Puzzle, Theory, and Evidence from Nineteenth–Century Europe," *World Politics* 57: 70–98.

Chapter 6

Second-Generation Fiscal Rules for the United States

INTRODUCTION

The economic shocks of the past two decades yielded mixed attitudes toward rules-based fiscal policy. The 2008 financial crisis saw many developed countries abandon or circumvent their fiscal rules, allowing debt to grow at unsustainable rates. But some countries reacted to the financial crisis by reforming their fiscal rules to make them respond more effectively to economic shocks, while achieving a sustainable debt trajectory. Economists refer to them as "Second-Generation" fiscal rules. A similar pattern is now emerging from the aftermath of the original coronavirus pandemic. Countries with effective fiscal rules were able to respond to this economic shock without massive increases in debt and are now reducing debt from the high levels incurred during the pandemic. However, countries with ineffective fiscal rules incurred unprecedented levels of debt during the pandemic and are projected to grow debt at rates that are unsustainable (Poulson et al. 2022).

Unfortunately, the United States is in the latter category of high debtor countries. In this study, we describe the 1980s and 1990s "Great Moderation" in monetary and fiscal policies. Approaching the Great Moderation, many U.S. policy makers concluded that debt was rising at an unsustainable rate and that only effective fiscal rules could restore sustainable debt levels. The Balanced Budget and Emergency Control Act of 1985, also known as the Gramm-Rudman-Hollings Act, created the first statutory limits on federal spending. That act set statutory deficit targets enforced by automatic across-the-board spending reduction, referred to as sequestration. The Budget Enforcement Act of 1990 replaced the deficit limits in the Deficit Control Act with annual limits on discretionary spending and controls over the annual increase in debt, calculated by adding together, for each fiscal year, increases in direct spending and decreases in revenue, a process referred to as "pay-as-you-go." Those fiscal rules closed the fiscal gap and reduced the debt/GDP ratio. In the 1990s, the economy experienced rapid economic growth, and with these fiscal rules in place the budget was balanced, and debt was restored to a sustainable level (Merrifield and Poulson 2016a, 2017b).

Over the past two decades, however, the economic shocks felt in this period undermined support for the fiscal rules, and the United States abandoned the fiscal rules enacted during the Great Moderation and responded to the financial crisis and the coronavirus pandemic with massive debt growth. Under existing law, the United States will increase the debt/GDP ratio to one of the highest levels in the developed world. The failure to maintain a sustainable debt trajectory reflects fundamental flaws in our fiscal rules and fiscal institutions. The challenge is to restore another Great Moderation in fiscal and monetary policies.

A CONSENSUS SUPPORTING A GREAT MODERATION IN MACROECONOMIC POLICY

The National Commission on Fiscal Responsibility and Reform

(National Commission on Fiscal Responsibility and Reform 2010)

Following the financial crisis in 2010, two major task forces were created to address the debt crisis. The National Commission on Fiscal Responsibility and Reform was appointed by President Obama and chaired by former Senator Alan Simpson (R-WY), and Erskine Bowles, former Chief of Staff to President Clinton. The Commission drafted the Simpson-Bowles plan in 2010 and updated the plan in 2013. The plan was endorsed by a majority of the Commission but failed to reach the super-majority required to submit the plan to Congress. Key recommendations in the plan included:

1. Raise revenues to 21 percent of GDP.
2. Reduce spending to 21 percent of GDP.
3. Reduce debt to 60 percent of GDP by 2023.
4. Reduce debt to 40 percent of GDP by 2035.
5. Reduce tax rates.
6. Broaden the tax base by eliminating most tax deductions and credits.
7. Cap all discretionary spending.
8. Eliminate some procurement projects and low-priority programs.
9. Stabilize Socials Security finances.

The Domenici-Rivlin Task Force (Bipartisan Policy Center 2010)

Following the 2008 financial crisis, the Bipartisan Policy Center created the second Task Force. Former Senate Budget Committee chairman Pete Domenici (R-NM) and Alice Rivlin, director of the Congressional Budget Office (CBO), chaired the Task Force. The Domenici-Rivlin Plan was published in 2010 and updated in 2012. The Task Force recommendations included the following:

1. Stabilize federal debt below 60 percent of GDP.
2. Reduce spending to 23 percent of GDP.
3. Raise revenue to 21 percent of GDP.
4. Broaden the tax base by eliminating many deductibles, exclusions, preferences, and credits.
5. Freeze domestic discretionary and defense spending.
6. Moderate spending growth on health care.
7. Put Social Security on a sustainable footing.
8. Increase benefits for the lowest lifetime wage earners.
9. Decrease benefits for top 25 percent of wage earners.

Solutions Initiative

(Peter P. Peterson Foundation 2019)

The Peter P. Peterson Foundation's Solution Initiative brought together leading policy organizations from across the political spectrum to propose plans to achieve long-term fiscal sustainability.

Comprehensive plans were proposed in 2011, 2012, 2015, and 2019. These organizations proposed a wide range of fiscal policy reforms to put the nation on a more sustainable fiscal path. While differences in the fiscal policy reforms reflected the different policy priorities of the authors, there was bipartisan agreement that the nation must close the fiscal gap and reduce the debt/GDP ratio. The following graph shows the projected debt/GDP ratio in each of the plans.

Figure 6.1 shows the trend in the debt/GDP ratio in each of these plans compared to the CBO long-term forecast in 2019. The CBO long-term forecast projected that the debt/GDP ratio would rise to more than 200 percent by midcentury. The trend proposed by all of these plans projected a ratio below 100 percent. The debt/GDP ratio projected by midcentury in these plans varied from 40 percent to 100 percent. The consensus was not only that the nation should close the fiscal gap but also that the debt/GDP ratio should be reduced well below 100 percent. The assumption was that these sustainable

PETER G. PETERSON FOUNDATION   Solutions Initiative 2019: Projected federal debt

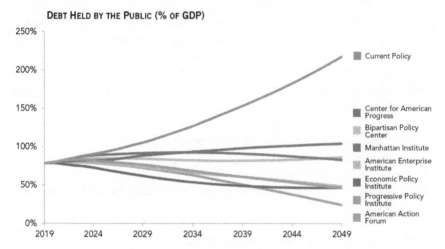

Figure 6.1   Solutions Initiative 2019: Projected Federal Debt. *Source*: Peter G. Peterson Foundation, Solutions Initiative, 2019.

debt levels could be achieved while addressing the major fiscal challenges facing the nation.

The recommendations of these different task forces reflected a consensus in both the private and the public sector that the United States should return to the Great Moderation in monetary and fiscal policies and that the statutory rules enacted during the Great Moderation should again constrain fiscal policy. The consensus prior to the impact of the coronavirus pandemic was the United States was on track to restore the Great Moderation. For example, the Center on Budget and Policy Priorities maintained that much of the Simpson-Bowles Plan had been achieved and that the nation was on track to achieve the deficit and debt targets set in statutory fiscal rules (Kogan 2012). However, that report used some fiscal gimmicks to make it seem like Congress did more fiscal consolidation than it did. A more accurate assessment of fiscal policy in these years was provided by the Committee for a Responsible Federal Budget (CFRFB). CFRFB noted that Congress and the president never agreed on the "grand Bargain" proposed in Simpson-Bowles. But substantial deficit reduction was achieved through a piecemeal approach. CFRFB estimated that three-fifths of the deficit reduction proposed in Simpson-Bowles was achieved. Unfortunately, these savings came primarily from near term cuts in discretionary spending. CFRFB projected that after 2015 deficits would rise rather than fall and that the debt would continue to grow. The problem was that Congress made little progress in fulfilling the tax policy reforms and entitlement reforms proposed in Simpson-Bowles.

CFRFB concluded that Congress failed to address the nation's most pressing fiscal challenge: the large and growing cost of Social Security, Medicare, and Medicaid.

IS THE CONSENSUS SUPPORTING A GREAT MODERATION IN MACROECONOMIC POLICY DISAPPEARING?

Unfortunately, this restoration of fiscal discipline was short-lived. Recent statutory legislation weakened and suspended the discretionary spending caps. Tax cuts were enacted, not offset by spending reductions, requiring suspension of pay-go rules. Entitlement programs and other mandatory spending claimed a growing share of federal spending. Rules-based fiscal policy was abandoned to pursue unprecedented deficit spending, which led to our ongoing unsustainable debt growth.

In 2021, the field of play has changed and the goal post for fiscal policy in the United States has shifted. This change reflects the impact of the coronavirus pandemic, but it also reflects a fundamental change in the consensus regarding fiscal policy in the United States.

America's Fiscal and Economic Outlook

(Peter P. Peterson Foundation 2021)

In 2021, the Peter P. Peterson Foundation asked a group of experts from think tanks across the political spectrum to express their views on how America's unsustainable long-term fiscal outlook impacts the economy, budget, risk exposure, and global leadership. The scholars were also asked how fiscal policy could address some challenges to capitalism including disparities in economic security and opportunity, climate change, health and retirement security, evolving global threats, and infrastructure needs.

Most experts pay lip service to close the fiscal gap but argue that this should not be at the expense of new spending programs to meet the challenges facing the U.S. William Gale from the Brookings Institute expresses this view explicitly.

> Second, the economy is more important than the budget. Saving the budget but hurting the economy would be a pyrrhic victory. In addition, although the COVID-related package added $4.2 trillion (about 19 percent of 2021 GDP) to the federal debt and federal debt is expected to continue to rise for the next several decades, the "debt problem" seems less urgent today than in the past. Low current and projected interest rates provide "elbow room" and time that

can be used to pursue important public initiatives. (Peter P. Peterson Foundation 2021: 1–7)

Several of the scholars in the Peterson survey argue that we should close the fiscal gap while meeting the new challenges facing the nation, but these scholars are in the minority. For example, James Poterba refers to the difficulty in making "the fiscal policy adjustments that would stabilize the debt/GDP ratio" (Peter P. Peterson Foundation 2021: 1–6). He notes that to stabilize the debt/GDP ratio at 100 percent in 2050 would require either a significant increase in revenue or a reduction in spending.

Brian Riedl also notes that

If Congress begins gradually phasing in budget reform over the next few years, it can stabilize the debt close to the current level of 100 percent of GDP and preserve much more long-term fiscal space for other priorities. This path also requires forgoing major new federal initiatives today, because even those "paid for" with new taxes may use up the limited number of plausible tax increases that are otherwise needed to bring current federal programs into long term sustainability. (Peter P. Peterson Foundation 2021: 1–6)

Dana Peterson and Lori Murray make the point that fiscal responsibility should be a priority while meeting other budgetary challenges. "The net savings required to make our debt grow more slowly than our economy (instead of vise-versa) and ultimately reverse the growth of the debt to GDP, should be tackled alongside the cost of new spending on budget bills" (Peter P. Peterson Foundation 2021: 1–7).

Fiscal Policy in the 117th Congress (2021–2022)

The change in the playing field and shift in the goal post for fiscal policy are most evident in legislation passed in the 117th Congress (Congressional Budget Office 2021a, 2021b, 2021c, 2021d). The Committee for a Responsible Federal Budget (CFRFB 2021b) estimates that the bipartisan infrastructure investment and jobs act will add $400 billion to deficits over the next decade. CFRFB (2021c) estimates that the House Build Back Better Act (H.R. 5376) would add $750 billion to the deficit over the next five years and about $160 billion over ten years.[1] The majority in Congress supports fiscal policies that will significantly increase deficits and increase the ratio of debt to GDP well over the 200 percent projected by the CBO under current law (CFRFB 2021a). The legislation enacted in the 117th Congress will result in debt levels comparable to that in Japan by midcentury.

Restoring the Great Moderation in fiscal policy requires closing the fiscal gap. Closing the fiscal gap requires new fiscal rules to stabilize the debt/GDP ratio, and progress on debt reduction is unsustainable without a well-crafted cap on spending growth. There is of course controversy regarding a sustainable level and trajectory of debt/GDP. A debt/GDP ratio of 100 percent would appear to be an upper limit, while more ambitious plans would reduce that ratio well below 100 percent (Peter P. Peterson Foundation 2019).

DESIGNING NEW FISCAL RULES

There has been a dramatic rise in the number of countries enacting new fiscal rules. In 1990, only a handful of countries had the new fiscal rules; by 2015, ninety-two countries had new rules in place (Lledo et al. 2017).

There is an extensive literature on the design of fiscal rules, and no other organization has been more influential in analyzing fiscal rules than the International Monetary Fund (IMF) (Alesina and Tabellini 1990; Alesina and Drazen 1991; Debrun et al. 2018; Persson and Tabelini 2000; Von Hagen 1991; Von Hagen and Harden 1995; Kopits and Syzmanski 1998; Kopits 2001; International Monetary Fund (IMF) 2009, 2018a, 2018b).

The 2008 financial crisis caused many countries to circumvent or drop their fiscal rules. However, following the financial crisis some of those countries refined their rules to make them more effective constraints on fiscal policy. The IMF refers to them as Second-Generation fiscal rules. The IMF maintains that there is now a consensus based on this experience that is the basis for optimal design of fiscal rules. In addition to its extensive research, the IMF has codified this optimal design in two publications "How to Select Fiscal Rules" and "How to Calibrate Fiscal Rules: A Primer" (Lledo et al. 2017, 2018).

IMF studies use econometric models to measure the impact of fiscal rules on budgets and aggregate economic activity and to simulate the impact of economic shocks (International Monetary Fund 2009). The simulation analysis uses Keynesian fiscal multipliers designed to capture the impact of fiscal policies in the short run. Those multipliers embody the assumption that fiscal rules impose a tighter fiscal stance that has a negative impact on output in the short run.

There are two basic problems with the IMF methodology for analyzing the impact of fiscal rules. (1) Keynesian fiscal multipliers are controversial (Cogan et al. 2013) even for simulated short-run effects, more so for designing fiscal rules for long-term fiscal sustainability; (2) the IMF uses static rather than dynamic scoring.

The IMF methodology uses static scoring to measure the impact of fiscal rules and fiscal policy. As the IMF notes, their approach may miss valuable information on how the economy would behave over a forecast period. In particular, using IMF methodology "there is no feedback from fiscal policy

changes to macroeconomic variables, in particular GDP." The IMF notes
that their analysis assumes that growth is constant over the long run, but "in
reality growth and the interest growth differential vary with the level of debt"
(International Monetary Fund 2009, 2018a, 2018b, 2018e; Schick 2010;
Schaechter et al. 2012; and Wyploz 2013).

The IMF surveys alternative methodologies in measuring the impact of
fiscal rules and fiscal policies on aggregate economic activity (IMF 2018a,
2018b). An alternative to Keynesian modeling is political economy model
first introduced in the work of Alesina and Tabellini (1990). That study was
the first to find evidence that fiscal consolidation policies could have a positive impact on economic growth in the long term. Several features of these
political economy models capture the supply side effects of fiscal policies.
The models capture the feedback from fiscal policy changes on macroeconomic variables, most importantly GDP. Fiscal consolidation policies that
constrain the growth of government spending are accompanied by higher
rates of economic growth, which over a long period of time results in significantly higher levels of GDP. In contrast to the Keynesian models, the political
economy models utilize dynamic scoring rather than static scoring to capture
these feedback effects.

A Political Economy Model for the United States

In this study, a political economy model is designed to measure the impact of
fiscal rules and fiscal policy on U.S. budgets and aggregate economic activity (the formal model is appended). The study uses scenario analysis first
introduced by Debrun et al. (2018) to simulate the impact of fiscal rules in
Israel, and then expanded in other IMF studies (International Monetary Fund
2009). Scenario analysis is forward-looking in simulating the impact of fiscal rules over a forecasting horizon. The simulated outcome with fiscal rules
is compared to a baseline, which in the IMF studies is the World Economic
Outlook. In this study, the baseline used for comparative purposes is the CBO
Long-Term Budget Outlook. Debt dynamics are compared with and without
new fiscal rules and fiscal policies in place.

In contrast to IMF studies, our analysis uses dynamic rather than static
scoring to capture feedback effects on macroeconomic variables. The
dynamic simulation analysis assumes an opportunity cost when resources
are shifted from the private to the public sector. Fiscal consolidation policies
that constrain the growth of government spending are accompanied by higher
rates of economic growth. The dynamic simulation model also captures the
supply side effects of changes in taxes in the long term. The feedback effects
of changes in fiscal rules and fiscal policies that result in fiscal consolidation
are captured in this dynamic simulation analysis. A combination of fiscal

rules and fiscal policies that downsizes the federal government and boosts economic growth is most likely to achieve sustainable debt in the long term. As Alesina and Tabellini (1990a) argue, fiscal consolidation may or may not negatively impact output in the short run, but the primary objective of fiscal consolidation policies is achieving sustainable debt levels in the long term. For a survey of the literature on the long-run relationship between debt and economic growth, see de Rugy and Salmon (2020).

A fundamental tradeoff is between commitment and flexibility in rule design. Rules may commit elected officials to follow a constrained fiscal policy in order to achieve a specific target, such as a spending limit designed to achieve a desired debt or deficit target. But the more stringent the rule, the less flexibility elected officials have in responding to economic shocks from recessions or emergencies (Yared 2018).

The theoretical and empirical literature on Second-Generation fiscal rules supports a hybrid approach to rule design (Eyraud et al. 2018). In a hybrid approach, a threshold is set for target levels of debt/GDP and deficit/GDP that trigger fiscal policy responses. The optimal target thresholds must be tight enough to achieve a sustainable fiscal policy, but not so tight that policy makers cannot respond to economic shocks. To be effective, the rules must limit discretionary fiscal policy and must be enacted in the context of status quo fiscal policies as the starting point for their adoption. This hybrid approach can resolve the tradeoff between commitment and flexibility in fiscal rule design.

DYNAMIC SIMULATION ANALYSIS OF FISCAL RULES IN ALTERNATIVE PROPOSALS

Sustained progress on the fiscal gap will require new fiscal rules, and a number of new bills have rules designed to achieve that objective. Private think tanks have also proposed new fiscal rules to close the fiscal gap. In the following analysis, we use the dynamic simulation model to estimate the impact of the proposed fiscal rules. We project the debt/GDP ratio and the budgetary impact of each of the plans. Both back cast and forecast simulations are estimated.

This analysis reveals how difficult it will be to achieve sustainable debt/ GDP levels in the coming decades. We simulate the effects of some clearly described fiscal rules that lack emergency provisions or don't specify long-run fiscal sustainability practices. For example, "The Penny Plan" doesn't specify how spending should address emergencies, and it doesn't specify how to keep spending growth sustainable after the five-year period seen to be adequate to achieve budget balance. We begin the description of our simulations with the two proposals with effects we can meaningfully back cast and forecast. In our back casts, the simulation indicates how economic and fiscal conditions would differ in 2019 from actual 2019 conditions had a fiscal rule been enacted in 1993 as part of the "Reinventing Government" initiative. In our forecast simulations, the fiscal rule takes effect for FY2022 and is simulated over the period 2022 to 2042.

The Kurt Couchman Fiscal Rule

(Couchman 2020)[2]

Description

Targeted spending can grow at the same rate as prior GDP growth. Prior GDP growth is the average growth rate over the five-year period before the budget year (which includes the still-unfolding current year). That is, if the average GDP growth is 4 percent, the budget year's spending can be 104 percent of the current year's spending. That spending cap growth rate declines by 0.1 percentage points (mild braking) if the debt-to-GDP ratio rose in the year before the current year. That reduction in spending growth following debt-to-GDP growth is cumulative. That is, following debt growth a year ago, budget year spending can only be 103.9 percent of the current year. If that happens again, it's 103.8 percent, then 103.7 percent, and so on.

Conversely, a falling debt-to-GDP ratio increases the spending growth rate but not above the average GDP growth rate. Emergency-designated spending reduces the spending cap over the following six-year period (or longer, if necessary, as the COVID responses would require).

Increasing the revenue baseline can immediately increase the spending cap (it's the PAY-GO principle and is required to be a neutral rule).

Back Cast: 1994–2019

Applying the Couchman Rule to just discretionary spending is useless. That would have yielded a slightly bigger 2019 spending level and debt than the actual spending level and debt. Even after rule-induced braking in some years, "limiting" discretionary spending growth to GDP growth yields slightly faster discretionary spending growth than occurred.

If we had limited total federal spending (discretionary + interest + mandatory [mostly entitlements]) growth to GDP growth, with mild braking after years in which the debt/GDP rises, starting in 1994, the 2019 debt-to-GDP ratio would have been 1.4 percent below its actual value. The actual 2019 publicly held debt to GDP ratio was 78.4 percent. With the Couchman Rule in effect starting in 1994, the debt/GDP in 2019 would have been 77.0 percent. However, the Couchman Rule would have yielded much less volatile spending growth. With a payback of emergency spending spread over the next six years, simulated spending during the Great Recession would have been much below actual spending.

You might have wondered, as we did, why the simulation showed the debt-to-GDP rising even though spending growth is equal to GDP growth, or slightly less in some years. In most of the years prior to the Great Recession, the Couchman Rule grew total spending faster than actual total spending—that slightly lowered GDP growth, and revenue growth. With the Great Recession total spending surge, 2019 Couchman Rule total spending is nearly $1 Trillion below actual 2019 spending.

Forecast: 2022–2042

Applying the Couchman Rule to the discretionary spending outlook yields a 2042 debt-to-GDP ratio of 1.429:10.5 percentage points below the CBO projection of 1.534. That's progress but still with debt/GDP well above rough consensus tolerance levels of 0.6; that is, debt held by the public at 60 percent of GDP. Again, note that the total debt has been over 130 percent of debt held by the public.

Applying the Couchman Rule to the total spending outlook yields a 2042 debt-to-GDP ratio of 0.846:69 percentage points below the CBO projection of 1.534. That leaves the 2042 debt-to-GDP ratio in the vicinity of consensus tolerance levels, which is with debt held by the public around 60 percent of GDP. Again, note that the total debt has been over 130 percent of debt held by the public. So, additional revenues, asset sales, and entitlement reform will be needed for further desired progress.

Note, also, that capping total spending growth leaves discretionary spending—funding for the actual tasks of the government—as a residual. That is, we find the sum available to fund federal government agencies by subtracting entitlement and interest spending from the total spending limit. Given the anticipated rapid growth in entitlement spending, it is almost surprising that the average change in that discretionary residual is positive, nearly one percent per year. More troublesome might be the significant fluctuations in the result of subtracting interest and entitlement spending from the total spending cap. For example, doing that cuts discretionary spending by 4 percent in 2028 increases it by 5 percent in 2029, and cuts it by nearly 3 percent in 2030.

Maximizing America's Prosperity (MAP) Act

(Braun, Brady 2019)

Description

MAP challenges the Congress to set spending and debt targets, as a share of GDP, but does not specify a target. MAP caps federal noninterest spending as a percentage of full employment GDP (also known as potential GDP). So, in the simulation, we explore the effects of credible targets, which we define to be targets that yield debt/GDP reduction without politically impossible reductions in discretionary spending growth.

Forecast: 2022–2042

Setting federal noninterest spending at 18 percent of potential GDP, we get a 2042 debt-to-the-public-to-GDP ratio of 100.2 percent well below the CBO-projected debt/GDP of 153.4 percent, but still well above the 60 percent rough consensus of debt/GDP tolerance. That constraint on total spending growth yields an annual average increase in discretionary spending of 1.53 percent, tough, but plausible. Setting federal noninterest spending at 17.5 percent of potential GDP, we get a 2042 debt-to-the-public-to-GDP ratio of 88.4 percent: still well above the 60 percent rough consensus of debt/GDP tolerance. This constraint on total spending growth yields a still plausible annual average increase in discretionary spending of 1.38 percent.

Republican Study Committee Plan

(Republican Study Committee 2021)

Even though the Republican Study Committee Plan does not specify a fiscal rule, we find the 2042 effect of their ambitious ten-year plan to cut entitlement spending by $6.7 trillion and cut discretionary spending by $4.8 trillion. For the simulation, we assume that those cuts are sustained for 2032–2042. That would reduce the 2042 ratio of the debt held by the public to GDP to 64 percent. Since emergency spending was not addressed, the actual debt/GDP ratio would be somewhat higher.

Of course, the challenge is to achieve approximately 17 percent reductions in annual discretionary spending and 33 percent reductions in entitlement spending. The lack of Democratic cosponsors for the bill suggests that the Republican Study Committee legislation is not politically viable.

Simpson-Bowles

(National Commission on Fiscal Responsibility and Reform 2010)

Description

Simpson-Bowles urged Congress to match reductions against a baseline, such as the CBO projections, with additional revenues. To see the maximum effect (for much-needed optimism), we assume that the additional revenues come from asset sales—a source that has no negative economic effects beyond some states' likely eventual need to manage mining boomtowns.

So, we use the M-P rule to generate reductions against the CBO baseline and then assume asset sales match the gap between CBO-projected discretionary spending and the simulated M-P rule-capped spending. The result is a 2042 debt at about half the CBO-projected level.[3]

The assumption that savings is generated entirely from federal asset sales is heroic to say the least, so we also conducted simulations of the Simpson-Bowles rules assuming revenue increase as an alternative. Assuming revenue increases yields a 2042 debt-to-GDP ratio of 72.3 percent. Using tax revenue in place of asset sale revenue causes the debt/GDP ratio to be higher. The revenue eases the degree of M-P rule-driven braking so that discretionary spending rises from 2022 to 2042 at an average rate of 1.5 percent per year.

Penny Plan

(Paul 2018)

Description

The authors of the Penny Plan assume that cutting total spending by 1 percent for five years will balance the budget and then it will stay balanced so that GDP growth will gradually reduce debt/GDP. We simulate the Penny Plan author's intent. We continue the 1 percent cuts until the budget balances, which is the entire 2022–2042 period. It comes close to balance in 2042.

Forecast: 2022–2042

If we assume that a 1 percent cut is feasible and desirable every year, the Penny Plan yields 2042 debt held by the public at 88.8 percent of 2042 GDP. So, even if we manage to cut total spending by 1 percent every year for twenty years, cash debt will still be nearly 90 percent of GDP.

Progressive Policy Institute (PPI)

(Ritz 2020a, 2020b)

This simulation awaits PPI updates of their 2019 plan to take into account the pandemic spending and the first year of the Biden administration.

It should be reiterated that, for improved accuracy, we revised the CBO projections to include the $1.9 trillion covid-response legislation. That will cause our statement of the (M-P revised CBO-projected) debt to differ from the published CBO projections. Probably, the CBO will issue another long-term outlook before PPI updates their 2019 plan.

Likely, a key element of that update will be the enactment into law of a climate change policy. A key part of the promised simulation will be a sensitivity analysis of key climate change uncertainties such as the revenue yield, and economic impacts, of a carbon tax.

CONCLUSION

Large, growing gaps between the borrowing costs of different nations are an early ominous sign of growing concerns about the U.S. federal government's ability to service its large and growing debt. Indeed, just the cash debt to the public, which is of greatest immediate concern, now tops GDP, with gross debt topping debt to the public by about another 30 percent. New-normal slower economic growth, and emerging inflation, indicates that noteworthy effects of the large U.S. cash debt, still growing at unsustainable rates, are occurring already. We emphasize cash debt because there are significant additional unfunded liabilities. *Greater tax burdens for our grandchildren are far from the only effects of large unfunded liabilities and a large and growing cash debt* (Merrifield and Poulson 2020a, 2020b).

Given the great difficulty, politically, of cutting programs without imminent or ongoing devastating crisis symptoms (default, hyperinflation) that we want to avoid, we foresee that progress on debt reduction can only be realized through a steady, slow process. It means that a credible debt reduction strategy must include a means to sustain it between administrations and over the business cycle. We assume that "means to sustain" will be fiscal rules that cannot be set aside by a simple majority vote. It is crucial to have effective fiscal rules in place to respond to an economic crisis, the current economic crisis provides a unique opportunity to enact effective fiscal rules. Since the Congress will not adopt a rule that prevents a rapid response to genuine emergencies, at least a super-majority requirement will be needed to prevent abuse of emergency spending to exceed the fiscal-rule-prescribed spending growth limit.

Elected officials and private citizens have attempted to chart a course that would return the nation to a Great Moderation in fiscal policy. Elected officials and policy experts from across the political spectrum have designed new fiscal rules and other plans for addressing the debt crisis. We use dynamic simulation analysis to measure the impact of the proposed fiscal rules on budgets and the economy and compare the simulation results for the different fiscal rules proposed by legislators and private organizations.

NOTES

1. This assumes that increased infrastructure spending will not become permanent; if it is a permanent increase this could add $3 trillion to the ten-year deficit impact of the legislation.

2. These simulations were estimated based on the 2020 version of the fiscal rule proposed by Couchman. Since then, he has modified and updated the proposal, and a more recent version has been introduced in Congress. See the chapter by Couchman in Poulson et al. (2022).

3. Using a public sector balance sheet approach, liquidating assets does not improve the government's overall solvency, but it does increase cash flow.

REFERENCES

Alesina, A., and G. Tabellini. 1990. "A Positive Theory of Fiscal Deficits and Government Debt," *Review of Economic Studies* 57: 4030414.

Alesina, A., and A. Drazen. 1991. "Why Are Stabilizations Delayed?" *American Economic Review* 81: 1170–1188.

American Action Forum. 2019. *PGPF-American Action Forum Solutions, 2019,* June 12.

Bank for International Settlements. 2011. "The Real Effects of Debt," BIS Working Papers No. 352, September.

Bipartisan Policy Center. 2010. *Domenici-Rivlin Debt Reduction Task Force Plan 2.0*, Washington DC. https://bipartisanpolicy.org/report/domenici-rivlin-debt-reduction-task-force-plan-20/

Blankart, C. 2000. "The Process of Government Centralization: A Constitutional View," *Constitutional Political Economy* 11(1): 27–39.

Blankart, C. 2011. *An Economic Theory of Switzerland*, CESifo DICE Report 3/2011.

Blankart, C. 2015. "What the Eurozone Could Learn from Switzerland," *CESfio FORUM* 16(2): 39–42.

Braun, M. 2019. *Maximizing America's Prosperity Act of 2019*, S. 2245, U.S. Congress, Washington, DC.

Cogan J., J. Taylor, V. Wieland, and M. Wolters. 2013. "Fiscal Consolidation Strategies," *Journal of Economic Dynamics and Control* 37(2): 404–421.

Committee for a Responsible Federal Budget. 2021a. *Analysis of CBO's March 21 Long term Budget Outlook*, March 4.

Committee for a Responsible Federal Budget. 2021b. *Infrastructure Plan Will Add $400 Billion to the Deficit, CBO Finds,* August 5.

Committee for a Responsible Federal Budget. 2021c. *Full Estimates of the House Build Back Better Act*, November 18.

Congressional Budget Office. 2015. *Why CBO Projects that Actual Output Will be Below Potential Output on Average*, February. cbo.gov/publication/49890

Congressional Budget Office. 2017. *Cost Estimate for the Conference Agreement on H.R. 1, a Bill to Provide for Reconciliation Pursuant to Titles II and V of the*

Concurrent Resolution on the Budget for the Fiscal Year 2018, December 15. cbo .gov/publication 53415

Congressional Budget Office. 2019. "The Effect of Government Debt on Interest Rates," Working Paper 2019-01, March.

Congressional Budget Office. 2020a. *The Budget and Economic Outlook 2020-2030,* January 28. cbo.gov/publication/56020

Congressional Budget Office. 2020b. *Interim Economic Projection for 2020 and 2021,* May 19. cbo.gov/publication/56351

Congressional Budget Office. 2020c. *Federal Debt a Primer,* March. cbo.gov /publication/56165

Congressional Budget Office. 2020d. *An Update to the Economic Outlook: 2020 to 2030,* July. cbo.gov/publication/56442

Congressional Budget Office. 2020e. *CBO's Economic Forecast: Understanding the Slowdown of Productivity Growth,* NABE Foundation 17th Annual Economic Measurement Seminar. cbo.gov/publication/56531

Congressional Budget Office. 2021a. *Long Term Budget Outlook,* March. cbo.gov /publication/56977

Congressional Budget Office. 2021b. *Re: Three Scenarios for the Budget as Specified by Senator Graham, Letter to Honorable Lindsey Graham, Ranking Member of the Committee on the Budget,* United States Senate, Washington DC, May 21.

Congressional Budget Office. 2021c. *Extended Budgetary Effects of H.R. 1319, The American Rescue Plan Act of 2021,* March 10. cbo.gov/publication/57056

Congressional Budget Office. 2021d. *Estimated Budgetary Effects of H.R. 5376, The Build Back Better Act, as Posted on the Website of the House Committee on Rules on November 3, 2021 (Rules Committee Print 117-18), as Amended by Yarmouth Amendment 112.* cbo.gov/publication 58366

Couchman, K. 2020. "Effective Fiscal Rules Build on Consensus," in *A Fiscal Cliff: New Perspective on the U.S. Debt Crisis,* edited by John Merrifield and Barry Poulson, Cato Institute.

Debrun, X., J. Ostry, T. Williams, and C. Wyless. 2018. "Public Debt Sustainability," in *Sovereign Debt: A Guide for Economists and Practitioners,* IMF Conference, edited by S. Abbas, A. Pienkowski, and K. Rogoff, International Monetary Fund, forthcoming, Oxford University Press.

Debrun, X., and L. Jonung. 2019. "Under Threat-Rules Based Fiscal Policy and How to Preserve it," *European Journal of Political Economy* March 57: 142157.

De Rugy, V., and J. Salmon. 2020. "Debt and Growth: Decade of Studies," Policy Brief, Mercatus Center, George Mason University, April 15.

Eyraud, L., X. Debrun, A. Hodge, V. LLedo, and C. Patillo. 2018. "Second Generation Fiscal Rules: Balancing Simplicity, Flexibility, and Enforceability," IMF Discussion Note SDN/18/04, April.

Feld, L., and G. Kirchgassner. 2006. "On the Effectiveness of Debt Brakes: The Swiss Experience," Center for Research in Economics Management and the Arts, Working Paper No. 2006-21.

International Monetary Fund (IMF). 2009. "Fiscal Rules—Anchoring Expectations for Sustainable Public Finances." *IMF Policy Paper,* International Monetary Fund, Washington, DC.

International Monetary Fund. 2013. "Staff Guidance Note for Public Debt Sustainability Analysis in Market-Access Countries," May.

International Monetary Fund (IMF). 2018a. "Fiscal Monitor: Managing Public Wealth," October 2018, 11–13.

International Monetary Fund (IMFb). 2018b. "Assessing Fiscal Space-An Update and Stock Taking," IMF Policy Paper, International Monetary Fund, Washington D.C.

Kogan, R. 2012. *What Was Actually in Bowles-Simpson- and How Can We Compare it with Other Plans*, Center on Budget and Policy Priorities, October 2.

Kopits, G. 2001. "Fiscal Rules: Useful Policy Framework or Unnecessary Ornament?" IMF Working Paper 01/145, International Monetary Fund, Washington, DC.

Kopits, G., and S. Symansky. 1998. "Fiscal Policy Rules," IMF Occasional Paper 162, International Monetary Fund, Washington, DC.

Kotlikof, L. 2015. *America's Fiscal Insolvency and its Generational Consequences*, Testimony to the Senate Budget Committee, February 25.

Lledó, V., S. Yoon, X. Fang, S. Mbaye, and Y. Kim. 2017. "Fiscal Rules at a Glance," 2015 IMF Fiscal Rules Database Background Note, International Monetary Fund, Washington, DC.

Lledo, V., P. Dudine, and A. Peralta-Alva. 2018. "How to Select Fiscal Rules: A Primer, International Monetary Fund," March 15.

Merrifield, J., and B. Poulson. 2016a. *Can the Debt Growth be Stopped? Rules Based Policy Options for Addressing the Federal Fiscal Crisis*, Lexington Books, New York, NY.

Merrifield, J., and B. Poulson. 2016b. "The Swedish and Swiss Fiscal Rule Outcomes Contain Key Lessons for the U.S.," *Independent Review* 21(2): 251–275.

Merrifield, J., and B. Poulson. 2016c. "Stopping the National Debt Spiral: A Better Rules for Solving the Federal Fiscal Crisis," Policy Brief, The Heartland Institute.

Merrifield, J., and B. Poulson. 2017a. "New Constitutional Debt Brakes for Euroland Revisited," *Journal of Applied Business and Economics* 19(8): 110–132.

Merrifield, J., and B. Poulson. 2017b. *Restoring America's Fiscal Constitution*, Lexington Books, New York, NY.

Merrifield, J., and B. Poulson. 2018. "Fiscal Federalism and Dynamic Credence Capital in the U.S.," *ERN Institutional and Transition Economics Policy and Paper Series* 10(16). November 28.

Merrifield, J., and B. Poulson. 2020a. *A Fiscal Cliff: New Perspectives on the Federal Debt Crisis*, Cato Institute.

Merrifield, J., and B. Poulson. 2020b. "How to Solve America's Debt Crisis in the Wake of the Coronavirus Pandemic," Heartland Institute, Policy Brief, April.

National Commission on Fiscal Responsibility and Reform. 2010. *The Moment of Truth*, White House, Washington DC, December.

Organization for Economic Cooperation and Development. 2013. "General Government Fiscal Balance," in *Government at a Glance* 2013, OECD Publishing, Paris.

Paul, R. 2018. *Chairman Paul's Penny Plan Budget: A Budget for Fiscal Year 2019*, Subcommittee on Federal Spending Oversight, April.

Persson, T., and G. Tabellini. 2000. *Political Economics: Explaining Economic Policy*, The MIT Press, Cambridge, MA.

Peter P. Peterson Foundation. 2019. *Solutions Initiative 2019 Charting a Sustainable Future*, June. www.pgpf.org

Peter P. Peterson Foundation. 2021. *America's Fiscal and Economic Outlook*, November. www.pgpf.org

Poulson, B. 1981. *Economic History of the United States*. Macmillan Publishing, New York.

Poulson, B., J. Merrifield, and S. Hanke, editors. 2022. *Public Debt Sustainability: International Perspectives*, Lexington Press, forthcoming.

Poulson, B., and M. Dowling. 1972. "The Climacteric in U.S. Economic Growth," *Oxford Economic Papers* 25(3), Nov.

Reinhart, C., and K. Rogoff. 2009. *This Time is Different: Eight Centuries of Financial Folly*, Princeton University Press.

Reinhart, C., K. Rogoff, and M. Savastano. "Debt Intolerance," *Brookings Papers on Economic Activity* 1(Spring 2003): 1–74.

Republican Study Committee. 2021. *Reclaiming Our Fiscal Future: Fiscal Year 2022 Budget*, Washington DC.

Riedl, B. 2019. *A Plausible Blueprint for Fiscal Sustainability*, Manhatten Institute, June 11.

Ritz, B. 2020a. *Create a Fiscal Switch to make Our Economy Resilient Against Recessions,* Progressive Policy Institute, July 10.

Ritz, B. 2020b. *Emergency Economics Framework for Fighting a Recession in 2020 and Beyond*, Progressive Policy Institute, March 17.

Schaechter, A., T. Kinda, N. Budina, and A. Weber. 2012. "Fiscal Rules in Response to the Crisis - Toward the "Next-Generation" Rules. A New Dataset." *IMF Working Paper 12/187,* International Monetary Fund, Washington, DC.

Schick, A. 2010. "Post-Crisis Fiscal Rules: Stabilizing Public Finance while Responding to Economic Aftershocks," *OECD Journal on Budgeting* 2010(2): 1–17.

Turner, D., and F. Spinelli. 2011. "Interest Rate Growth Differentials and Government Debt Dynamics," *OECD* Economics Department Working Papers, No. 919.

Von Hagen, J. 1991. "A Note on the Empirical Effectiveness of Formal Fiscal Restraints," *Journal of Public Economics* 44: 199–210.

Von Hagen, J., and I. J. Harden. 1995. "Budget Processes and Commitment to Fiscal Discipline," *European Economic Review* 39: 771–779.

Wall Street Journal. 2020a. "Federal Reserve Says It's Launching New Corporate Bond-buying Program," Tuesday June 16, 8A.

Wall Street Journal. 2020b. "Fed Looks to Put Cap on Treasury Yields," Friday June 12, B11.

Wall Street Journal. 2020c. "Fed Vows Low Rate for Years," Thursday June 11, A1–A2.

Wall Street Journal. 2020d. "More Aid Pushed for Cities and States," June 15, A3.

Wyplosz, C. 2013. "Fiscal Rules: Theoretical Issues and Historical Experience," in *Fiscal Policy after the Financial Crisis*, edited by A. Alesina and F. Giavazzi, University of Chicago Press, Chicago.

Yared, P. 2018. "Rising Government Debt and What to do about it," National Bureau of Economic Research Working Paper No. 24979, Cambridge MA.

Chapter 7

The Merrifield-Poulson Rules for Restoring a Great Moderation in Fiscal Policy

THE MERRIFIELD/POULSON (MP) FISCAL RULES

We propose second-generation fiscal rules for the United States. Appendix A has a detailed description of the proposed Merrifield/Poulson (MP) rules. The following summarizes the main features of the rules.

Flexibility is introduced in our proposed (MP) rules in a number of ways. For example, elected officials have the discretion to determine how stringently to apply the limit. In the long term, a spending limit must address the demand for government services, such as pension and health benefits for an aging population. Elected officials can adopt a spending limit multiplier set at unity in the medium term and then gradually adjust the multiplier upward to its long-run value as debt reduction goals are met.

We create that flexibility through debt and deficit brakes. Approaching debt and deficit threshold levels triggers lower limits on spending growth. A debt brake multiplier set at unity would apply a debt brake or deficit brake gradually near threshold levels. A debt brake multiplier greater than unity would apply the debt brake and deficit brake more stringently above the threshold levels.

Other fiscal rules complement our proposed deficit/debt brake. An emergency fund provides for emergencies such as natural disasters and military conflict. The MP rules provide for emergency fund deposits up to a specified cap and allow for deficits in the emergency fund in periods of financial crisis and recession (International Monetary Fund 2018a, 2018b). The MP rules address countercyclical government services demand growth with a higher spending cap equal to half the amount of revenue declines.

In the long run, once the fiscal gap is closed, deficits in the emergency fund must be offset by surpluses in the primary budget in the near term. As in the Swiss case, deficits in the emergency fund must be balanced by surpluses within a fixed time frame. Our emergency fund design is similar to the notional account used in Switzerland to achieve budget balance in the near term. The rules constraining the emergency fund could be suspended in the case of a war. An alternative would be to extend the payback period rather than suspend the rules during periods of emergency such as war (Lledó et al. 2017).

Some countries have enacted fiscal rules with a "golden rule" that exempts government capital expenditures from the spending limits. We propose a version of the golden rule that would retain the integrity of the fiscal rule. Investment spending spurs economic growth, so some countries exempt it from spending caps, and also allows debt financing. But even with a clear formal definition of investment, an exemption creates a loophole we want to avoid. So, the MP rules create regular savings to fund countercyclical investment beyond what the ex-ante fiscal limits allow.

The capital investment fund proposed in the MP rules is patterned after the Swiss model (Merrifield and Poulson 2016b; Poulson et al. 2022). In periods when economic growth is above the long-term average rate of economic growth, a portion of revenue is set aside in the capital investment fund. In periods of slower economic growth, money from the capital fund finances additional infrastructure investments. This method of allocating the capital funds based on the rate of economic growth assures a steady growth in infrastructure investment in the long run.[1]

The MP rules funnel money into emergency and capital funds (programmed savings) and cap discretionary spending growth at a multiple of population growth plus the inflation rate, or less, when there is debt- and deficit-induced braking of spending growth. Total spending is then discretionary spending plus emergency and capital fund deposits, plus interest, plus entitlement spending. With debt much above the specified debt/GDP tolerance, the MP rules freeze discretionary spending.

Our deficit/debt brake is designed for the U.S. economy's unique institutions. The proposed fiscal rules are simulated for the United States over the forecast period 2022–2042, based on parameters unique to the U.S. economy over this time period.

It is important to contrast the proposed MP fiscal rules, with other fiscal rules proposed for the United States. We propose a combination of interrelated fiscal rules designed to achieve multiple targets, including a deficit/GDP ratio and a debt/GDP ratio. The long-term goal is a sustainable debt-to-GDP ratio. Once a sustainable debt level exists, the proposed rules approximate a cyclically balanced budget, with surpluses in high growth periods offsetting deficits in periods of economic contraction.

The flaw in current U.S. fiscal policy is the failure to set long-term goals and to incorporate those goals in a true budget process. Some have argued that it is unrealistic to set long-term goals and impose fiscal rules to achieve those goals. They argue that Congress already struggles with short-term budgets and that Congress is not able to hold to long-term goals. But this is an argument for continuing a fiscal policy process relying on the discretionary policies that created the debt crisis. Continuing to muddle along with current discretionary fiscal decision-making processes and policies is not a viable option.[2]

Critics will argue that a fiscal rules package will be seen as too complicated—difficult to enact and to implement. We simulate the proposed fiscal rules to show how they can be implemented to achieve the multiple targets. We maintain that a combination of fiscal rules is a prerequisite for fiscal stabilization in the United States over the long term.[3] The challenge is to design fiscal rules that are credible and politically achievable and sustainable.

DYNAMIC SIMULATION ANALYSIS OF THE MP RULES

We use a dynamic simulation analysis to measure the impact of the proposed rules on the budget and on the U.S. economy. The dynamic simulation model and the simulation analysis are discussed in detail at the website objectivep olicyassessment.org/vetfiscalrules and in Merrifield and Poulson (2017b; Poulson et al. 2022). The simulation results provide insight into the role that fiscal rules can play in achieving debt sustainability.

We use the national income accounting methodology adopted by the OECD. Our GDP, personal income, population, inflation, and fiscal data are from standard sources, including the Congressional Budget Office (CBO), Office of Management and Budget, Department of Commerce, and Department of Labor. The National Bureau of Economic Research produced our income elasticity of federal revenue data. Lacking an official source for "emergency spending" and inability to cobble together reliably complete annual emergency spending estimates from separate sources, we estimated emergency spending data, as the TARP revenue-adjusted difference between the planned deficit, or surplus, and the typically much larger change in the national debt. Simulation results and sensitivity analysis of the major parameters of the model are available at the website objectivepolicyassessment.org/ vetfiscalrules.

The design of fiscal rules must take into account the unique fiscal institutions of each country, and that is especially true for the United States. Budget process rules in the U.S. Congress are unlike that in any other country. The rules assume that changes in tax rates are binding over a ten-year forecast period. At the end of the ten-year period, the tax rates are assumed to revert to the tax rates prior to this policy change.[4]

Congress can propose that the new tax rates become permanent, but the assumption is that the tax rules are non-binding in a future Congress. Some provisions of the 2017 tax law (Tax Cuts and Jobs Act) are temporary while others are permanent. For a discussion of how this legislation impacts the budget, see Congressional Budget Office (2017). The dynamic simulations in this study are based on the Congressional Budget Office forecast and incorporate these assumptions.[5]

The following discussion summarizes the results of the simulation analysis. Two different types of simulation analysis are conducted, a backcast for 1994 to 2019 and a forecast for 2022 to 2042. The backcast simulation asks what the impact of rules-based fiscal policies would have been over the historical time period. A brief summary of the simulation results for the backcast is provided, because the empirical results show that with the MP rules in place the United States would have been able to close the fiscal gap and stabilize the debt/GDP ratio at a sustainable level. However, that is not true for the forecast simulation. With the MP rules in place over the forecast period the fiscal gap is closed at a debt/GDP level well above that which is considered sustainable. This evidence reveals how difficult it will be after two decades of rapid spending growth and debt fatigue to address the debt crisis. Therefore, the simulation results for the forecast period are discussed in some detail. This is followed by a scenario analysis exploring alternative policy options to reduce the debt/GDP to sustainable levels.

Backcast 1994–2019

With the MP rules in place in the United States over this historical period, the simulated debt/GDP ratio at the end of the period, in 2019, is 60.4 percent. This compares to the actual debt/GDP ratio in that year of 78.4 percent. Thus, rules-based fiscal policy over the historical time period would have closed the fiscal gap at a sustainable debt/GDP ratio. More importantly, it would have put debt on a sustainable trajectory with a falling debt/GDP ratio. This is not surprising because similar rules-based fiscal policies have, in fact, restored sustainable debt in other countries over this period. For example, Switzerland has had a debt brake in place for three decades. Over this period Switzerland cut the debt/GDP ratio to less than 40 percent, well below the debt sustainability level (Feld and Kirchgassner 2006; Blankert 2015). Other European countries such as Sweden, Germany, and the Netherlands have had similar success (Merrifield and Poulson 2016a, 2016b, 2017b; Poulson et al. 2022).

Forecast 2022–2042

The analysis includes two forecast scenarios. The first scenario is the long-term forecast by the CBO. This CBO long-term forecast is our baseline for comparison with the alternative simulation scenario with the MP fiscal rules in place. That simulation assumes the CBO baseline scenario combined with the M-P fiscal rules and measures the impact of fiscal rules on the economy over the forecast period ending in 2042. That simulation assumes that the unusually high level of spending in response to the covid pandemic does not become the base against which the MP spending limit is applied. We set the base for the simulation scenario at the FY 2019 spending level; thus FY 2022 spending is that base adjusted for three years of inflation plus population growth. All values are in nominal dollars for comparison with CBO long-term forecasts.

Debt

Figure 7.1 compares the debt forecast by the CBO, with debt simulations with the fiscal rules in place. The CBO forecasts an increase in debt from $21 trillion to $75 trillion over the next two decades. As a share of GDP, the CBO forecasts an increase from 100 percent to 151 percent.

The fiscal rules significantly reduce the growth in debt compared to the CBO forecast. With the fiscal rules in place, debt increases to $47 trillion by the end of the forecast period in 2042. As a share of GDP, debt increases to 94 percent by the end of the period.

With the fiscal rules in place over the forecast period the fiscal gap is closed, and the debt/GDP ratio is on a downward trajectory. However, at the end of the period the debt/GDP ratio is at current levels, which many consider

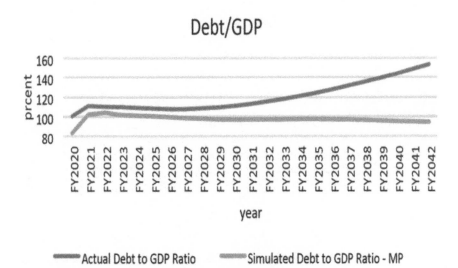

Figure 7.1   Debt/GDP (percent). *Source:* Authors' calculations.

to be well above a sustainable debt level. Thus, the simulation analysis reveals how difficult it will be to address the debt crisis at this point in time, even with effective fiscal rules in place. Later we will explore alternative simulation scenarios with fiscal policies that could lower the debt/GDP ratio to levels that are considered to be sustainable.

Deficits

Figure 7.2 compares the deficits forecast by the CBO, with deficit simulations with the fiscal rules in place. In the CBO forecast deficits decrease over the next decade and then increase significantly in the following decades. Deficits are estimated at 4.0 trillion dollars in 2020 and are projected to increase to 4.8 trillion dollars by the end of the period. The CBO estimates deficits as a share of gross domestic product fall from about 20 percent in 2020 to 10 percent at the end of the period.

With the fiscal rules in place deficits are reduced, but not eliminated. By the end of the period deficits are reduced to roughly 1.5 trillion dollars, or 5 percent of GDP. The fiscal rules do put the country on a trajectory to reduce deficits as a share of gross domestic product.

Government Spending

Figure 7.3 compares the total government spending forecast by the CBO with spending simulated with the fiscal rules in place. The CBO projects that total government spending will more than double, from 7 trillion dollars in 2020 to

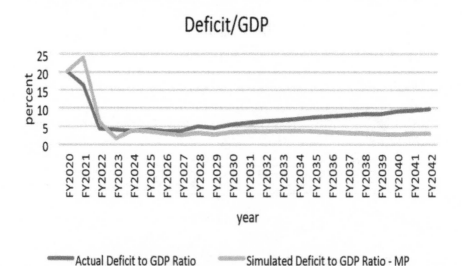

Figure 7.2   Deficit/GDP (percent). *Source*: Authors' calculations.

Spending/GDP

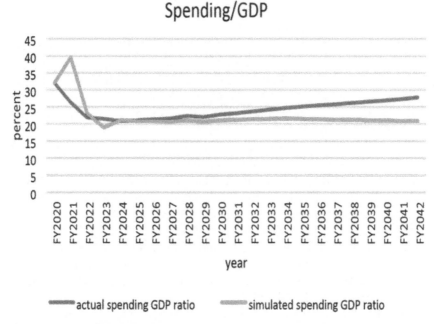

actual spending GDP ratio   simulated spending GDP ratio

Figure 7.3 Spending/GDP (percent). *Source*: Authors' calculations.

$14 trillion dollars at the end of the period. As a share of GDP, total spending will fall from 32 percent to 28 percent.

With the fiscal rules in place simulated total government spending grows to 10 trillion dollars at the end of the period. As a share of GDP total spending falls to 21 percent. The simulations reveal how difficult it will be to reduce government spending in the coming decades, even with fiscal rules in place. Some have argued that government spending should be reduced relative to the private sector by setting a cap of 20 percent or less on total government spending as a share of GDP. Note that even with effective fiscal rules in place, simulated total government spending as a share of GDP exceeds that cap throughout the forecast period.

The CBO forecasts that noninterest discretionary spending will fall over the next decade and then increase over the remaining period. At the end of the period discretionary spending is about or at the same level as at the beginning of the period, 5 trillion dollars.

With the fiscal rules in place, discretionary spending falls by half over the next few years and then rises slowly to 3 trillion dollars by the end of the period. The fiscal rules impose a very stringent constraint on the growth of discretionary spending, compared to that forecast by the CBO.

Economic Growth

Figure 7.4 compares the nominal GDP growth rate forecast by the CBO with that simulated with the fiscal rules in place. The CBO forecasts a high rate of economic growth, 6 percent, in 2021. The rate of economic growth is then forecast to fall to 3.5 percent by the end of the period. With the fiscal rules in place the growth rate falls to 3.8 percent by the end of the period. The modestly higher economic growth with the fiscal rules in place is accompanied by modestly higher growth in federal revenues.

The economic shocks that the United States has experienced in recent decades have clearly contributed to a climacteric or retardation in economic growth. As the CBO notes, actual GDP has been about half a percent below potential GDP and this is projected to continue in the long run. During and after each economic shock actual output has fallen short of potential output to a greater extent and for longer time periods than actual output has exceeded potential output during economic booms. Retardation in economic growth is especially evident in the aftermath of the coronavirus pandemic recession (Congressional Budget Office 2015, 2017, 2019, 2020a, 2020b, 2020c, 2020d, 2020e, 2021a, 2021b, 2021c).

The CBO long-term forecasts include the probability of shocks of various sizes over the forecast period. However, if the economy experiences another economic shock comparable to the financial crisis in 2008, or the coronavirus pandemic in 2020, we should anticipate further retardation in economic growth in the coming decades. The rising debt burden will make

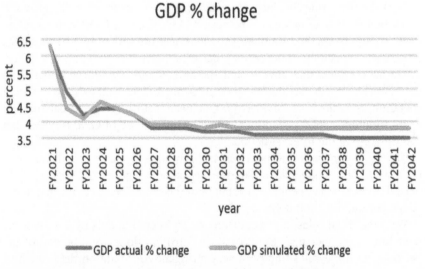

Figure 7.4   GDP (percentage change). *Source*: Authors' calculations.

it even more difficult for the government to respond to these economic shocks.

The MP rules provide that a portion of federal revenues be earmarked for an emergency fund. With this emergency fund the government would have resources to address an economic shock, such as the financial crisis in 2008, and the coronavirus pandemic in 2019. In other words, these fiscal rules would provide the federal government with more fiscal space to respond to economic shocks. Whether or not the government would have the fiscal space to avoid defaulting on the debt is an open question.

ALTERNATIVE SCENARIO ANALYSIS

Rules-based fiscal and monetary policy is designed to close the fiscal gap and reduce debt to sustainable levels. Our simulation analysis reveals that with the MP fiscal rules in place the United States is able to close the fiscal gap at current levels but is not able to reduce the debt/GDP ratio to levels considered sustainable over the forecast period. Even with these stringent fiscal rules in place the nation will be at risk of debt default for the foreseeable future, especially if we experience another major economic crisis.

This simulation analysis will certainly be discouraging to folks committed to restoring a "Great Moderation" in fiscal policy and sustainable levels of national debt. But that is no reason not to enact rules-based fiscal policies to address the debt crisis. The question then is what alternative fiscal policies could achieve these objectives. To answer this question, we simulate several scenarios with alternative fiscal policies over the forecast period.

The consensus estimate of a sustainable debt ratio is 60 percent for developed countries (Merrifield and Poulson 2016a, 2017b; Poulson et al. 2022). There is also a consensus that when the debt/GDP ratio reaches 90 percent, a country begins to experience retardation in economic growth (Reinhart and Rogoff 2009; Reinhart et al. 2003; Riedl 2019; Kotlikof 2015, de Rugy and Salmon 2020). We use these two benchmarks in simulating alternative fiscal policies over the forecast period. All of the scenarios assume that the MP fiscal rules are in place over the entire period.

The empirical results of these alternative fiscal policy scenarios are presented in table 7.1. The matrix shows the debt/GDP ratio in 2042 with these alternative fiscal policies in place. The scenarios that reduce the debt/GDP ratio below 90 percent are shown in bold.

Economic Growth

The simulation analysis with the MP rules in place assumes the average annual rate of growth incorporated in the CBO long-term forecast. Higher

Table 7.1   Debt/GDP in 2042 with Alternative Fiscal Policy Scenarios (percent)

Extra Econ Growth (percent)	Additional Annual Savings (billion dollars)			
	$0 (%)	$200 (%)	$400 (%)	$600 (%)
0.0	109.4	100.5	90.4	**79.5**
0.5	102.1	93.2	**83.9**	**74.0**
1.0	94.3	**86.2**	77.5	68.5
1.5	**86.9**	79.4	71.5	63.2
2.0	**79.9**	73.0	65.5	58.1

Source: CBO Long-Term Forecast 2021 and estimates by authors.

rates of economic growth will of course reduce the ratio of debt to gross domestic product. In this scenario analysis, we estimate the debt/GDP ratio assuming higher rates of economic growth. The first column in the matrix shows the assumed higher rates of economic growth compared to that forecast by the CBO. The second column shows simulated debt/GDP in 2042 with the MP fiscal rules and higher rates of economic growth assuming no additional savings from alternative fiscal policies.

Ceteris paribus, to reduce the debt/GDP ratio below 90 percent would require growth rates 1.5 percent higher than that forecast by the CBO. Even with growth rates 2.0 percent higher the debt/GDP ratio is still well above the 60 percent level. Such higher growth rates have never been achieved in the United States in the long term. These simulation results suggest that the United States cannot grow its way out of the debt crisis.

Additional Annual Savings with Alternative Fiscal Policies

Alternative fiscal policies to solve the debt crisis could require downsizing the federal government and earmarking the savings to reduce the federal debt. The other columns in the matrix show the debt/GDP ratio in 2042 assuming different rates of additional annual savings from downsizing the federal government, ranging from $200 billion to $600 billion.

Assuming the growth rate projected by the CBO, additional annual savings of $600 billion would be required to reduce the debt/GDP ratio below 90 percent by the end of the period.

The question posed in this simulation analysis is what alternative fiscal policies could reduce debt to a sustainable level. There is only one alternative fiscal policy that reduces the debt/GDP ratio below 60 percent. The sustainable debt level is reached with $600 billion in additional annual savings from alternative fiscal policies, combined with a 2 percent higher growth rate. All other alternative fiscal policies generate debt/GDP ratios above the sustainable level at the end of the period.

Downsizing the Federal Government

Generating annual savings of $600 billion from alternative fiscal policies downsizing the federal government is a formidable task indeed. In this analysis, there are two potential sources of saving of sufficient magnitude to reduce the debt by this magnitude, entitlement reform, and federal asset sales.

The CBO also explores the magnitude of potential savings from entitlement reform and other reforms (Congressional Budget Office 2021a). The estimates from this scenario analysis are in general consistent with the CBO estimates. The CBO also emphasizes what a formidable challenge it would be to generate significant savings from these reforms.

In the current political climate, it is highly unlikely that the federal government would enact the reforms required to achieve sustainable levels of debt. The last time that the federal government generated significant savings from entitlement reform was during the Reagan administration. Neither political party now supports reform of entitlement programs sufficient to generate annual savings of 600 billion dollars.

There is a precedent for generating savings through federal asset sales and leasing in the eighteenth and nineteenth centuries. Massive amounts of land and other resources were transferred from the federal government to the private domain. But the closing of the frontier in the late nineteenth century ended this era of privatization (Poulson 1981). There has been some privatization of federal assets under recent administrations, but these policies generated modest savings, and the savings were not earmarked to reduce debt.

Reducing the debt/GDP ratio to sustainable levels with alternative fiscal policies to downsize the federal government appears to be unattainable in the current political climate.

CONCLUSION

Our simulation analyses reveal how challenging it will be for the United States to achieve sustainable debt levels. Enacting the MP rules combined with policies to promote higher rates of economic growth and downsizing of the federal government could achieve this objective, but these alternative fiscal policies appear to be infeasible in the current political climate.

The noncrisis scenario is for continued, deepening debt fatigue. That is the scenario forecast by the CBO under current law. The political cause of debt fatigue in the United States is that suggested by Xavier Debrun, "Lack of domestic support for fiscal discipline, which leads to destabilizing budget cycles when fiscal fatigue sets in" (Debrun et al. 2019, 16).

We refer to the deepening debt fatigue scenario as the "Japan disease." Having accrued one of the highest debt/GDP ratios ever recorded, Japan has already experienced debt fatigue for three decades. Each economic shock in that period caused a sharp increase in an already high debt/GDP ratio. It happened because the Japanese government responded to these economic shocks with a series of fiscal stimulus packages. The Bank of Japan monetized this debt, and with fiscal dominance the bank must keep interest rates at or below 0 percent. Over most of this period, Japan failed to achieve the benchmarks set for fiscal and monetary policy. Even inflation rates have remained stubbornly below the target rate. Japan has seen much slower than usual growth in output and employment and is projected to continue to experience that debt fatigue in the coming decades.

There remains an alternative path for the United States to pursue that would yield sustainable levels of debt; a path that is becoming an ever rougher road. Following the precedent set in European countries, the United States could enact effective fiscal rules to restrain the growth in government spending and reduce deficits in the long term. However, the simulation analyses reveal that after two decades of debt fatigue-inducing monetary and fiscal responses to major economic shocks, this will be a formidable task indeed.

Imposing effective fiscal rules would require a major downsizing of the federal government compared to that forecast by the CBO. Discretionary spending would have to be nearly frozen at current levels. Total federal spending would have to be reduced far below that forecast by the CBO. This would require fundamental reforms to constrain the cost of entitlement programs, which are the major source of increased federal spending. Given the debt fatigue that has occurred over the past two decades, the United States seems unlikely to pursue this difficult alternative path.

Deterioration in dynamic credence capital in the United States means that the most likely noncrisis scenario is that forecast by the CBO. The federal government will continue to expand relative to the private sector, with much of the growth in government spending financed by borrowing. By mid-twenty-first century, U.S. federal debt will increase relative to GDP to levels comparable to that in Japan.

Over the next few decades, the growth in federal debt burdens will expose the country to greater risk of debt default and or hyper-inflation, especially if the United States experiences another major economic shock. The United States will not likely default on the federal debt in the near term. The most likely outcome is that the United States will continue along the current path, with more debt fatigue, inflation, and further retardation in economic growth.

However, in the long term, there is another outcome suggested by the climacteric in economic growth experienced by the United States in the early twentieth century (Poulson and Dowling 1972). The major economic shocks of that era culminated in the decade-long Great Depression, in which virtually every country devalued their currency, and many countries defaulted on their debt. Such a collapse of the international economy is increasingly possible as more countries experience debt fatigue and retardation in economic growth. This is a dismal outlook for the world economy, but one that becomes more relevant the longer that major debtor countries such as Japan and the United States delay addressing their debt crisis. In the final chapter of this book, we end on a more optimistic note by exploring some institutional changes that could allow the United States to change course and enact rules-based fiscal policies to address the debt crisis.

NOTES

1. Since most infrastructure spending is financed privately or by state governments, a disbursement from the capital fund could be linked to planned or scheduled capital expenditures in the states, e.g. highway construction.

2. Given the intense lobbying focused on discretionary spending, implementation of the fiscal rules would likely require institutional reforms in the budget process discussed in the final chapter of this book.

3. Note that our simulation analysis of alternative fiscal rules focusing on a single target that have been introduced in Congress shows that fail to achieve the desire fiscal sustainability (see previous chapter).

4. When tax cuts are enacted through reconciliation, the rules prohibit increasing net deficits outside of the budget window. Provisions that reduce revenue tend to sunset to dodge a point of order in the Senate under the Byrd rules, but sometimes they sunset earlier. Strictly speaking, almost no statute is binding on a future Congress, although in practice most continue for long periods without substantive change, reflecting inertia in the budget process.

5. We should note that the simulations are based on the CBO projections using the "current law" baseline which is more optimistic than the "alternative fiscal scenario" which assumes various expiring provisions/programs continue. Note also that the CBO measures of debt do not include off-budget liabilities of the federal government such as lending for education and housing programs.

REFERENCES

Blankart, C., 2015, "What the Eurozone Could Learn from Switzerland," *CESfio FORUM* 16(2): 39–42.

Congressional Budget Office, 2015, *Why CBO Projects that Actual Output Will be Below Potential Output on Average*, February.

Congressional Budget Office, 2017, *Cost Estimate for the Conference Agreement on H.R. 1, a Bill to Provide for Reconciliation Pursuant to Titles II and V of the Concurrent Resolution on the Budget for the Fiscal Year 2018*, December 15.

Congressional Budget Office, 2019, *The Effect of Government Debt on Interest Rates*, Working Paper 2019-01, March.

Congressional Budget Office, 2020a, *The Budget and Economic Outlook 2020–2030*, January 28.

Congressional Budget Office, 2020b, *Interim Economic Projection for 2020 and 2021*, May 19.

Congressional Budget Office, 2020c, *Federal Debt a Primer*, March.

Congressional Budget Office, 2020d, *An Update to the Economic Outlook: 2020 to 2030*, July.

Congressional Budget Office, 2020e, *CBO's Economic Forecast: Understanding the Slowdown of Productivity Growth*, NABE Foundation 17th Annual Economic Measurement Seminar.

Congressional Budget Office, 2021a, *Long Term Budget Outlook*, March.

Congressional Budget Office, 2021b, Re: Three Scenarios for the Budget as Specified by Senator Graham, Letter to Honorable Lindsey Graham, Ranking Member of the Committee on the Budget, United States Senate, Washington DC, May 21.

Congressional Budget Office, 2021c, Extended Budgetary Effects of H.R. 1319, The American Rescue Plan Act of 2021, March 10.

Debrun, X., and L. Jonung, 2019, "Under Threat-Rules Based Fiscal Policy and How to Preserve It," *European Journal of Political Economy* March 57: 142157.

De Rugy, V., and J. Salmon, 2020, "Debt and Growth: Decade of Studies," Policy Brief, Mercatus Center, George Mason University, April 15.

Feld, L., and G. Kirchgassner, 2006, "On the Effectiveness of Debt Brakes: The Swiss Experience," Center for Research in Economics Management and the Arts, Working Paper No. 2006–21.

IMF Conference, edited by S. Abbas, A. Pienkowski, and K. Rogoff, International Monetary Fund, forthcoming, Oxford University Press.

International Monetary Fund, 2013, "Staff Guidance Note for Public Debt Sustainability Analysis in Market-Access Countries," May.

International Monetary Fund (IMF), 2018a, *Fiscal Monitor: Managing Public Wealth*, October 2018, pp. 11–13.

International Monetary Fund (IMFb), 2018b, Assessing Fiscal Space-An Update and Stock Taking, IMF Policy Paper, International Monetary Fund, Washington D.C.

Kotlikof, L., 2015, *America's Fiscal Insolvency and its Generational Consequences*, Testimony to the Senate Budget Committee, February 25.

Lledó, V., S. Yoon, X. Fang, S. Mbaye, and Y. Kim, 2017, "Fiscal Rules at a Glance," 2015 IMF Fiscal Rules Database Background Note, International Monetary Fund, Washington, DC.

Merrifield, J., and B. Poulson, 2016a, *Can the Debt Growth be Stopped? Rules Based Policy Options for Addressing the Federal Fiscal Crisis*, Lexington Books, New York, NY.

Merrifield, J., and B. Poulson, 2016b, "The Swedish and Swiss Fiscal Rule Outcomes Contain Key Lessons for the U.S.," *Independent Review* 21(2): 251–275.

Merrifield, J., and B. Poulson, 2017, *Restoring America's Fiscal Constitution*, Lexington Books, New York, NY.

Poulson, Barry, 1981, *Economic History of the United States*, Macmillan Publishing, New York.

Poulson, B., J. Merrifield, and S. Hanke, editors, 2022, *Public Debt Sustainability: International Perspectives*, Lexington Press, forthcoming.

Poulson, B., and M. Dowling, 1972, "The Climacteric in U.S. Economic Growth," *Oxford Economic Papers* 25(3), Nov.

Reinhart, C., and K. Rogoff, 2009, *This Time is Different: Eight Centuries of Financial Folly*, Princeton University Press.

Reinhart, C., K. Rogoff, and M. Savastano, 2003, "Debt Intolerance," *Brookings Papers on Economic Activity* 1(Spring): 1–74.

Riedl, B., 2019, *A Plausible Blueprint for Fiscal Sustainability*, Manhattan Institute, June 11.

Chapter 8

Institutional Reforms to Restore a "Great Moderation" in Monetary and Fiscal Policy

The Friedman Solution

INTRODUCTION

In the current political climate restoring a "Great Moderation" in macro-economic policy appears to be an insurmountable task. Over half a century ago, Milton Friedman proposed rules-based monetary and fiscal policies to achieve a Great Moderation in macroeconomic policy. His proposals have even more relevance for our generation as we attempt to chart a path for macroeconomic policies in the wake of the coronavirus pandemic. In this study, we trace the evolution of Friedman's ideas and how they can provide a path forward.

In the years after World War II, Keynesian macroeconomics became more widely accepted in the economics profession, and eventually within the policy community. Keynesians argued that fiscal policies could be fine-tuned to achieve optimum levels of output and employment. Friedman was perhaps the most important voice challenging this reliance on discretionary fiscal policies to stabilize the economy over the business cycle. Friedman argued that rules-based monetary and fiscal policies should be used to constrain the government and allow the price system to allocate resources efficiently.

In an exchange with Friedman, Walter Heller expressed the consensus view, criticizing his proposed rule calling for the money stock to be increased at a constant rate. Friedman responded that:

> The reason why that (the rule for steady monetary growth) doesn't rigidly lock you in, in the sense in which Walter was speaking, is that I don't believe that money is all that matters. The automatic pilot is the price system. It isn't per-fectly flexible, it isn't perfectly free, but it has a good deal of capacity to adjust.

If you look at what happened to this country when we adjusted to post World War II, to the enormous decline in our expenditures, and the shift in the direction of our resources, you have to say that we did an extraordinarily good job of adjusting, and that this is because there is an automatic pilot. But if an automatic pilot is going to work, if you are going to have the market system work, it has to have some basic stable framework. (Friedman and Heller 1969, 28, 78)

Early in his career, Friedman advocated a cyclically balanced budget, with monetization of deficits and demonetization of surpluses, with budget balance over the business cycle (Friedman 1948). By the 1950s, however, Friedman had become a monetarist. He argued that the equation of exchange provides a superior explanation of aggregate economic activity to that offered by the Keynesians.

"If you want to control prices and incomes, they (the conclusions) say, in about as clear tones as empirical evidence can speak, control the stock of money per unit of output." He concluded that "the primary task of our monetary authorities is to provide economic stability by controlling the stock of money . . . Monetary policy should be directed exclusively toward the maintenance of a stable level of prices" (Friedman (1952) 1969, 170).

In their monumental empirical study, "A Monetary History of the United States" (1963), Friedman and Schwartz documented that historically every absolute decline in the stock of money was followed by a deep depression. Their monetarist analysis of the "Great Depression" offered an alternative to the Keynesian interpretation. The Fed's monetary policies in the 1930s were destabilizing, contributing to the length and severity of that business cycle.

Friedman hypothesized that monetary policy cannot affect real variables, referred to as the "natural rate" hypothesis. He challenged the assumption of a "Phillips Curve" tradeoff between inflation and unemployment, a key argument in the Keynesian analysis (Friedman (1968) 1969). He argued that in periods of sustained inflation, the public's expectations would adjust to the higher rates of inflation, eliminating any tradeoff between inflation and unemployment. During the stagflation of the 1970s, this monetarist interpretation gained greater traction within the economics profession. Friedman criticized the stop-and-go monetary policies pursued during the 1960s and 1970s, and he made the case for rules versus discretion in the conduct of monetary policy. Validation of Friedman's views came in 1979 when FOMC chairman Volcker committed the Fed to stable growth of the money supply to constrain inflation (Friedman (1979) 1983).

The high point in rules-based monetary policy in the United States came in the 1990s, a period referred to as the Great Moderation. In that decade, Paul Volcker was successful in maintaining stable growth in the money supply resulting in price stabilization and significantly lower interest rates. The effectiveness of monetary policies was conditional on new fiscal rules enacted in that period. These statutory fiscal rules were effective in constraining the growth in federal spending. By the end of the 1990s, the budget was balanced, and debt sustainability was achieved. The rules, proposed by John Taylor and others, expanded on Friedman's ideas for rules-based monetary and fiscal policy. They were not enacted as formal rules, comparable to the formal rules adopted within the European Community at that time. In the U.S. rules set guidelines for the conduct of monetary and fiscal policy, and the actual policies pursued approximated these guidelines. The monetary and fiscal rules enacted in the United States during the Great Moderation are referred to as indicative rules.[1]

While Friedman's contributions to rules-based monetary policy are well documented, less well known are his contributions to rules-based fiscal policy. He was part of a group of scholars at the University of Chicago, including Antonin Scalia, who supported a Balanced Budget Amendment to the U.S. Constitution. His ideas were a major influence in the adoption of a balanced federal budget plank in the Republican Party platform (Merrifield and Poulson 2016a, 2017b).[2]

Friedman also took an active role in the efforts to enact tax and expenditure limits (TELs) at the state and local level (Merrifield and Poulson 2021). When Ronald Reagan was governor of California in the 1970s, he and Friedman toured the state in support of Prop One, the nation's first state TEL. While Prop One failed narrowly at the polls, it set the stage for the tax revolt in California and throughout the nation. Later in that decade California enacted, through citizen initiative, the Jarvis Amendment, limiting property taxes and the Gann Amendment, a state TEL. The Jarvis Amendment continues to constrain property taxes in California. The Gann Amendment imposed an effective constraint on the growth of state spending, limiting it to the growth in population plus inflation. However, in the late 1980s the California legislature was successful in weakening the effectiveness of the Gann Amendment.

Friedman took an active role in supporting TELs in other states as well. He supported the efforts of citizens in Colorado and Wisconsin to design and implement effective state TELs. In Colorado, he opposed the efforts by state legislators to weaken the Taxpayer Bill of Rights (TABOR). In Wisconsin, he supported a stringent tax and spending limit similar to TABOR introduced in that state legislature and opposed alternative weaker measures. Over the years, thirty-two states have enacted some form of TEL. Most of these measures have proven to be ineffective constraints on the growth in state spending. When TELs are designed and enacted by legislators as statutory measures, they tend to be weak, ineffective, and easily circumvented. That is why Friedman took an active role in support of citizen and taxpayer organizations helping them design and enact effective state TELs. When the preferences of elected officials differ from that of citizens, direct democracy provides an opportunity for citizens to enact fiscal rules through the initiative process to protect their rights. The TELs enacted through citizen initiative are more likely to be effective, especially when they are incorporated in the state constitution (Merrifield Poulson 2021).

At the turn of the twenty-first century, it seemed that Friedman's vision for rules-based monetary and fiscal policy was becoming a reality. At the state level well-designed fiscal rules, such as the TABOR Amendment in Colorado, were copied in other states to effectively constrain the growth in state government. At the national level, statutory fiscal rules ended the deficits and debt accumulation of prior decades. Monetary policies approximated the indicative targets implicit in Taylor Rules. The public choice literature, expanding on Friedman's early ideas, provided the rationale for this rules-based approach to fiscal and monetary policy.

Over the past two decades, however, the United States has largely abandoned this rules-based approach to macroeconomic policy. While there is a broad consensus across the political spectrum on the need to restore a Great Moderation on macroeconomic policy, each year our nation drifts further from rules-based monetary and fiscal policy. This is not for lack of trying. Each year new legislation is proposed in Congress to enact more stringent fiscal rules, but these measures often fail to receive the votes required for passage, and some measures fail to be reported out of committee. Usually, these bills do not get a vote at all, and they are almost never reported out of committee. For decades Congress has debated resolutions calling for an amendment to the constitution requiring a balanced budget, and other provisions imposing greater fiscal discipline. But these efforts have failed to receive the super-majority vote required for Congress to propose amendments (Poulson et al. 2022).[3]

In 2022, in the wake of the coronavirus pandemic, the nation seems to have drifted even further from rules-based monetary and fiscal policy. The reality is that statutory fiscal rules have failed to impose fiscal discipline, and the nation continues to pursue heterodox monetary policies long after these policies were enacted in response to economic crises.

The fatal flaw in our current fiscal and monetary rules is unbounded discretion. Indicative rules set targets for fiscal and monetary policy but leave it up to elected officials (or appointed officials in the case of the Fed) to implement those policies. There is an extensive literature on why elected or appointed officials choose to pursue macroeconomic policies inconsistent with the preferences of citizens. One explanation focuses on time inconsistency, when governments are not able to make binding commitments about future policy. Effective fiscal and monetary policies must solve this commitment problem. Rules imply commitment, while discretion implies its absence; with effective rules a government can tie the hands of its successor and improve outcomes (Stokey 2003).

The literature on time inconsistency assumes a rational welfare maximizing government. Friedman (1948) offered an alternative explanation for failed macroeconomic policies. Policy makers may be misguided, greedy, or myopic. Rules-based fiscal and monetary policies must offer protection for citizens from elected or appointed officials who are self-interested and respond to pressure groups, or who are simply misinformed. This alternative assumption regarding the motives of elected and appointed officials would become the foundation for a new public choice literature.

Whatever the explanation, it is clear that our monetary and fiscal policies are failing. Indeed, the U.S. economy in 2022 has many of the problems encountered in 1979 prior to the Great Moderation. The United States has experienced two decades of slower economic growth, and that retardation in growth is projected to continue in the coming decades. Two major economic shocks have been accompanied by greater volatility in output and employment, followed by slow economic recovery. After years of financial market repression, the rate of inflation now exceeds the indicative targets set by the Fed.

The solution is to restore rules-based monetary and fiscal policy. But, we can no longer rely on the indicative rules enacted during the Great Moderation; the United States needs "second-generation" fiscal and monetary rules. This will require some fundamental reforms in our fiscal and monetary institutions. To be effective, formal rules must be incorporated in constitutional and statutory law, as they have been within the European Union (Poulson et al. 2022).

WHAT HAVE WE LEARNED FROM SECOND-GENERATION FISCAL RULES?

Fiscal Authorities must pursue two tasks. They must pursue fiscal policies to stabilize output and employment in the short term and maintain the fiscal discipline required for debt sustainability in the long term (International Monetary Fund 2013; Bank for International Settlements 2011; Debrun et al. 2018; Debrun and Jonung 2019; Organization for Economic Cooperation and Development 2013). The fiscal policies used to stabilize the economy over the business cycle may include both discretionary and non-discretionary policies, that is, automatic stabilizers. Theory and analysis show that the consequence of time inconsistency is that fiscal authorities have a bias toward deficits and debt. Fiscal authorities may sacrifice fiscal discipline in responding to short-term economic shocks; the result is persistent deficits and debt accumulation that undermine long-term debt sustainability (Alesina and Tabellini 1990; Persson and Svensson 1989; Alesina and Passalacqua 2015).

During the Great Moderation of the 1980s and 1990s, fiscal authorities in the United States were able to use indicative fiscal rules to achieve debt sustainability. Indicative fiscal rules set targets for deficits and debt as guideposts for fiscal authorities in order to achieve debt sustainability. While sanctions and enforcement mechanisms were incorporated in the rules, the primary enforcement mechanism was the political cost of failing to meet the targets. Fiscal authorities were able to close the fiscal gap, while responding to economic instability over the business cycle (Merrifield and Poulson 2016a, 2017b; Poulson et al. 2022).

In responding to economic shocks over the past two decades, fiscal authorities in the United States have failed to achieve debt sustainability. The fiscal framework relying on indicative fiscal rules has largely collapsed. Perhaps the best evidence for this is the Biden budget proposed for FY 2023 (Office of Management and Budget 2022). That budget projects that in coming decades the United States will incur deficits and accumulate debt greater than that incurred during recent economic shocks. Over the past two decades, a clear distinction has emerged between the group of countries that have closed the fiscal gap, that is, stabilized and reduced the debt/GDP ratio, and high debtor countries that have failed to do so. The United States now falls within the group of high debtor countries.

Some empirical studies have attempted to estimate the debt/GDP ratio at which a country begins to experience retardation in economic growth. The study by Reinhart and Rogoff (2009) estimated the level for a broad cross-section of developed countries at 90 percent. That study has been challenged in other studies, and some question whether such a threshold debt/GDP level even exists (Reinhart et al. 2003).[4] It is important to distinguish this literature from the studies that estimate the debt/GDP ratio at which a country is exposed to risk of default. As noted earlier, there is considerable controversy regarding the sustainable debt/GDP level. Empirical studies show that different countries are exposed to risk of default at different debt/GDP levels. Developing countries may experience default at much lower debt/GDP ratios than developed countries (Poulson et al. 2022).

The consensus in this literature is that the United States and other high debtor countries are now at risk of default and must close the fiscal gap to achieve sustainable debt/GDP levels (Peter G. Peterson Foundation 2019, 2021). We maintain that closing the fiscal gap in the United States now requires formal fiscal rules, sometimes referred to as hard fiscal law, rather than indicative fiscal rules. The new fiscal rules must impose explicit ex-ante constraints on deficits and debt on a long-term basis. The rules must have a strong legal basis, with strict sanctions and enforcement procedures. The fiscal rules that we propose are grounded in the transversality condition, which states that the present value of the debt/GDP ratio must remain finite

(Wypolsz 2005, 71). That condition provides a theoretical basis for setting the target debt/GDP ratio required for debt sustainability. In practical terms, the fiscal authority must commit to target debt/GDP ratios below a level that is considered unsustainable.

The new fiscal rules that we proposed address the main criticisms of hard fiscal law. Flexibility is built into the rules to provide for stabilization in fiscal policy over the business cycle. The rules prioritize emergency preparedness and provide for capital expenditures through a capital investment fund to stabilize capital expenditures in the long term. The rules create incentives for enacting reforms in mandatory as well as discretionary programs.

There is a broad consensus across the political spectrum that the nation must close the fiscal gap and restore sustainable fiscal policy (Peter G. Peterson Foundation 2019, 2021). There is also broad support for a normalization of monetary policy based on orthodox monetary tools (Poulson et al. 2022). Restoring a Great Moderation in macroeconomic policy will now require some fundamental reforms in our monetary and fiscal institutions. In this study, we focus on three of these institutional reforms: budget process reform, independent monetary and fiscal institutions, and incorporating fiscal rules in the constitution. To meet this challenge, it is important to build on the experience of other countries that have been successful in enacting this second generation of fiscal and monetary rules.

REFORMING THE BUDGET PROCESS

The Balanced Budget and Emergency Deficit Control Act of 1985, also referred to as the Gramm-Rudman-Hollings Act, launched a Great Moderation in macroeconomic policy. The act set a crucial precedent in the budget process. Congress committed to balancing the budget within a set time frame. Balancing the budget would, ceteris paribus, close the fiscal gap at that debt/GDP ratio. That legislation also set another important precedent, requiring Congress to reduce deficits each year to close the fiscal gap. The act, as amended, imposed spending caps and created new enforcement mechanisms in the budget process, that is, sequestration and pay-go, to enforce the budget rules.

Unfortunately, over the past two decades these fiscal rules have been suspended or abandoned altogether. Our analysis of recent fiscal legislation reveals that the budget process is broken (Merrifield and Poulson 2016a, 2017b; Poulson et al. 2022). We can no longer allow Congress to pursue discretionary fiscal policies that are unconstrained by fiscal rules. New fiscal rules must be enacted to restore the rules-based budget process created by the Balanced Budget and Emergency Control Act of 1985. Fortunately, Congress has now responded to this challenge, and the following discussion supports these legislative proposals.

S. 2765 the Bipartisan Congressional Budget Reform Act

S. 2765 could receive the bipartisan support required for passage of this legislation (U.S. Congress. 2019–2020). The act requires procedural reforms to introduce greater transparency and accountability in the budget process. The act would enable Congress to restore a budget process in which debt limits and caps on discretionary spending are again effective constraints on fiscal policy. The reporting requirements in the legislation would record when proposed legislation has a budgetary impact in violation of fiscal rules. The concurrent budget resolution would again set the framework for the budget process. Among other modifications the act includes provisions that:

> require biennial congressional budget resolutions, instead of the annual budget resolutions required under current law;
>
> retain the existing annual appropriations process;
>
> require a budget resolution to specify a target for the ratio of the debt held by the public to the gross domestic product
>
> (GDP) for each year covered by the resolution;
>
> require the debt-to-GDP target to be enforced using a reconciliation process that requires deficit reduction legislation to be considered using expedited legislative procedures; allow a budget resolution to include the amount of tax expenditures;
>
> provide for automatic adjustments of the debt limit and statutory discretionary spending limits to conform to the levels in the budget resolution;
>
> modify the procedures for considering budget resolutions in the Senate;
>
> allow budget resolutions that have bipartisan support and meet specified requirements to be considered in the Senate using expedited procedures;
>
> modify and establish budget points of order that may be raised against legislation;
>
> rename the Committee on the Budget of the Senate as the Committee on Fiscal Control and the Budget of the Senate; and
>
> expand reporting requirements for congressional committees, the Office of Management and Budget, the Congressional Budget Office, and the Government Accountability Office. (U.S. Congress. 2019–2020)

Special interests will continue to call for suspension and circumvention of fiscal rules. We propose several amendments to S. 2765 to strengthen enforcement provisions of the legislation. Implicit in S. 2765 is the assumption that the enforcement provisions of the Balanced Budget and Emergency Deficit Control Act of 1985 as an amendment would be retained going forward. Thus, the enforcement mechanisms of sequestration and pay-go would be retained. We recommend that this be made explicit, with the added provisions that a super-majority vote in both houses of Congress be required to suspend these rules.

An Advisory Fiscal Council (AFC)

The rules that we propose will require fundamental reforms in our fiscal institutions. We propose that the United States create an independent fiscal agency to implement a rules-based fiscal policy. To understand the role of an independent fiscal agency it is important to understand the limitations of the Congressional Budget Office (CBO).

The CBO originated with a conflict between Congress and President Nixon and the passage of the 1974 Congressional Budget Act (Congressional Budget Office 2021b). President Nixon threatened to withhold Congressional appropriations for programs inconsistent with his policies. This conflict over presidential impoundments led Congress to create a new budget process, including the CBO, to provide Congress with objective, impartial information about budgetary and economic issues.

The CBO is an advisory agency attached to Congress, with a director appointed by the president and approved by Congress. The director is jointly recommended by the budget chairs, traditionally alternating between the House and the Senate, to the Speaker of the House and the president pro tempore of the Senate. The CBO provides budget analysis on some legislative proposals, measuring the budgetary cost of specific legislation. As an advisory authority, the CBO is constrained by archaic rules incorporated in the budget process over the years. For example, the Byrd Rule restricts what can be included in reconciliation legislation in the Senate. The rule prohibits provisions that are viewed as "extraneous" to the budget. The Byrd Rule prevents a reconciliation bill from containing non-budgetary provisions that supporters might otherwise wish to have an easier path to passage. Other rules restrict the CBO's analysis of the budgetary impact of legislation to a ten-year time frame. Legislators then draft legislation to have a modest impact on the budget over that ten-year time frame, and a major budgetary impact beyond that time frame. The result is biased information in which the budgetary cost of legislation is not accurately reflected in near-term budget projections. This can lead to misguided fiscal policy. Another controversial rule is one that limits the use of dynamic scoring in measuring the long-term budgetary impact of taxes and spending. The CBO does dynamic scoring for major legislation that has a measurable impact on the macroeconomy, as supplemental information to the conventional static scoring. Over the years, economists have recommended reforms in these budget rules and in the role of the CBO, but few of those reforms were enacted.

The CBO has fulfilled its mandate and played an important role in improving transparency in fiscal policies. That role was especially important during the Great Moderation of the 1980s and 1990s when statutory rules-imposed constraints on fiscal policy to achieve balanced budgets and debt sustainability. Over the past two decades, however, those statutory rules have proven to be ineffective in achieving these objectives. The CBO continues to perform its role in providing objective impartial information to Congress. But, as Congress has chosen to suspend and circumvent statutory rules, neither the fiscal rules nor the CBO has had much impact on discretionary fiscal policy. The discretionary fiscal policies pursued by Congress have deviated even further from fiscal policies consistent with budget balance and debt sustainability. As mandatory spending increasingly dominates total spending, the role of legislators and the CBO in the budget process has fallen.

The experience in the United States reveals that the effectiveness of an independent fiscal agency depends upon the design of fiscal rules and the commitment of elected officials to the fiscal rules. During the Great Moderation, the statutory rules were effective and the CBO performed an important role in the transparency and accountability for fiscal policies consistent with the rules. But the statutory rules are poorly designed, and Congress has waived and adjusted them regularly. As a result, the role of the CBO in providing accurate information producing transparency and accountability is limited, and the reputational cost to elected officials who choose to ignore the fiscal rules is minimal (Inman 1996).

The experience of the European countries suggests that it will take better fiscal rules and institutional reforms, including an independent fiscal agency, to create rule enforcement pressure. Most importantly, it will require elected officials committed to the rules and public support for rules-based fiscal and monetary policy (Debrun et al. 2009; Dehaan et al. 2004; Debrun and Jonung 2019; Poulson et al. 2022).

We propose that the United States create an Advisory Fiscal Council (AFC) (model legislation for an AFC is contained in Appendix B). To understand the role of an AFC, it is important to distinguish this from an Independent fiscal Council (IFC) (IMF 2013, 2014). The role of an IFC would be similar to that of the Federal Reserve Board. IFC members would be unelected experts appointed by the president with a fixed term. Just as the Federal Reserve Board has the mandate to implement monetary policy, an IFC would have the mandate to implement fiscal policy. An IFC could set a target for the debt/GDP ratio, and a time frame for achieving that target. Annual deficits would have to be consistent with that target. The IFC could also be given the mandate to pursue countercyclical fiscal policies. Once the fiscal gap is closed, the IFC could have the mandate to balance the budget in the near term, that is, over the business cycle. The budget proposed by the president and the final budget approved by Congress would then have to be consistent with this balanced budget mandate. The IFC would be accountable to Congress, just as the Federal Reserve Board is accountable to Congress.

While economists have made a strong case for an IFC, especially in high debtor countries, such an independent fiscal authority would be inappropriate for the United States. Delegating fiscal policy to an IFC would be an infringement of the separation of powers clause in the U.S. Constitution. The constitution vests fiscal power in Congress and specifically prohibits some delegation of such power to an independent fiscal authority. It is highly unlikely that citizens would allow a delegation of such power because of the precedent this would set for other delegated powers. The literature on the "Imperial Presidency" suggests that citizens are already concerned about the growing fiscal power of the presidency and the abdication of power by Congress.

Another reason for rejecting an IFC is the track record of the Federal Reserve Board over the past two decades. The Federal Reserve Board is often viewed as a group of highly qualified experts willing to pursue monetary policies in the public interest, even when this conflicts with the priorities of elected officials. While that view of the Federal Reserve Board may have applied during the Great Moderation in monetary policy, it does not apply over the last two decades. Just as the Federal Reserve Board has failed to solve the time inconsistency problem, we should expect an IFC to fail to solve this problem in fiscal policy.

An Advisory Fiscal Council (AFC) in the United States, on the other hand, would play a role similar to that of the Fiscal Responsibility Council in Sweden. Sweden's Fiscal Responsibility Council is an AFC that has been effectively integrated into their fiscal framework for decades. It has played a crucial role in implementing the new fiscal rules enacted in Sweden over this period. The Fiscal Responsibility Council was created by statutes that delegate limited fiscal powers from parliament. There does not appear to be conflict between this delegation of fiscal powers and the Swedish Constitution. The Swedish Fiscal Responsibility Council has served as a model for similar independent fiscal authorities in other countries and could serve as a model for the United States as well. Such a limited delegation of fiscal powers to an AFC would not conflict with the separation of powers provisions of the constitution, nor our democratic principles (Merrifield and Poulson 2016b, 2017a).

Some economists argue that the proposed role of an Advisory Fiscal Council (FAC) could be fulfilled by existing fiscal institutions, including the CBO, the General Accounting Office, and the Federal Accounting Standards Board (FASAB) (Couchman 2022). However, there are several reasons why these fiscal institutions are not up to the task, and why an AFC is needed. The AFC would be charged with tasks that are not performed by existing institutions.

A major task would be implementing and monitoring new fiscal rules. This role for the AFC is essential in holding legislator accountable for meeting fiscal rules targets. If new fiscal rules are incorporated into the constitution, this role will be especially important. Constitutional fiscal rules would allow citizens and state legislators to monitor federal fiscal policies, and for the courts to determine whether or not federal fiscal policies are consistent with the constitution as amended. This would require changes in Article 1, Section 1, of the Constitution, which state that "All Legislative Powers herein vested shall be vested in a Congress of the United States."

It is important to emphasize that the AFC proposed for the United States would complement the rules-based fiscal policies that we propose. Some studies have proposed AFCs as a substitute for fiscal rules (Wyplosz 2005; Debrun et al. 2009). These studies suggest that the cost of fiscal rules, that is, loss of flexibility in pursuing countercyclical fiscal policy, justifies the creation of an AFC less constrained by fiscal rules. We maintain that high debtor counties, such as the United States, must be constrained by fiscal rules in order to close the fiscal gap and pursue sustainable fiscal policies in the long term. An AFC would complement the rules-based fiscal policy in achieving these objectives and could be integrated into such a fiscal framework in the United States, just as it has been in Sweden.

The AFC would be charged with major reforms in the budget process in the United States.

Recommendations for reform should include institutional changes in the budget process that will enable the country to address the debt crisis.

The AFC would be charged with recommendations for improved transparency and accountability in measuring the full cost of government programs. Of major importance are comprehensive measures of total government debt including off-budget debt such as unfunded liabilities in entitlement programs and liabilities incurred for student debt, housing, and other federal programs.

The magnitude of debt incurred in recent decades will impose a heavy burden on future generations. A major task for the AFC would be intergenerational accounting. Addressing the debt crisis by reforming entitlement programs will impose different burdens on current and future generations. The AFC would be charged with analyzing the potential impact on different cohorts of the population of reforms to close the fiscal gap in the long term.

Current fiscal rules at both the national and subnational levels are failing to achieve sustainable fiscal policies in the long run. A major task of the AFC would be analysis of the problems in current fiscal rules. The Council would be charged with recommending improvements in fiscal rules, and also exploring the potential fiscal impact of new fiscal rules similar to those enacted in other countries.

INDEPENDENT MONETARY INSTITUTIONS

Monetary theory and analysis show that the consequence of time inconsistency is that monetary authorities exhibit an inflationary bias. Monetary authorities are expected to perform two tasks: achieving price stability in the long term and stabilizing output and employment in the near term. When confronted with high unemployment or public indebtedness, monetary authorities tend to respond with inflationary policies (Kydland and Prescott 1977; Wyplosz 2005).

In the stagflation experienced during the 1970s, it was clear that the Federal Reserve was failing to perform either task. Their response to the contractionary impact of oil price shocks was to give up on price stability. The Fed monetized deficits and in effect became a hostage to expansionary fiscal policy. Those policies were accompanied by double-digit interest rates and rates of inflation (Poulson et al. 2022).

The stagflation experienced during the 1970s led to institutional reforms designed to restore the independence of the Fed, and to new monetary policies. Influenced by the work of Milton Friedman and other monetary economists, the Fed adopted monetary aggregate growth rules. In the long term, price stability was restored as the primary objective of monetary policy, and orthodox tools of open market operations were again used to achieve that objective. Over the last two decades of the twentieth century, those institutional reforms and monetary policies were successful in restoring low rates of inflation, while fulfilling the Fed's role in stabilizing output and employment over the business cycle. Similar reforms were enacted in other industrialized countries to restore independent monetary authorities. Most central banks used inflation targeting to give them the flexibility to respond to business cycles, while achieving price stability in the long term (Poulson et al. 2022).

At the end of the twentieth century, many economists concluded that these institutional reforms had solved the time inconsistency problem in monetary policy. In the United States and other countries, indicative monetary rules rather than rigid formal rules were perceived to be effective. This meant that monetary authorities did not commit to an explicit set of monetary rules, but rather exercised discretion in approximating a rules-based monetary regime. Wyplosz (2005) concluded that:

> The explicit aim was to replace necessarily arbitrary rules with incentives; short run discretion was controlled by long run discipline. Bound by clear objectives and the accountability of their actors, independent central banks have escaped the time inconsistency problem. They do not commit to specific predetermined actions, as the "rules school" used to prescribe, they are simply free of the inflation bias. (Wyplosz 2005, 67)

This Great Moderation in monetary policy was short-lived. Over the past two decades, the Fed has responded to economic shocks with nonorthodox discretionary monetary policies. Short-run stabilization policy now takes precedence over long-term price stabilization. The Fed is now committed to achieving full employment in the near term, even if this is accompanied by inflation well above the target range. Fed independence has again been sacrificed as the monetary authorities responded to each economic shock. Massive amounts of new debt have been monetized by the Fed's purchase of Treasury and other securities. As the Fed has drifted further from the Great Moderation, it is difficult to find many economists who think that it has solved time inconsistency problems (Poulson et al. 2022).

The Fed is now attempting to normalize monetary policy by increasing the discount rate. But given the acceleration of inflation and evidence that higher inflation is now built into expectations, it will be difficult for the Fed to commit to stable prices. If normalization of monetary policy requires the Fed to increase the discount rate to 6 percent, as occurred during the Great Moderation of the 1990s, there is a low probability that the Fed will reach that target. It is not likely that normalization of monetary policy will be achieved before the country encounters another economic crisis, as occurred during the past decade

In the coming decade, the negative impacts of nonorthodox monetary policy will be played out. In the long term, the CBO forecasts higher interest rates and rates of inflation, accompanied by retardation in economic growth (Congressional Budget Office 2022). President Biden's 2022 budget proposal is surprisingly consistent with this gloomy forecast (Office of Management and Budget 2022). Neither of these forecasts assumes that the United States will experience another major economic shock over this period. A major economic shock could test the limits of expansionary fiscal and monetary policies in the coming years. It is not clear that the nation has the fiscal or monetary space to continue pursuing the macroeconomic policies it has pursued over the past two decades.

Restoring the Great Moderation in monetary policy will require second-generation monetary rules, and institutional reforms for those rules to be effective. Since the path-breaking work of John Taylor, economists have explored the second generation of monetary rules as a framework for monetary policy (Poulson et al. 2022; Merrifield and Poulson 2017a). Taylor-type monetary rules would require the Fed to commit to an explicit set of rules setting bounds on discretionary monetary policy ex-ante. Price stability would again be restored as the primary objective of monetary policy, with the Fed playing only a supporting role in stabilizing output and employment over the business cycle. In the long term, the Fed would downsize the portfolio of securities it has accumulated over the past two decades. The

Fed would also abandon nonorthodox monetary policies, such as payment of interest on excess reserves. Orthodox monetary policies, relying on open market operations, would again be used to achieve the targets set in these monetary rules.

Pursuing second-generation monetary rules will require institutional reforms to restore the independence of the Fed. Monetary policy can no longer be held hostage to the U.S. Treasury. A more formal separation of powers is needed for the Fed to pursue monetary policy within the framework of Taylor-type rules. This separation of powers could be made explicit by Congress reforming the statutory rules establishing the authority of the Fed. Citizens may perceive that restoration of Fed independence is sufficiently important to be incorporated as an amendment to the constitution. Such an amendment could be proposed either by the Congress or by the states through an Article V amendment convention.

A BALANCED BUDGET AMENDMENT REVISITED

The Economic Rationale for Constitutional Fiscal Rules

To understand the economic rationale for constitutional fiscal rules, we begin with some assumptions in neoclassical economics. The basic assumption is the Coase Theorem (Coase 1960). The theorem holds that the political process will yield an equilibrium in transactions such that no exchange that can benefit some group of people without hurting others goes unconsummated. The literature on political economy explores why a political process might fail to achieve this Pareto optimum outcome. Political institutions encounter problems of time inconsistency, asymmetric information, and other transaction costs (Alesina and Tabellini 1990; Inman 1996; Kyland and Prescott 1977; Persson and Svensson 1989).

The fact that Congress cannot reach an agreement on a concurrent budget resolution suggests that all of these flaws are inherent in the budget process. Enforceability of a budget agreement is complicated when legislators have an incentive to renege on the agreement, and when they have less incentive to reach an agreement in the first place.

The economic shocks experienced over the past two decades have magnified the problem of agreeing on a budget. A robust response to these economic shocks required emergency expenditures. Once budget constraints were relaxed in response to economic shocks, it has proven difficult to return to a rules-based budget process. The major economic shocks experienced over the last two decades introduced greater uncertainty and risk in the budget process compared to that during the Great Moderation. The enforcement powers of the fiscal rules enacted during the Great Moderation have proven to be less effective in recent years.

The budgets negotiated in recent years are best described as an incomplete contract, using the terminology of the new economic theory of the firm (Wyplosz 2005). A contract is complete when it incorporates provisions covering every circumstance considered relevant to the transaction. That assumes that every future circumstance is knowable, and contractual obligations can be made contingent on future events. Economic shocks in recent years have made it more difficult for elected officials to predict future circumstances, or draft a budget providing for future contingencies. The outcome of this process is not a budget, but rather a document that requires continuous negotiation. Legislators are reluctant to abide by fiscal rules that a future legislature might weaken or suspend. The constitutional fiscal rules enacted in other countries are designed to overcome these problems and restore a rules-based budget process.

In Appendix C, model legislation is provided for the Balanced Budget Amendment and an Expenditures Limitation Act. The legislation is modeled after the amendment incorporated into the Swiss Constitution through a referendum approved by 85 percent of Swiss citizens. The proposed amendment requires the federal government to bring expenditures into equilibrium with revenues in the near term. The Balanced Budget Amendment to the constitution would impose a more binding constraint on the fiscal policies of the federal government. Unlike statutory fiscal rules, a constitutional rule could only be superseded by another constitutional amendment. Elected officials who choose to disregard the proposed Balanced Budget Amendment to the constitution would be perceived by citizens as having betrayed the public trust. These elected officials would then face the wrath of citizens in the political process (Merrifield and Poulson 2017; Poulson et al. 2022).

The Balanced Budget Amendment that we propose is based on our own constitutional history. A Balanced Budget Amendment submitted to the voters for ratification should be simple, straightforward, and easily understood by citizens in the ratification process. This would follow the precedent set in the original U.S. Constitution, and in amendments to the Constitution. In the federal constitution, a premium is placed on parsimonious language. The result is a relatively short document, compared to state constitutions, laying out broad principles and leaving it up to Congress to enact enabling legislation consistent with these broad principles. This precedent should be a guide in designing and enacting new fiscal rules. Under Article V, the balanced budget could be proposed either by Congress or by the states through an article convention. It would then be submitted to the states for ratification, either by the state legislature or a state convention.

Critics often cite the difficulties of enforcement as a reason to oppose a Balanced Budget Amendment to the constitution. It is true that in other

OECD countries, a Balanced Budget Amendment to the constitution has not always been enforced. That is why many of these countries, such as Switzerland, have enacted new fiscal rules to include both constitutional and statutory provisions, to impose the fiscal discipline required for expenditures to match revenues in the near term. Indeed, the European Union now mandates that all member countries enact such fiscal rules (Merrifield and Poulson 2017; Poulson et al. 2022).

The model legislation also provides for an Expenditures Limitation Act as enabling legislation to fulfill the constitutional mandate to bring expenditures into equilibrium with revenues in the near term. The "Necessary and Proper Clause" of the constitution gives Congress the power to build out constitutional powers and provisions through implementing legislation. The proposed enabling legislation is also modeled after the Swiss debt brake. The act is proposed as a statutory measure with explicit fiscal targets that must be met and includes measures required to meet these targets spelled out in some detail. Experience with this type of fiscal rule in Switzerland and other OECD countries reveals that reliance on explicit targets is required to balance the budget in the near term. The fiscal rules must provide transparency and accountability to assure that constraints on fiscal policies are effective. With these fiscal rules in place, it is clear when the balanced budget requirement is violated, and who is responsible for the violation, for example, an overreaching executive branch, a profligate legislature, or an activist judicial branch of government (Merrifield and Poulson 2016b, 2017a, 2017b).

GROWING DYNAMIC CREDENCE CAPITAL
BY RESTORING A GREAT MODERATION
IN MACROECONOMIC POLICY

Restoring a Great Moderation in macroeconomic policy will require bipartisan support. The experience in Switzerland reveals that there is multiparty support for balanced budget rules and debt limits (Blankart 2011, 2015; Feld and Kirchgassner 2006).

There are many reasons for the success of balanced budget rules and debt limits in Switzerland. The language of their balanced budget rule is simple, straightforward, and easily understood by citizens, as well as elected officials. Citizens know that in their household budgets, they must equate expenditures with income over time; failure to do so results in bankruptcy. In Switzerland, citizens play a unique role in their federalist system. Citizens as well as elected officials can propose amendments to the constitution. Their Balanced Budget Amendment was enacted through a referendum, with support from 85 percent of their citizens.

Swiss debt brakes were first enacted at the Cantonal level. They were triggered by the bankruptcy of a municipal district. Swiss courts interpreted their bankruptcy law such that municipalities could not require bailouts from their Cantonal government. This no bailout rule sent the right signal to municipal and Cantonal governments. Balanced budget rules and debt limits were then enacted by municipal and Cantonal governments to avoid bankruptcy.

Balanced Budget Rules and debt limits were later enacted at the federal level in Switzerland. Elected officials perceived that as a small independent country with limited financial resources, they could not afford to expose the nation to default on their debt. With the new fiscal rules in place, they were able to cut the debt/GDP ratio by more than half.

As the Swiss government closed the fiscal gap and reduced the debt/GDP ratio, bipartisan support for their fiscal rules increased. Swiss citizens perceived that governments at all levels were pursuing prudent fiscal policies, and they gained confidence in their fiscal institutions. Swiss economists refer to this as growing dynamic credence capital.

In the United States, it is fair to say that the country is now experiencing declining dynamic credence capital (Merrifield and Poulson 2018). Citizens perceive that the federal government is pursuing imprudent monetary and fiscal policies. These policies have resulted in two major inequities—intergenerational inequality and interregional inequality. As citizens and elected officials challenge these inequities, this can establish the basis for bipartisan support for balanced budget rules and debt limits in this country, just as it did in Switzerland.

Intergenerational inequality is growing as unsustainable growth in debt shifts the economic burden of government to future generations (Kotlikoff 2015). The accumulation of debt, and especially the unfunded liabilities in federal entitlement programs, which are the most rapidly growing source of that debt, exposes the country to the risk of default and threatens the long-term viability of entitlement programs. As the trust funds used to finance Social Security and Medicare are exhausted, future generations will pay higher taxes that are then transferred directly to beneficiaries of those programs. Intergenerational conflict is already evident and will increase as the entitlement programs absorb more of the federal budget. Future generations will ask the obvious question: why did our grandparents not pay the taxes required to finance their pension and health care benefits? Bipartisan support for balanced budget rules and debt limits is most likely to come from younger generations. But, as intergenerational conflicts over entitlement programs grow, so will a consensus supporting reform of those programs. Fewer citizens will support the intergenerational transfers of wealth now built into these programs.

Future generations will also bear the burden of economic stagnation due to increased debt burdens. The CBO forecasts that as the debt/GDP ratio grows, this will result in fewer economic opportunities for future generations. The CBO also projects that increasing debt burdens will expose the country to greater economic instability. Economic recessions have the greatest impact on the least skilled, low-wage workers. The CBO forecasts do not anticipate another major economic shock, but increased debt burdens mean that the nation has less fiscal space to respond to such shocks. In short, future generations will confront a less dynamic economy characterized by retardation in economic growth and great economic instability. Slower growth in job opportunities will hit the least skilled and lower-wage workers the most, which means growing disparities in income and wealth distribution across income classes. Few citizens would wish to leave such a legacy to future generations.

The other major inequity resulting from the growth in federal debt is regional inequality. In most states, elected officials have learned to live with fiscal rules designed to prevent bankruptcy. These rules can be traced back to the 1830s and 1840s when a number of states did go bankrupt. Every state but Vermont has constitutional rules mandating a balanced budget and limiting debt. In recent decades, many states have also enacted TELs. There is great variance in the effectiveness of these state TELs. There are some states, such as Illinois, that have failed to enforce their fiscal rules; and some municipal governments, such as Chicago, expose their citizens to bankruptcy. These zombie governments have become increasingly dependent upon federal government bailouts. But most state and local governments attempt to enforce their fiscal rules and in recent years have enacted reforms to strengthen those rules. Perhaps the best example of this success is the state of Utah (Merrifield and Poulson 2021). Utah has been balancing the state budget and limiting debt for decades. In recent years, Utah has enacted fiscal reforms to achieve those objectives. When unfunded liabilities in government employee pension and OPEB plans increased at an unsustainable rate, Utah legislators enacted reforms to bring those expenditures under control. Just like their Swiss counterparts, Utah legislators have significantly reduced state debt relative to state gross product in recent years. Citizens in Utah and other prudent states are asking the obvious question: if we have forced our elected officials to learn to live with balanced budgets and debt limits, why are we paying taxes to the federal government that are used to bailout states such as Illinois and cities such as Chicago that do not enforce their fiscal rules, and continue to incur unsustainable levels of debt?

The successful reforms enacted in Utah reveal bipartisan support for balanced budget rules and debt limits. Elected officials in Utah convinced their citizens that unfunded liabilities in government pension and OPEB plans were not only absorbing greater shares of the state budget, but they were threatening the long-term viability of those plans. Police, firefighters, and other public sector unions supported reforms designed to preserve the viability of their pension and health care plans, and with bipartisan support, including the support of public sector unions, Utah legislators were able to enact the reforms. With fiscal rules in place, Utah has been able to balance the budget and limit debt, setting an example for other states.

Because elected officials in Utah and other states have been living with balanced budget rules, debt limits, and TELs, they are the most qualified to design and enact such rules for the federal government. At this point in time, Congress has neither the experience nor the inclination to design and enact such rules. This is precisely the dilemma anticipated by the founding fathers when they incorporated Article V in the Constitution. They anticipated that Congress would find it difficult to impose such constraints and that special interests could dominate fiscal decisions in ways that threaten the stability of the democratic system. They designed Article V so that citizens and their elected representatives in the states, as well as Congress, could propose amendments to the constitution. We should expect that a campaign by citizens and state elected officials to incorporate a balanced budget rules and debt limits into the constitution will motivate Congress to propose such an amendment, if for no other reason than to preserve their prerogative in proposing amendments.

A campaign to enact balanced budget rules and debt limits in the constitution would have an educational impact on U.S. citizens, just as it did in Switzerland. Switzerland is one of the most diverse multilingual countries in the world. Swiss citizens were able to overcome their differences to support an amendment incorporating balanced budget rules and debt limits in their constitution. When U.S. citizens understand that they have the power under Article V to correct the flaws in federal fiscal rules and fiscal policies, we should expect broad bipartisan support for the proposed amendment.

The growing debt crisis in the United States has been accompanied by declining credence capital. Citizens know that unconstrained growth in debt is the result of flawed fiscal rules and fiscal policies. A campaign to incorporate balanced budget rules and debt limits in the constitution can reverse this decline. Building bipartisan consensus in support of the amendment could also diminish the partisanship and polarization we observe in Congress (Guldenshuh 2021).

SWORDS TO PLOUGHSHARES

The American journalist Tom Brokaw's book *The Greatest Generation* is a tribute to the citizens who responded to the challenge of the Great

Depression and World War II. After a decade in which they experienced the worst depression in our history, citizens in the United States and other democratic nations joined forces to defeat fascism. Just as important as that victory was the success of that generation in restoring a peacetime economy. Financing the war required unprecedented deficit spending and debt accumulation, but after the war the country returned to the "Old Time Religion" of balanced budgets and debt stabilization. With normalization of fiscal and monetary policy, the debt/GDP ratio was reduced to prewar levels. The country was able to downsize from a wartime economy to a peacetime economy in a relatively short period of time.

As Milton Friedman argued, the market system proved to be remarkably resilient in adjusting to these structural changes (Friedman and Heller 1969). Keynesian economists predicted that the post-war economy would return to the economic stagnation experienced during the Great Depression. In fact, the post-war economy experienced rapid economic growth and productivity change. As Friedrich Hayek argued, the return to private markets created incentives for an efficient allocation of resources and entrepreneurial activity (Boettke 2019). By the 1990s, during the Great Moderation, it appeared that Friedman and Hayek had won this battle of ideas. With the end of the cold war, the United States was again able to normalize macroeconomic policy, setting the stage for rapid economic growth and productivity change.

Over the past two decades, the nation has again been confronted with economic shocks and military conflicts. The financial crisis in 2008 and the coronavirus pandemic in 2020 required unprecedented fiscal and monetary coordination. The Russian invasion of Ukraine has again raised the specter of cold war, with a sharp discontinuous increase in defense spending in democratic nations responding to this military crisis. Citizens in the United States and other democratic nations have met these challenges, but a greater challenge will be to downsize government and normalize fiscal and monetary policy in the long term.

The indicative fiscal and monetary rules enacted during the Great Moderation have proven to be ineffective. Other counties have shown that second-generation fiscal rules are now required to impose fiscal discipline and solve the debt crisis, but the United States has not enacted effective fiscal and monetary rules. U.S. citizens have not imposed discipline on elected officials as prior generations did. We have abandoned the Old Time Religion of balanced budget and debt stabilization and continue to experience debt fatigue in the long term. Restoring Jeffersonian principles will require this generation of citizens and their elected representatives to balance the budget and pay off the debts they have incurred.

NOTES

1. The success of macroeconomic stabilization policies in the 1990s reflected not just effective fiscal and monetary rules. As Friedman argued, this was an era in which we relied on markets and the price system to allocate resources, and a broader set of government policies limited the role for government in the economy. The decade of the 1990s was a period of rapid economic growth and productivity change, reflecting the impact of this broader set of policies.

2. It is important to distinguish between these early balanced budget proposals and the second-generation fiscal rules discussed in this book. The latter refers to a balancing of the budget over the business cycle, or structural balance. Structural balance also requires a combination of fiscal rules designed to achieve long-term targets for debt sustainability. Second-generation fiscal rules require institutional changes to gain political support and viability for the rules in the long term.

3. For a discussion of other government policies that impact the economy during the Great Depression, see Poulson (1981).

4. For a discussion of the literature on debt and economic growth, see de Rugy and Salmon (2020).

REFERENCES

Alesina, A., and G. Tabellini. 1990. "A Positive Theory of Fiscal Deficits and Public Debt," *Review of Economic Studies* 57: 403–414.

Alesina, A., and A. Passalacqua. 2015. "The Political Economy of Public Debt, in *Handbook of Macroeconomics*," J. Taylor and H. Uhilg editors, Elsevier.

Bank for International Settlements. 2011. "The Real Effects of Debt," BIS Working Papers No. 352, September.

Blankart, C. 2011. *An Economic Theory of Switzerland*, CESifo DICE Report 3/2011.

Blankart, C. 2015. "What the Eurozone Could Learn from Switzerland," *CESfio FORUM* 16(2): 39–42.

Boettke, P. 2019. "F.A. Hayek: Economics, Political Economy, and Social Philosophy," *Great Thinkers in Economics*, Thirwall, A.P. editor, Mercatus Center, George Mason University.

Coase, R. 1960. "The Problem of Social Cost," *Journal of Law and Economics* 3(1): 1–44.

Congressional Budget Office. 2020a. *The Budget and Economic Outlook 2020-2030*, January 28.

Congressional Budget Office. 2020b. *Interim Economic Projection for 2020 and 2021*, May 19.

Congressional Budget Office. 2020c. *Long Term Budget Outlook*, September.

Congressional Budget Office. 2021a. *The Budget and Economic Outlook*, Washington DC, (January).

Congressional Budget Office. 2021b. *Introduction to the CBO,* Washington DC.

Couchman, K. 2022. Comments on *Restoring a Great Moderation in Macroeconomic Policy* (mimeo).

Debrun, Xavier, David Hauner, and Manmohan S. Kumar. 2009. "Independent Fiscal Agencies," *Journal of Economic Surveys* 23: 44–81.

Debrun, X., J. Ostry, T. Williams, and C. Wyless. 2018. "Public Debt Sustainability," in *Sovereign Debt: A Guide for Economists and Practitioners,* IMF Conference, edited by S. Abbas, A. Pienkowski, and K. Rogoff, International Monetary Fund, forthcoming, Oxford University Press.

Debrun, X., and L. Jonung. 2019. "Under Threat-Rules Based Fiscal Policy and How to Preserve it," *European Journal of Political Economy* March 57: 142–157.

DeHaan, J., H. Berger, and D. Jansen. 2004. "Why Has the Stability and Growth Pact Failed?" *International Finance* 7: 235–260.

De Rugy, V., and J. Salmon. 2020. "Debt and Growth: Decade of Studies," Policy Brief, Mercatus Center, George Mason University, April 15.

Feld, L., and G. Kirchgassner. 2006. "On the Effectiveness of Debt Brakes: The Swiss Experience," Center for Research in Economics Management and the Arts, Working Paper No. 2006-21.

Friedman, M. 1948. "A Monetary and Fiscal Framework for Economic Stability," *American Economic Review* 38(3): 245–264.

Friedman, Milton. 1956. "The Quantity Theory of Money—A Restatement," in *Studies in the Quantity Theory of Money,* edited by Milton Friedman, The University of Chicago Press, Chicago, 3–21.

Friedman, Milton. 1960. *A Program for Monetary Stability*, Fordham University Press, New York.

Friedman, Milton. 1962. "Should There Be an Independent Monetary Authority?" in *In Search of A Monetary Constitution,* edited by Leland B. Yeager, Harvard University Press, Cambridge, MA.

Friedman, Milton. 1969. "The Optimum Quantity of Money" [1969]; "The Role of Monetary Policy" [1968]; "Price, Income, and Monetary Changes in Three Wartime Periods" [1952]; "The Supply of Money and Changes in Prices and Output" [1958]; "Money and Business Cycles" [1963]; "In Defense of Destabilizing Speculation" [1960], in *The Optimum Quantity of Money and Other Essays,* edited by Milton Friedman, Aldine Publishing Company, Chicago.

Friedman, Milton. 1977. "Nobel Lecture: Inflation and Unemployment," *Journal of Political Economy* 85(3): 451–472.

Friedman, Milton. 1983. "Why Inflation Persists" [1977]; "Inflation and Jobs" [1979], in *Bright Promises, Dismal Performance: An Economist's Protest,* edited by William R. Allen, Harcourt, Brace, Jovanovich, New York.

Friedman, Milton, and Walter W. Heller. 1969. *Monetary vs. Fiscal Policy*, W. W. Norton, New York.

Friedman, Milton, and Anna J. Schwartz. 1963. *A Monetary History of the United States, 1867–1960*, Princeton University Press, Princeton, NJ.

Guldenshuh, D. 2021. *Article V Convention Legislative Report*, The Heartland Institute.

Inman, R. 1996. "Do Balanced Budget Rules Work? U.S. Experience and Possible Lessons for the EMU." Working Paper 5838, National Bureau of Economic Research.

International Monetary Fund. 2013. "Staff Guidance Note for Public Debt Sustainability Analysis in Market-Access Countries," May.

Kotlikoff, L. 2015. "America's Fiscal Solvency and its Generational Consequences," Testimony in the Senate Budget Committee February 25.

Kyland, L., and E. Prescott. 1977. "Rules Rather than Discretion: The Inconsistency of Optimum Plans," *Journal of Political Economy* 85(3): 473–491.

Merrifield, J., and B. Poulson. 2016a. *Can the Debt Growth be Stopped? Rules Based Policy Options for Addressing the Federal Fiscal Crisis*, Lexington Books, New York, NY.

Merrifield, J., and B. Poulson. 2016b. "The Swedish and Swiss Fiscal Rule Outcomes Contain Key Lessons for the U.S," *Independent Review* 21(2): 251–275.

Merrifield, J., and B. Poulson. 2017a. "New Constitutional Debt Brakes for Euroland Revisited," *Journal of Applied Business and Economics* 19(8): 110–132.

Merrifield, J., and B. Poulson. 2017b. *Restoring America's Fiscal Constitution*, Lexington Books, New York, NY.

Merrifield, J., and B. Poulson. 2018. "Fiscal Federalism and Dynamic Credence Capital in the U.S," ERN *Institutional and Transition Economics Policy and Paper Series* 10(16). November 28.

Merrifield, J., and B. Poulson. 2020. *Fiscal Cliff: New Perspectives on the Federal Debt Crisis*, Cato Institute.

Merrifield, J., and B. Poulson. 2021. "Debt Sustainability in the States," Paper prepared for the American Legislative Exchange Council annual meeting Salt Lake City Utah, July.

Office of Management and Budget. 2021a. *The President's FY 2022 Discretionary Request*, whitehouse.gov/omb/budget.

Office of Management and Budget. 2021b. *Budget of the U.S. Government Fiscal Year 2022*. Washington DC, whitehouse.gov/omb/budget.

Office of Management and Budget. 2022. *Budget of the U.S. Government Fiscal Year 2023*. Washington DC, whitehouse.gov/omb/budget.

Organization for Economic Cooperation and Development. 2013. "General Government Fiscal Balance" in *Government at a Glance* 2013, OECD Publishing, Paris.

Persson, T., and L. Svensson. 1989. "Why a Stubborn Conservative Would Run A Deficit: Policy with Time Inconsistent Preferences," *Quarterly Journal of Economics* 104: 325–345.

Peter G. Peterson Foundation. 2019. *Solutions Initiative: Charting a Sustainable Future*, www.pgpf.org.

Peter G. Peterson Foundation. 2021. *Comprehensive Plans to Address the National Debt*, www.pgpf.org.

Poulson, B. 1981. *Economic History of the United States*, Macmillan, New York.

Poulson, B., S. Hanke, and J. Merrifield, editors. Forthcoming 2022. *Public Debt Sustainability: International Perspectives*. Lexington Press, Lanham, MD.

Reinhart, C., and K. Rogoff. 2009. *This Time is Different: Eight Centuries of Financial Folly*, Princeton University Press.

Reinhart, C., K. Rogoff, and M. Savastano. 2003. "Debt Intolerance," *Brookings Papers on Economic Activity* 1(Spring): 1–74.

Stokey, N. 2003. "Rules versus Discretion After Twenty Five Years," NBER Macroeconomics Annual 2002, Vol. 17.

U.S. Congress. 2019-2020. *Bipartisan Budget Reform Act*, 116th Congress.

Wall Street Journal. 2020. "Federal Reserve Says It's Launching New Corporate Bond-buying Program," Tuesday June 16, 8A.

Wyplosz, C. 2005. "Fiscal Policy: Institutions versus Rules," *National Institute Economic Review*, No. 191, July.

Appendix A

MP RULES EQUATIONS

$$\text{AGDP}_t = \left(\left(\left(\text{GDP}_t/\text{GDP}_{t-1}\right) - \text{GRCHG} - \text{RECESS}_t\right) * \text{AGDP}_{t-1}\right) + \text{AGDP}_{t-1}$$

Where: GDP = CBO GDP projections.

AGDP = GDP adjusted for recession (RECESS) or changes in economic growth (GRCHG).

$$\text{ADEF}_t = \left(\text{TOTDEBT}_t - \text{TOTDEBT}_{t-1}\right) * \left(-1\right)$$

Where: ADEF = actual deficit.

TOTDEBT = total debt

$$\text{ENDOGCH}_t = \left(\left(\left(\text{RTOTREV}_{t-1} - \text{ASSET}\right)/\text{RGDP}_{t-1}\right) - \left(\left(\text{RTOTREV}_{t-2} - \text{ASSET}\right)/\text{RGDP}_{t-2}\right)\right)$$

Where: ENDOGCH = endogenous dynamic scoring factor

RTOTREV = simulation-revised total revenue.

ASSET = revenue generated from asset sales.

RGDP = simulation-revised GDP

$$GA_t = IF\left(EXOGTAXCH_t = 0,\ \left(RMTR * ENDOGCH_t\right),\ \left(RMTR *\right.\right.$$
$$\left.\left.\left(EXOGTAXCH_t *(-1)\right)\right) + \left(RMTR * ENDOGCH_t\right)\right) + 1$$

Where: GA = dynamic scoring-based growth adjustment: GDP RGDP
RMTR = research-based connection between tax rates and growth
ENDOGCH = exogenous (user-chosen) dynamic scoring factor

$$RGDP_t = \left(RGDP_{t-1} + \left(\left(AGDP_t - AGDP_{t-1}\right) * GA_t\right)\right)$$
$$+ \left(OCR * \left(RDEF_{t-1} - ADEF_{t-1}\right)\right)$$

Where: OCR = research-based opportunity cost rate
for moving resources from the private to public sector.

$$INCTXRT_t = \left(REVELAST * \left(INCTAX_t / AGDP_t\right)\right)$$
$$- \left(EXOGTAXCH_t * REVELAST\right)$$

Where: INCTXRT = average income tax rate
REVELAST = elasticity relating income tax revenue to GDP
INCTAX = personal + corporate income tax revenue

$$RGFREV_t = \left(GFREV_t * \left(1 - SRLS_t\right)\right) + \left(\left(RGDP_t - AGDP_t\right)\right.$$
$$\left.* PISH * \left(INCTXRT_t + MTXRT_t\right)\right)$$

Where: PISH = personal income share of GDP
RGFREV = simulation-revised general fund revenue
SRLS = static revenue effect of exogenous tax rate change
MTXRT = tax rates except income, MED, and SS.

$$
\begin{aligned}
\text{DEBTBRK}_t = \text{IF}(&\text{RDEBTGDP}_{t-1} < (\text{TOLPROX} * \text{DEBTTOL}), \\
& 0, \text{IF}\big(\big((\text{RDEBTGDP}_{t-1}/\text{DEBTTOL} \\
& * (\text{RDEBTGDP}_{t-1} - (\text{TOLPROX} * \text{DEBTTOL}))\big)\big) \\
& * \text{DEBTBRT} > 1,1,\big((\text{RDEBTGDP}_{t-1}/\text{DEBTTOL}) \\
& * (\text{RDEBTGDP}_{t-1} - (\text{TOLPROX} \\
& * \text{DEBTTOL}))\big)\big) * \text{DEBTBRT}\big))
\end{aligned}
$$

Where: DEBTBRK = debt-based drop in cap on GF spending growth
RDEBTGDP = simulation-revised Debt-to-GDP ratio.
TOLPROX = proximity to debt-tolerance level (DEBTTOL) that initiates braking.
DEBTBRT = debt-based braking multiplier [rate].

$$
\begin{aligned}
\text{DEFBRK}_t = \text{IF}(&\text{RDEFGDP}_{t-1} < (\text{TOLPROX} * \text{DEFTOL}), 0, \\
& \text{IF}\big(\big((\text{RDEFGDP}_{t-1} / \text{DEFTOL} * \\
& (\text{RDEFGDP}_{t-1} - (\text{TOLPROX} * \text{DEFTOL}))\big)\big) \\
& * \text{DEFBRT} > 1, 1, \big((\text{RDEFGDP}_{t-1} / \text{DEFTOL}) * \\
& (\text{RDEFGDP}_{t-1} - (\text{TOLPROX} * \text{DEFTOL}))\big)\big) \\
& * \text{DEFBRT}\big))
\end{aligned}
$$

Where: DEFBRK = deficit-based drop in cap on GF spending growth
DEFBRT = deficit-based braking multiplier [rate].

$$
\begin{aligned}
\text{CCSP}_t = \text{IF}(&\text{RTOTREV}_t > \text{RTOTREV}_{t-1}, 0, \\
& \text{IF}\big(\big((\text{RTOTREV}_{t-1} - \text{RTOTREV}_t) * 0.9\big) \\
& > (\text{RTOTREV}_{t-2} - \text{RTOTREV}_{t-1}), 0, \\
& \big(\text{CCREVSH} * (\text{RTOTREV}_{t-1} - \text{RTOTREV}_t)\big)\big)\big)
\end{aligned}
$$

Where: CCSP = countercyclical spending adjustment when revenue drops.
CCREVSH = degree of adjustment.

$$\begin{aligned}
\text{RGFSPwoINT}_t = \text{IF}\Big(\big(1 + \big((1 - \text{DEFBRK}_t - \text{DEBTBRK}_t) * \text{POPINF}_t\big)\big) > 1, \\
\big(\text{RGFSPwoINT}_{t-1} - \text{CCSP}_{t-1}\big) \\
*(1 + \big((1 - \text{DEFBRK}_t - \text{DEBTBRK}_t) \\
*\text{POPINF}_t))), \text{RGFSPwoINT}_{t-1} \\
-\text{CCSP}_{t-1}\big) + \text{CCSP}_t
\end{aligned}$$

Where: RGFSPwoINT_t = simulation-revised general fund spending without interest.

POPINF = population growth rate + inflation rate.

$$\begin{aligned}
\text{KFDEP}_t = \text{IF}\big(\text{REALPI10CHG}_t < \text{REALPICHG}_t, \\
\text{GDYRDEP}_t, \big((-1)* \big(\text{KMAXSH} * \text{KFBAL}_{t-1}\big)\big) \\
+\big(\big((1 - \text{KMAXSH}) * \text{KFBAL}_{t-1}\big) * \text{INTRT}_t\big)\big)
\end{aligned}$$

Where: KFDEP = capital fund deposit or withdrawal

REALPI10CHG = average real income change over the last ten years.

REALPICHG = real income change over the last year.

GDYRDEP = Good year deposit.

KFBAL = capital fund balance at the beginning of the fiscal year.

KMAXSH = maximum one-year withdrawal.

$$\begin{aligned}
\text{EFBAL}_t = \text{IF}\big(\big((\text{EFMAXDRT} * \text{RGFSPwoINT}_t) + \text{EFBAL}_{t-1} - \text{EFSP}_t\big) \\
> \text{EFCAP}_t, \text{EFCAP}_t, \text{EFBAL}_{t-1} - \text{EFSP}_t \\
+\big(\text{EFMAXDRT} * \text{RGFSPwoINT}_t\big)\big)
\end{aligned}$$

Where: EFMAXDRT = Maximum Deposit rate for the Emergency Fund

EFBAL = Emergency Fund Balance

EFSP_t = Emergency Fund Spending; User provided with 1/24th of 1994–2017 as the default.

EFCAP = Emergency Fund Balance Cap

$$\text{EFDEP}_t = \text{IF}\Big(\big((\text{EFMAXDRT} * \text{RGFSPwoINT}_t) + \text{EFBAL}_{t-1} - \text{EFSP}_t\big)$$
$$> \text{EFCAP}_t, \text{EFCAP}_t - \text{EFBAL}_{t-1} + \text{EFSP}_t,$$
$$\big(\text{EFMAXDRT} * \text{RGFSPwoINT}_t\big)\Big)$$

Where: EFDEP = Emergency Fund Deposit

$$\text{RTOTSP}_t = \text{SSMEDSP}_t + \text{RGFSPwoINT}_t + \text{INT}_t + \text{KFDEP}_t + \text{EFDEP}_t$$

Where: RTOTSP = simulation-revised total spending
SSMEDSP = Social Security + Medicare Spending
INT = Interest on the Debt

Appendix B

MODEL LEGISLATION FOR AN
ADVISORY FISCAL COUNCIL (AFC)

An AFC, herein referred to as the Council, shall be appointed to help implement the Balanced Budget Amendment and Expenditures Limitation Act. The Council is appointed by and reports to the Congress. Congress shall appoint one of the eight Council members for a non-renewable three-year term every two years.

The Council is responsible for assessing the extent to which the Balanced Budget Amendment and Expenditures Limitation Act are implemented. The Council has the responsibility to monitor fiscal policy and legislation that have a financial impact to assure that total expenditure and total revenue are in equilibrium in the near term. In addition to monitoring fiscal policy and legislation with a financial impact, the Council has a broader mandate to assess the macroeconomic conditions and macroeconomic policy.

Section (1) Setting Fiscal Targets

The Council is charged with setting the different fiscal targets imposed by these laws and determining the extent to which those targets are met. The targets include long-term as well as short-term fiscal targets over multiple budget years. When fiscal targets are not met, the Council is charged with recommending remedial fiscal measures that will bring fiscal policy in line with the targets. The Council is also charged with measuring the impact of legislation on these targets.

Section (2) Assessing Current Macroeconomic Conditions

The Council is charged with assessing current macroeconomic conditions, including the coordination of fiscal and monetary policy. The Council shall provide reports to Congress on a timely basis over the budget year. Of primary importance is the mandate that near-term expenditures be brought into equilibrium with long-term revenues; the Council shall provide an Annual Report to Congress on this mandate.

Section (3) Budget Process Reform

The Council is charged with recommending budget process reforms that will enable the country to address the debt crisis. In cooperation with the Federal Accounting Standards Board the Council is charged with recommendations for improved transparency and accountability in measuring the full cost of government programs. Of major importance are comprehensive measures of total government debt including off-budget debt such as unfunded liabilities in entitlement programs.

Section (4) Intergenerational Accounting

The magnitude of debt incurred in recent decades will impose a heavy burden on future generations of Americans. Addressing the debt crisis by reforming entitlement programs will impose different burdens on current and future generations. The Council is charged with implementing intergenerational accounting, including the analysis of the potential impact of entitlement reforms on different cohorts of the population.

Section (5) Assessing the Impact of Fiscal Policies on Long-Term Economic Growth

Lon-term fiscal sustainability will require high and sustained rates of economic growth. The Council is charged with assessing the impact of tax and expenditure policies on long-term economic growth. The Council will recommend to Congress investments to promote high rates of economic growth, including but not limited to investments in research and development, infrastructure, and human capital.

DISCUSSION

Fiscal rules must be designed to resolve tradeoffs in credibility, flexibility, and simplicity. Current fiscal rules lack effective enforcement mechanisms;

new fiscal rules must provide for more effective enforcement. Other countries have introduced Councils to monitor and help enforce their fiscal rules. The United States should introduce an AFC to provide greater transparency and accountability in the budget process. The challenge in the design of fiscal rules is not only to satisfy the balanced budget principle but also to prepare for future emergencies and major economic shocks such as those experienced over the past few decades. Finally, the fiscal rules must enable the country to address long-term challenges, investing in research and development, infrastructure, and human capital. Elected officials must prepare for long-term demographic changes and the impact of an aging population on pension and health plans. They must meet these long-term changes while pursuing fiscal policies with intergenerational fairness.

The AFC is responsible for assessing the extent to which the proposed Balanced Budget Amendment and Expenditures Limitation Act are implemented. The Council is appointed by the president but reports to the Congress. The Council is charged with setting the different fiscal targets imposed by these laws and determining the extent to which those targets are met. The targets include long-term as well as short-term fiscal targets over multiple budget years. When fiscal targets are not met, the Council is charged with recommending remedial fiscal measures that will bring the fiscal policy in line with the targets. The Council is also charged with measuring the impact of legislation on these targets. Finally, the Council is charged with assessing current macroeconomic conditions, including the coordination of fiscal and monetary policy. The Council shall provide reports to Congress on a timely basis over the budget year. Of primary importance is the mandate that long-term expenditures be brought into equilibrium with long-term revenues; the Council shall provide an Annual Report to Congress on this mandate.

Appendix C

MODEL LEGISLATION FOR A BALANCED BUDGET AMENDMENT AND EXPENDITURES LIMITATION ACT

There is an extensive literature exploring fiscal rules in other countries. In recent years, many of these studies have focused on the Swiss Debt Brake, arguably the most effective fiscal rules enacted in any country. The Swiss Debt Brake combines a constitutional balanced budget rule with a statutory Expenditures Limit. The fiscal rules that we propose are modeled after the Swiss Debt Brake (Merrifield and Poulson 2017; Poulson et al. 2022).

BALANCED BUDGET AMENDMENT

Summary

The Balanced Budget Amendment is designed to address the federal debt crisis. In recent decades the federal government has incurred debt at an unsustainable rate and is projected to continue to do so in coming years. This amendment requires that total expenditure be brought into equilibrium with total revenues in the near term. It also provides for countercyclical fiscal policy by permitting limited deficits during periods of recession and requiring surpluses in periods of economic expansion. Thus, the amendment achieves both sustainability of public finances in the near term and more stable public finances over the business cycle.

Section (1). The federal government shall hold its expenditures and revenues in near-term equilibrium.

Section (2). The federal government shall set the maximum amount of expenditures each year required to hold expenditures and revenue in equilibrium in the near term.

Section (3). The maximum amount of expenditures in (2) may be exceeded for emergency expenditures with a two-thirds vote of approval in both houses of Congress.

Section (4). If actual expenditures in any year exceed the maximum allowable expenditures in paragraphs (2) and (3), the excess expenditures shall be compensated in the following years.

Section (5). Details are determined by statutory law.

Explanation

Section (1)

Total government expenditures must be brought into equilibrium with total revenues in the near term. The flaw in the budget process is unconstrained growth in federal expenditures. The formal and informal rules that constrained expenditures historically are no longer effective. This constitutional provision makes explicit the mandate to constrain total expenditures to equal total revenues in the near term.

Section (2)

To bring total expenditures into equilibrium total with revenues in the near term, this provision imposes an Expenditures Limit each year. The design of the Expenditures Limit is left to statutory law. But the Expenditures Limit must be designed to equate total expenditures with total revenues in the near term.

Section (3)

This section provides for emergency expenditures conditional upon a super-majority vote of both houses of the legislature. Emergencies are unexpected developments beyond the control of government. They include, but are not limited to, natural disasters, military emergencies, fiscal crises, and pandemics. Congress must budget for emergencies and equate total expenditures and total revenues in the near term.

Section (4)

This provision makes clear how Congress must satisfy both provisions (2) and (3). If total expenditures, including emergency expenditures, exceed total revenues in any year, those excess expenditures must be offset by surplus revenue in subsequent years.

Section (5)

This Balanced Budget Amendment requires enabling legislation. The amendment sets constitutional parameters for that statutory law. Ultimately the Supreme Court must hold the other branches of government responsible for upholding these constitutional parameters in statutory law.

Expenditures Limitation Act

Summary

The Expenditures Limitation Act is enabling legislation required for the federal government to bring total expenditures into equilibrium with total revenues in the near term. The act imposes a limit on annual total expenditures. The Expenditures Limit is adjusted when deficits and/or debt approach tolerance levels. The act also provides for an Emergency Fund and a Capital Investment Fund. An amortization fund and Compensation Account are created to assure that total expenditures are brought into equilibrium with total revenues in the near term. An Advisory Fiscal Council is created to help implement the Balanced Budget Amendment and the Expenditures Limitation Act.

Section (1) Expenditures Limit

The maximum annual growth in total expenditures, herein referred to as the Expenditures Limit, shall be determined by Congress consistent with the Balanced Budget Amendment. The Expenditures Limit is the product of the sum of inflation plus population growth, adjusted to reflect long-run trends in federal revenues and expenditures. Congress shall take the Adjusted Expenditures Limit into account in dealing with all legislation with a financial impact.

Section (2) Adjusted Expenditures Limit

The Adjusted Expenditures Limit is the Expenditures Limit after adjustment for the Deficit Brake and Debt Brake. In no case shall the Adjusted Expenditures Limit fall below 0.

Section (3) Deficit Brake

To ensure that equilibrium is maintained between total expenditures and total revenues in the near term, Congress shall impose a Deficit Brake. A Deficit Brake shall be imposed in any year when the actual deficit/GDP ratio approaches a deficit/GDP tolerance level equal to (3) percent of GDP. The

Deficit Brake reduces the Expenditures Limit proportional to the distance between the actual deficit/GDP level and the deficit/GDP tolerance level.

Section (4) Debt Brake

To ensure that equilibrium is maintained between total expenditures and total revenues in the near term, Congress shall impose a Debt Brake. The Debt Brake shall be imposed in any year when the total debt/GDP ratio approaches a debt/GDP tolerance level equal to (100) percent of GDP. The Debt Brake reduces the Expenditures Limit proportional to the distance between the actual debt/GDP ratio and the debt/GDP tolerance level.

Section (5) Emergency Fund and Capital Investment Fund

The actual expenditures in a given year may exceed the Adjusted Expenditures Limit in the event of an emergency. An emergency is an extraordinary development that cannot be controlled by the federal government, including but not limited to natural disasters, military emergency, and financial crises. Congress shall annually appropriate an Emergency Fund deposit that is the lesser of the Emergency Fund limit (__) percent of total expenditures, or the Emergency Fund limit minus the Emergency Fund balance. Emergency Fund expenditures require a declaration of emergency by Congress and a two-thirds vote of approval for the emergency expenditures in both houses of Congress.

The actual expenditures in a given year may exceed the Adjusted Expenditures Limit to fund capital investment. Congress shall appropriate a Capital Investment Fund deposit in any year when the actual rate of growth in GDP exceeds the trend rate of growth in GDP. The trend rate of growth in GDP is calculated as the average annual rate of growth in GDP over the prior ten years. Debits to the Capital Investment Fund can only occur in years when the actual rate of growth in GDP is below the average annual rate of growth in GDP. Funds can be expended from the Capital Investment Fund for investment projects approved by a majority vote of both houses of Congress.[1]

Section (6) Amortization Account

Receipts and expenditures reported in the Emergency Fund and Capital Investment Fund shall be credited or debited to an Amortization Account managed outside the ordinary budget. A deficit in the Amortization Account in the previous budget year shall be offset within the next six budget years through a reduction in the Adjusted Expenditures Limit. If the deficit in the Amortization Account increases by more than (0.5) percent of total expenditures, the offsetting period may be reset by Congress with two-thirds approval in both houses. The obligation to balance the Amortization Account shall be deferred until any deficit in the Compensation Account is eliminated. The magnitude of the savings required to balance the Amortization Account and Compensation Account shall be decided by Congress on an annual basis when approving the ordinary budget.

Section (7) Compensation Account

At the end of each budget year, when financial statements have been approved, the actual total expenditures shall be compared to allowable total expenditures for that year. If the actual total expenditures are higher or lower than the allowable total expenditures for that year, the deviation shall be debited or credited to a Compensation Account managed outside the ordinary budget. A deficit in the Compensation Account shall be offset over the course of several years through a reduction in the Adjusted Expenditures Limit. If the deficit exceeds (6) percent of total expenditures in the prior year, the excess shall be eliminated within the next three budget years.

Explanation

Sections (1) and (2)

The key component of the Expenditures Limitation Act is a limit on the annual rate of growth in federal expenditures. The Expenditures Limit is equal to the product of the sum of inflation plus population growth and the Expenditures Limit multiplier. Congress shall adjust the Expenditures Limit based on long-term trends in federal revenues and expenditures. The objective is to bring total expenditures into equilibrium with total revenues in the near term. For example, federal finances will be impacted by a demographic shock as the baby boom generation enters retirement and demands Social Security and Medicare benefits. Based on these long-term projections Congress will need to maintain a lower Expenditures Limit in the near term and adjust the Expenditure Limit upward in the long term. Congress will also need to reform these entitlement programs; but even with reforms, the Expenditures Limit will need to reflect these trends in the demand for government services. Interest on the public debt is also projected to increase in the long term. The Expenditures Limit also needs to be adjusted to reflect the impact of these interest costs on the public debt.

Sections (3) and (4)

The flaw in current fiscal rules is that they fail to prevent deficits and the accumulation of debt from one business cycle to the next. The Deficit Brake and Debt Brake are designed to prevent this accumulation of debt. When deficits approach the deficit/GDP tolerance level the Deficit Brake is triggered.

When debt approaches the debt/GDP tolerance level the Debt Brake is triggered. The Adjusted Expenditures Limit reflects the constraints imposed on expenditures by the Deficit Brake and Debt Brake.

Section (5)

Money is allocated to an Emergency Fund when the actual fund is below the Emergency Fund cap. A portion of the surplus revenue is allocated to the Emergency Fund. The Emergency Fund is available to finance emergency expenditures, such as natural disasters, military emergencies, and financial crises. In periods of recession and revenue shortfall, the Emergency Fund is used to offset revenue shortfalls. Surplus revenue in periods of expansion can offset deficits in periods of recession, providing for more stable growth in expenditures over the business cycle.

In periods when economic growth exceeds the long-term trend in growth a portion of the surplus revenue is allocated to the Capital Investment Fund. In periods of slower growth, the Capital Investment Fund is used to finance additional investment expenditures. In this way, fuller utilization is achieved in the capital goods industry, and the federal government benefits from greater efficiency and bargains in capital investment. Capital investments also help to sustain federal expenditures in periods of recession.

Section (6)

The Emergency Fund and the Capital Investment Fund are accounted for separately from the ordinary budget. The Amortization Account serves as a control parameter for these funds, recording expenditures and receipts. If either of these funds incurs deficits, the deficits must be paid off over the course of the subsequent six budget years by means of surpluses in the ordinary budget. If the deficits are foreseeable, the necessary savings can be made in advance.

Section (7)

In the long term, after the fiscal gap is closed, a Compensation Account is created. At the end of the budget year, the total expenditures and total revenue are calculated. Surplus revenue is first allocated to the Emergency Fund and the Capital Investment Fund. Any additional surplus revenue is credited to the Compensation Account, separate from the ordinary budget. If total expenditures exceed total revenue the excess is charged to the Compensation Account. Compensation Account deficits must be eliminated in subsequent years. Additional Surpluses in the Compensation Account are used to reduce the public debt.

DISCUSSION

The proposed Balanced Budget Amendment addresses the problem of time inconsistency in fiscal policy. The problem with the current law is that if Congress reaches an agreement on a budget that equates total expenditures with total revenues in the near term, there is nothing to prevent a future Congress from pursuing fiscal policies that violate the balanced budget principle. Fiscal policies during the "Great Moderation" of the 1980s and 1990s were constrained by fiscal rules consistent with the balanced budget principle that has not been true over the past two decades.

There is no foolproof way to guarantee that Congress will pursue fiscal policies consistent with the balanced budget principle, but incorporating this principle in constitutional law will further this objective. Evidence at both the subnational and national level supports the thesis that when the balanced budget principle is incorporated as constitutional law, elected officials are more likely to uphold the principle.

Support for the balanced budget principle is furthered by the procedure of incorporating it as constitutional law. Enacting the Balanced Budget Amendment will be a learning experience involving citizens as well as elected officials in discussion and debate regarding the balanced budget principle, and the laws required to satisfy this principle. Article V of the Constitution provides two amendment procedures. Congress with a two-thirds vote of approval for a resolution may propose an amendment. The states may also propose an amendment with two-thirds of the states approving the resolution. Thus far, amendments have only been approved through the Congressional amendment process; the states have failed to achieve the two-thirds supermajority requirement to submit a resolution for approval.

However, the debt crisis has set the stage for approval of a Balanced Budget Amendment proposed by the states. The debt crisis is precisely why Article V was incorporated into the constitution. Anticipating that elected officials would find it hard to impose constraints on themselves, especially when it comes to fiscal issues, the founding fathers incorporated the provision that citizens and their elected representatives in the states can also propose an amendment.

Elected officials at the state and local levels have centuries of experience in living with the balanced budget principle. Every state but one has balanced budget provisions in their state constitution. Most states also have constitutional provisions limiting debt. Many states have also incorporated new fiscal rules, such as tax and expenditure limits, in their constitution. A Balanced Budget Amendment in the federal constitution should be informed by this learning experience of citizens and their elected representatives with the balance budget principle at the state and local level.

Elected officials at the federal level will also gain from the experience of enacting a Balanced Budget Amendment to the U.S. Constitution. A citizen-led effort should motivate Congress to take a critical look at the flaws in current fiscal rules and budget procedures. It should also motivate Congress to seek the bipartisan support required for Congress to propose such an amendment. As in the past, when it appeared that a citizen-led effort to enact an amendment to the constitution appeared likely to be successful, Congress was motivated to act in order to preserve its prerogatives in proposing amendments to the constitution.

NOTE

1. As noted in the text, funding for capital investments may involve transfers to the states. Currently money is transferred to the states via formula grants under titles 23 and 49 of the United States Code at appointed times. The proposed legislation would require enabling legislation conforming to this code.

Index

About the Authors

Barry W. Poulson is emeritus professor of economics at the University of Colorado. He has been visiting professor at several universities including the Universidad Autónoma de Guadalajara, University of North Carolina, Cambridge University, Konan University, and Universidad Carlos Tercera. He is the author of numerous books and articles in the fields of economic development and economic history, has served as president of the North American Economics and Finance Association, and is an advisor to the Task Force on Tax and Fiscal Policy for the American Legislative Exchange Council. His current research focuses on fiscal policies and fiscal constitutions.

John Merrifield was on the faculty of the University of Texas at San Antonio for thirty-two years. He retired from teaching and faculty meetings to devote additional time to critical research issues and to have more time with his wife and "high-maintenance" teenage adopted boys. He is associate editor for the *Nonpartisan Education Review*, past editor for *Journal of School Choice*, and has authored or edited five books, fifty-six peer-reviewed journal articles, and several chapters in his primary teaching and research fields of education economics, public finance, urban and regional economics, and environmental and natural resource economics.

Lightning Source UK Ltd.
Milton Keynes UK
UKHW031953241022
411033UK00002B/101